Coast to Coast
on the
Ravenber Way
A walk across Northern England

Ron Scholes

with maps, drawings and photographs by the author

© Ron Scholes, 1997, 2003, 2011

First Published by Pentland Press in 1997
Second Edition by Landmark Publishing Ltd in 2003

Third Edition published by Sigma Leisure – an imprint of Sigma Press, Stobart House, Pontyclerc, Penybanc Road Ammanford, Carmarthenshire SA18 3HP

The rights of Ron Scholes as author of this work has been asserted by him in accordance with the Copyright, Design and Patents Act 1993.

British Library Cataloguing in Publication Data

A CIP record for this book is available from the British Library

ISBN: 978-1-85058-871-9

Typesetting and Design by: Sigma Press, Ammanford, Carms

Maps, photographs and drawings: © Ron Scholes

Cover photographs: main photograph: Wasdale Head, Cumbria below (left to right): Ravenglass, Cumbria; Riddlehamhope, Northumberland; Norham, Northumberland; Royal Border Bridge, Berwick, Northumberland

Printed by: Berforts Group Limited

Disclaimer: The information in this book is given in good faith and is believed to be correct at the time of publication. Care should always be taken when walking in hill country. Where appropriate, attention has been drawn to matters of safety. The author and publisher cannot take responsibility for any accidents or injury incurred whilst following these walks. Only you can judge your own fitness, competence and experience. Do not rely solely on sketch maps for navigation: we strongly recommend the use of appropriate Ordnance Survey (or equivalent) maps.

This book is dedicated to the Hanliensian Rambling Club of North Staffordshire; for many years of fellowship and companionship on local walks, and on the hills and mountains of this country.

Berwick-upon-Tweed

Norham

VALLEYS
OF THE
RIVERS
TILL AND
TWEED

Kirknewton

Wooler

NORTH
SEA

SCOTLAND

Alwinton

Rothbury

NORTHUMBERLAND
NATIONAL PARK

Elsdon

West
Woodburn

Wark

Hexham

Blanchland

Allenheads

Garrigill

NORTHERN
PENNINES

LAKE DISTRICT
NATIONAL PARK

Dufton

Askham

Wasdale Head

Ambleside

Ravenglass

IRISH
SEA

THE RAVENBER

A LONG DISTANCE WALKING ROUTE
ACROSS NORTHERN ENGLAND.

Suggested Sections — O
Main Route — •—•—•—
Alternative Routes — ▶—▶—▶—

Contents

Main Route Maps - M

Alternative Route Sections

Alternative Routes Maps - A

Ravenber Mileage Distance Table

Main Route

1. Ravenglass	miles	km
Irton Road	5¼	6.4
Illgill Head	4½	7.2
Wasdale Head	3¼	5.2
Total	13	20.8

2. Wasdale Head		
Styhead	2	3.2
Old Dungeon Ghyll	5½	8.8
Ambleside	8½	13.6
Total	16	25.6
Distance covered	29	46.4

3. Ambleside		
Troutbeck	2½	4.0
High Street	5½	8.8
Askham	10	16.0
Total	18	28.8
Distance covered	47	75.2

4. Askham		
Morland	8¾	4.0
Long Marton	6	9.6
Dufton	2	3.2
Total	16¾	26.8
Distance covered	63¾	102

5. Dufton	miles	km
Dunfell Hush	5½	8.8
Dorthgill	6½	10.4
Garrigill	3	4.8
Total	15	24
Distance covered	78¾	126

6. Garrigill		
Nenthead	3½	5.6
Coalcleugh	2¼	3.6
Allenheads	6	9.6
Total	11¾	18.8
Distance covered	90½	144.8

7. Allenheads		
Hangman Hill	6	9.6
Dye House	6½	10.4
Hexham	4	6.4
Total	16½	26.4
Distance covered	107	171.2

8. Hexham		
Newbrough	5½	8.8
Brocolitia	2¾	4.4
Wark	4¾	7.6
Total	13	208
Distance covered	120	192

9. Wark	miles	km
Tone Inn	5	8
Threeburn Mouths	6¾	10.8
Elsdon	4¾	7.6
Total	16½	26.4
Distance covered	136½	218.4

10. Elsdon		
Manside Cross	3½	5.6
Coquet Cairn	5	8
Rothbury	4½	7.2
Total	13	20.8
Distance covered	149½	239.2

11. Rothbury		
Thropton	3	4.8
Sharperton	6	9.6
Alwinton	3	4.8
Total	12	19.2
Distance covered	161½	258.4

12. Alwinton	miles	km
Border Gate	7¾	12.4
Mounthooly	6	9.6
Westnewton Bridge	5¾	9.2
Total	19½	31.2
Distance covered	181	289.6

13. Westnewton Bridge		
Sybil's Well	4¾	7.6
Etal	3¾	6.0
Norham	10½	16.8
Total	19	30.4
Distance covered	200	320.0

14. Norham		
Horncliffe	3½	5.6
Union Bridge	1¼	2.0
Berwick-upon-Tweed	5¾	9.2
Total	10½	16.8
Distance covered	210½	336.8

Foreword

RON SCHOLES HAS MUCH EXPERIENCE of long-distance walking as well as fell walking. He has walked through Wales from South to North; he has covered the Southern Uplands of Scotland; and in 1990, using his own route, he travelled solo from Cape Wrath to Land's End. During this long journey he had a rest day at Bainbridge in the Yorkshire Dales and AW and I went there to meet him. We were impressed by his well-organized plan and his stamina.

Now he has completed his own version of a coast-to-coast walk and what an attractive route it is. When reading the sections familiar to me, I have been reminded of happy days on the fells with A.W., and have been inspired by a desire to walk the parts of the route unknown to me. Many alternatives are shown and these could prove useful for those who may find the longer days a little too far. However, fell walkers will probably want to avail themselves of the proximity of the mountains in the early stages.

Ron has much of interest to say about places and terrain seen along his chosen route. These descriptions will provide good reading material during the evenings and will heighten appreciation of surroundings during the day's march.

Betty Wainwright

Author's Note

Alfred Wainwright, 1907 - 1991

My friendship with Alfred Wainwright began in the early 1970s, firstly through the medium of correspondence. His magical little *Pictorial Guides to the Lakeland Fells* were always a source of delight among members of the local rambling club. Routes up mountains and along ridges were constantly discussed, and his many humorous and pithy comments were chuckled over, until they became part of the language of rambling. I quote from his *Pictorial Guide to the Lakeland Fells, Book Three, The Central Fells*: Pavey Ark 5, Ascent via Jack's Rake: "Care should be taken to avoid falling down the precipice or sending stones over the edge! Falling bodies, human or mineral, may constitute a danger to unseen climbers on the rocks of scree below, or to the grazing sheep."

Secondly, after offering to give illustrated talks, plus help in other ways, for his favourite charity, Animal Rescue Cumbria, I was honoured to meet AW and Betty on many occasions; at events, at Kapellan and at their home in Kendal Green.

AW was always enthusiastic when the conversation turned to the question of routes across the Pennine and Scottish hills and, understandably, about the intimate details of coves, cols, crags and summits of his own Lakeland peaks. On one occasion I was very promptly taken to task for confusing Bannisdale and Bannerdale.

He was always interested in the subject of long-distance walks; the nature of the country to be traversed, accommodation, distances and likely problems to be encountered.

During work on his *Peak District Sketchbook*, I enjoyed the privilege of showing him some of the scenic attractions of my native Staffordshire Moorlands; the serrated craggy skylines of the Ramshaw Rocks and the Roaches – which he climbed; the long moorland ridge of the Morridge; the River Dane and the hamlet of Gradbach; the exquisite, very often unknown, delights of the Manifold Valley and the lovely village of Ilam; the Upper Dove, and the villages of Sheen, Longnor and Hollinsclough. He was enthusiastic about the sylvan qualities of the remote Cheshire village of Wildboarclough and the prominent hill of Shutlingsloe; but it was Three Shires Head, where

Staffordshire, Cheshire and Derbyshire meet, that particularly impressed him with its rugged charm and beauty.

He loved to drop in to a friendly teashop at the end of the day for a scone or teacake and a pot of tea. There was also the occasion when he was initiated into the mysteries of a local delicacy – the Staffordshire oatcake.

I shall always remember the pleasure AW gained when walking through the grounds of the Animal Rescue Shelter at Kapellan; his joy in strolling along the pathway through the wooded area down to the beck, amidst the daffodils, bluebells, wood anemones and violets. The daffodils, especially, are a tribute to a remarkable and fascinating character, who produced, among his many books, those little works of art devoted to his beloved Lakeland Fells.

Ron Scholes

Acknowledgements
I am grateful for the willing help that I received from many people during the compilation of this guide book: Forestry Manager, Rothbury, Northumberland; Northumberland National Park, Hexham; Rights of Way Officer, Cumbria County Council, Kendal; Northumberland County Council, County Hall, Morpeth.

My thanks to the staff of the Tourist Information Centres at Ambleside, Hexham, Rothbury and Berwick-upon-Tweed. Also to the staff of the local libraries, particularly at the Newcastle-upon-Tyne Central Library, Local History Section.

Notes

Rail Transport

This is available at both ends of the walk. Ravenglass is served by the Cumbrian coast route linking Carlisle to the north, and Barrow-in-Furness and Lancaster to the south. Berwick-upon-Tweed lies on the main east coast London to Edinburgh line.

The Route

Seasoned walkers will experience little difficulty in completing the main route as indicated by the fourteen stages. Taking into account the fact that there is limited accommodation at certain locations, the journey may require an extra day or two using some of the alternative routes. However, if leisure time is limited, then certain sections can be completed as and when personal circumstances permit.

Navigational Route Maps

The sketch maps indicate grid north and are drawn to a scale of 2¼ inches to one mile. Contours are at 250 foot intervals and heights are shown in feet, together with a reasonably accurate equivalent in metres.

Walkers will need to carry Ordnance Survey® maps to aid navigation, or to establish an overall picture of the surrounding landscape, and to find accommodation facilities off-route. It is essential that anyone attempting this long-distance walk should have the necessary map-reading and compass skills.

The Ordnance Survey®, Explorer and Outdoor Leisure Series, 2½ inches to the mile are listed at the beginning of each section. A small number of maps may be carried at one time to save weight, and those sheets needed for later stages may be collected at a forward accommodation address. The used maps may then be posted home.

Be aware that small points of directional information provided in the text such as the location of finger posts, waymarkers, stiles, gates etc., may be changed; it is possible that these items have been resited or removed.

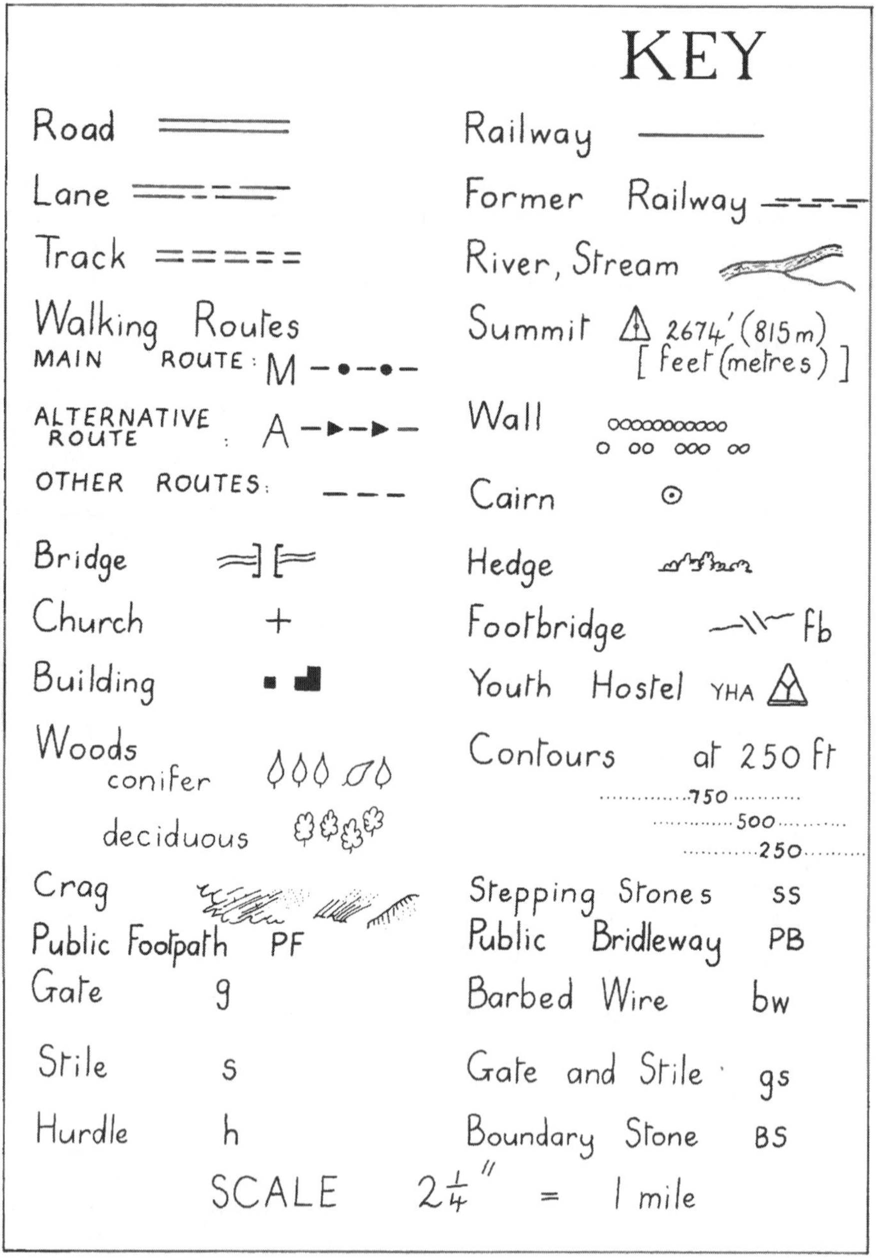

KEY

Road ═══

Lane ═══-══

Track ═════

Walking Routes
MAIN ROUTE: M —•—•—

ALTERNATIVE ROUTE: A —▶—▶—

OTHER ROUTES: — — —

Bridge ═] [═

Church +

Building ▪ ◾

Woods
conifer ◊◊◊ ⌀◊

deciduous 🌳🌳🌳

Crag

Public Footpath PF

Gate g

Stile s

Hurdle h

Railway ——

Former Railway —₌₌₌

River, Stream

Summit ⚠ 2674'(815m)
[feet (metres)]

Wall ∞∞∞∞∞∞
o oo ∞∞ ∞

Cairn ⊙

Hedge

Footbridge —\⌐ fb

Youth Hostel YHA ⚠

Contours at 250 ft
...............750...........
...............500...........
...............250...........

Stepping Stones SS

Public Bridleway PB

Barbed Wire bw

Gate and Stile gs

Boundary Stone BS

SCALE $2\frac{1}{4}''$ = 1 mile

Introduction

I FIND A LARGE-SCALE MAP just as exciting to read as a stirring account of adventures in the Gobi Desert. Although I am not likely to travel into the wilds of Central Asia, I can easily be transported to some outstanding tract of countryside that is part of Britain's beautifully varied landscape.

Rights of way, many following ancient routes, are part of our national heritage. They should be jealously guarded and above all should be walked, so that they do not become lost to succeeding generations of ramblers and hill walkers.

The walk described in the book follows existing rights of way in the form of footpaths, bridleways and tracks, making this cross-country route a challenging long-distance journey. The pleasure gained from planning an expedition, the degree of difficulty involved and the immense satisfaction achieved in completing it, is surely, part of the stuff of life.

Problems experienced along the way have been communicated to the footpath officers of the County Councils and National Parks who are responsible for a particular area. In some cases, new stiles and waymarkers have been installed, but the authorities have a large backlog of problems in the rights of way network, and Target Parishes have been identified for priority attention. It is important, therefore, to inform the footpath officers of difficulties met along the route, so that all parish footpaths receive equal consideration.

The objective in this book is Berwick-upon-Tweed on the Northumberland coast, a historical place to look around and very convenient for Holy Island, if the rigours of the completed walk force one to go into retreat. Otherwise it is a return home; but, if you cannot stop your legs from walking, there is the further challenge of the Southern Upland Way, which can be joined a few miles north in Scotland.

The walk commences at Ravenglass, which lies at the mouth of Eskdale's three lovely rivers, the Irt, Mite and Esk. It passes Lakeland's finest array of high peaks, encompassing Wasdale Head, traces the way used by Roman soldiers over the High Street Range, crosses the pastoral Eden Valley, climbs over the high Pennines, traverses the northern moors and heads on into the ancient kingdom of Northumbria. Beyond the Roman Wall lies the barrier of the Cheviot Hills, where reivers and mosstroopers once roamed. Finally, the walk ends on an idyllic note, as it follows the leafy valley of the River Till and along the banks of the mighty River Tweed, to reach Berwick-upon-Tweed, England's northernmost town.

The walk – whose title, the Ravenber, is clearly derived from the words 'Ravenglass' and 'Berwick' – is a journey which passes through two National Parks and other areas of outstanding natural beauty. It briefly touches the Cumbria Way and Pennine Way, and has the merit of sustaining the walker's interest with a splendid diversity of attractive scenery mountains, high hills, rolling moorland, expansive forests and lush river valleys. Not only is there much to see topographically, with the ever-changing terrain, there are also charming villages and towns and a wealth of fascinating history on the ground: for example, prehistoric sites, ancient highways and settlements, medieval farming patterns, fortified peles and bastle houses, motte and bailey earthworks, castles, old mine workings and defunct railway lines.

Some enthusiasts will endeavour to do it the hard way with backpack and tent, but lesser mortals will be satisfied with the hospitality of a comfortable night's lodging. The route is divided into sections with mileages to suit the proficient walker, and will finish each day at a point where accommodation facilities are usually available. However, it should be mentioned that there are other stages that constitute long days; it is with these in mind that alternative routes have been included. Also, in some of the places, accommodation is limited so wayfarers are advised to book a bed well in advance.   The walk is described from west to east in view of the prevailing winds. Some people may prefer to alter the sections in order to suit their own needs, or simply to use them as a basis for their own walking routes. Of course, there are walkers who may wish to savour the mountains of Lakeland at the end of the journey. The main route distance, 210½ miles (336.8 km), and the number of extra miles gained from other route options and alternative routes may be calculated by each individual.

Whatever the decision, either to take in an extra summit or to visit some other point of interest, the object is to accept the challenge of this long-distance walk, and to complete the crossing from one coastline to the other.

In the noisome world it will feel good to be alive as you tramp the many varied upland and valley miles. There are times when you will literally feel the silence, and will gladly appreciate the solitude to be found in the inner recesses and corners of the countryside. The experience will strengthen your character as well as your legs, and will imbue a desire to return; such is the appeal of these northern hills and dales.

1. Ravenglass to Wasdale Head

Map	OS 1:25000 Outdoor Leisure, English Lakes (SW) 6
Highest elevation	Illgill Head: West Cairn 1,978ft (603m) Summit Cairn 1,998ft (609m)
Height of ascent	2,799ft (853km)
Distance	13 miles (20.8km)
Terrain	Low undulating fells. Woodland, and a high level grassy ridge with magnificent views

RAVENGLASS IS TUCKED AWAY on Cumbria's west coast, and it is almost an adventure getting there in the first place for the start of the Ravenber Walk across northern England. Participants approaching from the south have the choice of the circuitous A595, or the use of Network Rail's west coast line. From the east, narrow scenic roads with challenging steep gradients cross the Wrynose and Hardknott Passes, and from the north, a more direct section of the A595 passes Sellafield's nuclear power plant.

Ravenglass, sheltered from the sea, lies at the heart of the trident-shaped estuary of the rivers Irt, Mite and Esk. The surrounding area has been touched by history over the centuries. Neolithic people used the coastal sand to smooth and polish the roughly hewn Langdale stone axe heads. In, Roman times, Ravenglass (Glannaventa) was strategically placed as the terminus for the vital road from east to west - the Tenth Highway. It became an important port, acting as a supply base for the forts and garrisons in the north of the country. A fort was constructed, but the site was partially destroyed by the coming of the main railway line.

The fine natural harbour was used by Celts, Vikings and Normans, and the settlement received its market charter in 1209.

During the seventeenth and eighteenth centuries Ravenglass became the natural outlet for Eskdale, with strings of packhorses and carts bringing in loads of wool, iron ore, slate and wad (graphite). At times, sailing ships secretly landed cargoes of tobacco, sugar, rum and weapons on the nearby dunes. Local farmers and yeomen welcomed this flourishing but illicit smuggling trade. Inland, reminders of those busy days are the attractive stone bridges to be found along Eskdale, and the old packhorse inns, such as Penny Hill (now a farm) and the Woolpack. It is interesting to note that there were regular sailings from Ravenglass to Liverpool until the end of the eighteenth century, when silting prevented access to all but shallow-draughted vessels.

The village lies just off the main road and is without through traffic. The single main street narrows, then widens, and is lined with a charming variety of colour-washed houses. The thoroughfare ends abruptly at a storm gate to keep out the high tides. The stony foreshore quickly turns to estuarine ooze, and across the water westwards lies the Ravenglass Gallery and Nature Reserve, a noted nesting site for black-headed gulls and terns; it is also packed with rare plants and animals.

To the south, the finger end of the Eskmeals Nature Reserve is one of the few remaining unspoiled sand-dune systems in Britain; it is rich

Ravenglass

in plant species and interesting wildlife communities. Further south is the prohibited area of the Eskmeals Gunnery Range.

Looking inland, one notices the backyard defences of the houses on the seaward side of the main street. Here and there, washing lines stretch out tautly towards supporting poles, and a few boats lean awkwardly on the sand. The foreground scene fits in perfectly, and the picture is complete with the background of distant Lakeland fells.

Discerning folk know Ravenglass as the headquarters of the Ravenglass and Eskdale Railway – known affectionately as La'al Ratty. This fascinating railway started life as a three-foot gauge in 1875, for the transportation of iron ore. The line struggled on until 1913 when it was closed completely, and then reopened with a fifteen-inch gauge track. Eventually decline set in again, and it was put up for sale, with the scrap-metal vultures waiting to pounce on the remains. However, in 1960, a group of enthusiasts raised the necessary funds and purchased the railway. Nowadays, regular services operate with carriages pulled by miniature steam engines on a beautiful seven-mile journey to the Eskdale terminus at Dalegarth near Boot.

Ravenglass is still a quiet place, relatively unspoilt and comparatively unaltered, apart from a large car park and a small modern housing estate. It maintains a relaxed and peaceful atmosphere; an ideal location for the start of an exhilarating walk across country from the mouth of one estuary to another.

It's time to go. But remember the coast-to-coast walking custom of dipping one's boots in the water – salt water preferably, not a pathside puddle!

Main Route

Pass through flood gates at the end of the main street, and bear left along the foreshore. Note a bridleway sign and notice board: CAUTION, TIDAL HIGH WATER FLOODS WHOLE OF FORESHORE AT TIMES. Continue along the foreshore passing an arrow marker. Keep left at a gate and walk on a narrow path passing beneath main line railway bridge. Turn right along a metalled lane. If the foreshore is flooded, from the main street, turn up the road at the Pennington Arms. Cross over a footbridge and proceed along a path to a metalled lane. Turn right and continue as indicated.

On the left-hand side of the lane stand the ruins of Walls Castle; a Roman bath house with the highest standing remains of a Roman

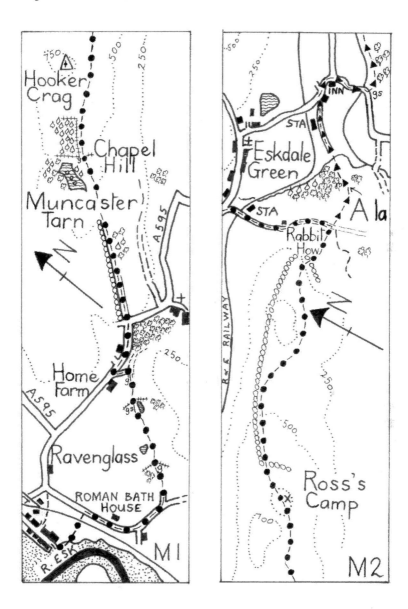

building in Britain. One room, possibly a changing room, has a niche in one wall for a small statue. Two of the rooms had hypocausts, and another had a solid floor which replaced an earlier hypocaust. Look for the well-preserved stretch of pink cement rendering. The baths stand at the north-east corner of the Roman fort, now cut by the railway and covered by dense woodland. Excavations have revealed that the fort was constructed in AD 130, and was garrisoned at intervals until AD 400. The barracks were built of timber, and defended by a turf rampart, which was strengthened by a stone wall in the third century.

Keep left at the track junction with arrow marker; ignore the first turning on the left and take the next turn left indicated by a footpath sign. Walk through a delightful wooded dell, passing a rock outcrop, to a gate. Beyond, the way opens out into parkland, note a clump of white foxgloves, and continue to a gate and step stile. Ahead is a NO ADMITTANCE notice, so bear left and follow the track past a farm building and a high stone wall to reach the A595 main road. Turn right, utilizing the pavement, and proceed up to a large car park opposite the entrance to Muncaster Castle.

The castle is the family home of the Duff-Penningtons, and if you have time to spare, the house and gardens are open to the public. The mansion, which grew up around a fourteenth-century pele tower erected on the Roman foundations of a look-out station, contains a fine collection of furniture, tapestries, paintings, books and china. The grounds and gardens, at their best in May and June, are renowned for a magnificent display of rhododendrons and azaleas. The terrace affords beautiful views along Eskdale – once described as Heaven's Gate by John Ruskin. Muncaster Castle is also a centre of the World Owl Trust.

Head uphill to a sharp bend in the road where two bridleways are signposted on the left. Keep straight on following the one to Muncaster Fell via Fell Lane, ascending gradually between stone walls. Continue on the same course looking back occasionally for glimpses of the sea and the Ravenglass estuary. The way comes to a small wooden gate before an area of rhododendrons; but ignore the gate on the left leading to Muncaster Tam. There is also a right of way going off to the right which descends to Chapels. Here is situated a 'pepperpot-shaped' tower erected in 1783 to commemorate the finding by shepherds of King Henry VI wandering after the Battle of Towton in 1461. He was taken to Muncaster Castle and sheltered there. As a token of gratitude the king gave his host a green glass bowl bearing the gold and enamel decoration 'The Luck of Muncaster', and with it the blessing that so long as the bowl was unbroken the family would prosper.

The main path bypasses the tarn, which is snugly sheltered by trees, and gently ascends Chapel Hill to a small gate. Looking southwards, there is the bulk of Black Combe rising above the sea. On reaching the end of a plantation keep straight on, with Hooker Crag, the highest point on Muncaster Fell, overlooking the path on its northern side.

Muncaster Fell is an isolated island of granite between the valleys of Miterdale and Eskdale. The underlying igneous rock, which is newer in age than the Borrowdale Series, makes a direct impact on the scenery and character of the area. In glacial times, Muncaster Fell was bounded to the north and to the south by glacial melt-water lakes. Today, the secluded tarn on Chapel Hill is the evidence of one of the overflow channels. The Fell's modest elevation commands vistas of great charm both seawards and inland, with heather, gorse, bracken and bilberry painting a joyous canvas of colour over its slopes.

The way ahead, indistinct in places, dips and bobs through an area of bracken to reach Ross's Camp. This is a huge raised flat slab of stone, inscribed and dated 1883 – a Victorian picnic table used by shooting parties. The grassy slopes rising behind the stone afford splendid views of the lengthening valley and the mountains beyond. The call of the Ravenber should be keenly felt at this point.

Eskdale is undoubtedly one of the loveliest of Lakeland's valleys. The flat lush floor coursed by the tree-lined curves of the River Esk, and patterned with pastures and farmsteads, is the stage for a backcloth of glorious fellsides. In the distance, the prominent shapely pyramid of Harter Fell catches the eye, and beckons tantalizingly to the dark mountain recesses of the upper dale.

Descend gradually to a gap in a wall and follow a side wall for a little way. A stone embankment is reached and the track climbs up to a rock cutting. From here a clear path slants downwards with a sighting of Eskdale Green in the foreground. Continue though a gate next to a sheep enclosure, then down past heathery covered outcrops to a gate and kissing gate. It is a short walk though gorse to a track junction and footpath signs at Rabbit How, GR 1393 9930. * (This is the departure point for the Alternative Route to Boot and Wasdale Head, also for Upper Eskdale and the high-level route options to Langdale; see pp. 29, 30, 32, 33, 34, 37, 38).

Bear left along the leafy bridleway to Forest How, and then along the metalled lane to Irton Road Station. Now, here's an opportunity to drool over those superb little trains of the Ravenglass and Eskdale

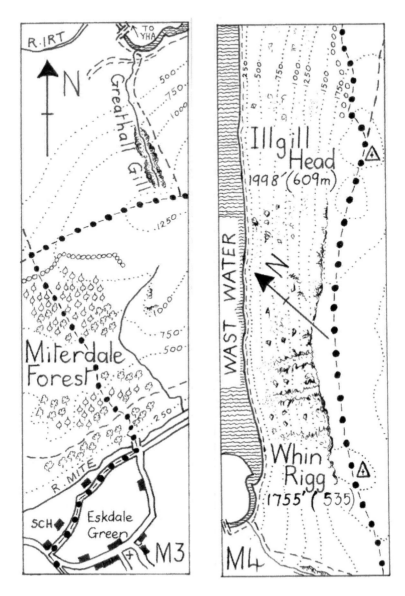

Railway. But first, put away all lurking thoughts about catching the next one back to Ravenglass. You have an objective to attain – Berwick-upon-Tweed! Accommodation is available locally in Eskdale Green and Boot, but it would be prudent to book a bed beforehand at any time during the Lakeland year. Continue down the lane to meet the Eskdale Green road. Bear left for a hundred yards and turn right on to a metalled lane that looks like a private drive – you are now in Miterdale. Pass a school on the left and then the entrance to Long Rigg Farm. Proceed through a gate and notice a dwelling and an excavated area on the left, probably the site of the former mill pond. Look for the sluice to the mill leat. At this point, the wooded mass of Miterdale Forest, the River Mite and the lane come together. Miterdale is a quiet unsung valley. Discerning visitors with time to spare should explore this almost secret fold in the hills.

Turn left at GR NY 143 009, through a gate opposite a track on the right. A marker post indicates a public bridleway to Irton Fell and Nether Wasdale. Cross over the packhorse bridge and climb gradually through an area of natural woodland. The way crosses a stream near rhododendron bushes and meets a track at right-angles. Go straight across and enter groves of mixed woodland with conifers. Proceed ahead, ignoring another track, and continue climbing to reach a gap in a wall and an area of conifers. Cross another track and aim slightly right to pass through another gap in a wall. The line of ascent passes a rock outcrop on the left and conifers on the right. Go on over another forest track and into a small clearing. You have now gained sufficient height to savour the view back across Eskdale to the surrounding fells.

Walk through a short boggy section to easier progress through pine trees. The edge of the forest is reached, and access to open country is via a small gate and step stile through a broken wall. Ahead is a cairn of stones. There are extensive views seaward, with the steam-billowing cooling towers of Sellafield Nuclear Power Plant very prominent. Walk forward for a few paces before veering right by a small cairn. Walkers intent on accommodation at Wast Water Youth Hostel should continue straight on for a descent into Wasdale; but bear in mind that it is a stiff climb up again on the following clay in order to return to the main route. The lakeside path beneath the screes is not recommended for people carrying full packs, or any packs for that matter. Be warned, there is a short section of huge piled-up boulders of prime obstacle course quality.

Back on the ridge at the small cairn, climb up the grassy slope to a ladder stile over a wall. Pass through an area dotted with boulders, descending a little to a broken wall, and spare a moment to glance down Greathall Gill, which is a spectacular gash in the fellside. The way proceeds easily via a succession of cairns to the top of Whin Rigg, 1,755ft (535m). The summit cairn is perched above the cliffs, and pinpoints the spot for an exciting view of Wast Water; it is also inevitable that one's gaze will quickly shift towards the lofty peaks at the eastern end of Wasdale. Descend gently, passing shallow pools, and peep down the awesome gullies that tumble down to the lake. The running buttresses and crags of the Screes fall spectacularly almost fifteen hundred feet into Wast Water – England's deepest lake, 258ft (78.6m), the home of brown trout and char.

In the evening when the western shore is settled into dusk, the Screes reflect the glow of the sky. Long after the surrounding fellsides have lost all trace of colour, the dark rocks, illuminated by the setting sun, project orange, red and purple silhouettes on to the brooding waters of the lake.

The walking is on grass, with an easy ascent following the escarpment to its highest point of Illgill Head, 1,998ft (609m). The summit, or better still the lower cairn, is an excellent belvedere for a magnificent view of Wasdale Head. The arc of mountains, the Scafells, Lingmell, Great Gable, Kirk Fell and Yewbarrow, forms an impressive backcloth to this, the finest of all Lakeland daleheads.

Bear left for a few yards to a broken wall which points directly down towards the head of the lake. Continue past a line of rock outcrops and walk along the north side of the wall which follows the line of Straighthead Gill. Aim slightly left, pass through the broken wall and cross the stream to join the path from Burnmoor. There is a cairn on the right indicating the course of this old corpse road. Pass some ruined buildings and follow the wall bordering the area of Fence Wood. The plantation contains conifers at first and then a tract of mixed woodland. Cross two streamlets by means of small footbridges and descend the stony track to a gate in a wall. Continue through two more gates, with the way becoming a pleasant grassy surface underfoot. The building on the right set in a copse of trees is Brackenclose, a Fell and Rock Climbing Club base. A permissive path to the Scafells leaves the track at this point.

Proceed over the wooden bridge crossing Lingmell Gill and turn right by the corner of a plantation. Walk alongside the fence to a gate and bear right along the track. On the left is the National Trust Wasdale Campsite; an attractive spot amongst leafy surroundings. There is a gate leading to the edge of the stone-littered bed of Lingmell Beck. Go along the bank for a few paces, and cross the shingle aiming for a gate and stile on the opposite side. Such is the vast amount of debris brought down by the beck in previous flood conditions that, normally, the water filters beneath the deep stone layer and you can walk over easily. But, after periods of continuous heavy rain, this crossing could prove to be a difficult obstacle.

Walk between gorse bushes and newly planted trees to a kissing gate. Negotiate a small stream by means of stepping stones, and continue along the track to a gate and stile. There are footpath signs here, and a notice indicating an alternative route by road, as the path is liable to flooding. Perhaps similar information could be displayed at the lake end of the path.

Now, it is only a short distance along the road to the hamlet of Wasdale Head.

At Wasdale Head there is the tremendous presence of the surrounding mountains. The green patches of pasture are intersected by stone walls, with a unifying huddle of buildings completing the picture. The whole grand scene is particularly beautiful when the dark fellsides are chequered with light and shade, and the sunlit cloud veils the tops.

The immense and laborious task of clearing the land of scrub and boulders, and the establishment of the original common field, was possibly undertaken by Norse settlers, who had sailed across from Ireland and the Isle of Man. Others are of the opinion that the land may have been cleared by settler-farmers between the tenth and thirteenth centuries. The internal field boundaries were probably built between 1750 and 1850 following Parliamentary legislation; it is likely that most of the walls in Lakeland were constructed about this time.

Some of the stone walls at Wasdale Head are fortress-like in appearance, being many feet thick; it is also evident that surplus stone was simply piled into separate dumps.

The small, agile Herdwick sheep is at home amongst the crags and high fells; it has the ability to thrive on poor pasture, and a well-known characteristic of remaining on its own 'heaf', or the area of fellside where it was weaned. However, other breeds may be found throughout Lakeland, namely Swaledale, Scots Blackface, Teeswater and Rough Fell. One of the fascinating aspects of sheep farming in this area is the link with those early Norse colonists in the marking of sheep. Various ear or 'lug' marks, were used to distinguish a farmer's lawful ownership of his animals. The word lug is derived from lög, a law. Other names can be linked with the early Scandinavian settlers; for instance, a male or female lamb before shearing is known as a 'hogg' or 'hogget', and a yearling ewe is called a 'gimmer'.

At the end of the nineteenth century, Wasdale was famous for Will Ritson; a farmer, the landlord of the Wasdale Head Inn and a noted raconteur and wit. He was an expert in the local dialect, and his exaggerated tales told whilst keeping a straight face made him a renowned character both locally and further a field. A competition is still held annually to find 'The Biggest Liar in the World'.

Just a short walk across the fields from the inn is the small, low-structured stone building of St Olaf's Church; it is reckoned to be the smallest church in use in England. Note the roof beams, said to have come from wrecked Viking ships; also, the tiny sketch of the Napes Needle on the south window. This rock pinnacle is part of the Great Napes, an awe-inspiring rock buttress high on the southern flank of Great Gable. Printed beneath the illustration are the words:

I will lift up mine eyes unto the hills
from whence cometh my strength

Some of the victims of climbing accidents lie in the compact yew-shaded graveyard. The awesome rock architecture facing north and east below the summit of Scafell has offered severe challenges to rock climbers ever since the early years of the sport.

Wasdale Hotel

The available accommodation at the Wasdale Head Inn and in nearby farms is often stretched to capacity, so Ravenber walkers are advised to book a bed well in advance. There is an outdoor equipment shop near to the inn, and a campsite just beyond the road. If all accommodation is taken and one is not equipped for camping, there is Wast Water Youth Hostel at the western end of the lake – a two-and-a-half-mile tramp along the lakeside road.

The Wasdale Show is usually held at the beginning of October, when such events such as sheep judging, fell racing and hound trailing attract many visitors to the dale.

Alternative Route

Rabbit How to Boot
Maps M2; A1a, p.21; A1b, p.31

Leave the main route at point GR 1393 9930. From the stile and gate, bear left across the field and contour round towards Bankend Wood. Turn left at the angle of the wall and follow the wall down the pasture to reach a gap. Cross the beck to a gate and stile, and proceed by way

Map	OS 1:25000 Outdoor Leisure, English Lakes (SW) 6
Distance	Rabbit How to Boot 3 miles (4.8km)
Note	Ravenglass to Rabbit How – Main Route 5 miles (8.0km)
Terrain	Easy walking. Lovely riverside surroundings. A delightful short ramble

of a leafy walled track to come alongside the Little Ratty railway line. Continue down the track to reach the road and turn right. Force yourself past the King George IV inn, which boasts a stock of over a hundred different malt whiskies, and carry on to Forge Bridge spanning the River Esk. Look over the parapet and admire the river's stony bed with its deep, clear, blue-green pools.

Turn left at the bridleway sign and follow the pleasant track, passing through two stiles, to reach a footbridge on the left crossing the river. Ignore it, and continue straight ahead to two gates, taking the right-hand one with a stile. Proceed alongside the wall through the meadow to another stile. Pass a ruined building on the right and walk on a length of cobbled path, then a slabbed section before a gate. The riverside surroundings are supremely idyllic, blessed with stands of hazel, sycamore, larch and cypress, including some very fine large specimens – a most attractive approach to Boot. Follow the wall to a gate and on to another area of mature woodland. Beyond the wall to the left lies Dalegarth Hall, with its rounded chimneys more traditionally typical of Westmorland. The way approaches a track with a gate and stile, where it is straight ahead for Boot and Upper Eskdale and right to Stanley Gill. If you have time to spare turn right and walk to a gate giving access to Stanley Gill Wood.

Follow the stream up a wooded ravine, where three bridges cross the stream as the ravine narrows. Beyond the third bridge there is a glimpse of Stanley Force, but a scramble up the left-hand side will give an uninterrupted view of this lovely waterfall. Return by the same route.

From the gate and stile close by Dalegarth Hall it is only a short distance to an impressively long footbridge across the wide bed of

Stanley Gill. Beyond, you can continue for a short distance, and then turn down towards the river Esk for an adventurous crossing over stepping stones. However, a note of caution is offered. The height of water is often above the level of the stones, which can be very slippery; but there is one advantage – the stepping stones do lead directly across the river to a very accommodating graveyard! A more prudent alternative is to continue along the river bank, and on to a footbridge constructed on the girders of the former iron ore mines railway across the gorge at Gill Force. At the far end of the bridge, look for a small plaque set into the handrail, in memory of Geoffrey Berry, Secretary of the Friends of the Lake District, photographer and author. The path follows the old railway track bed for a little way and continues to the church of St Catherine. This is a neat, low, seventeenth-century building of local Eskdale granite, which fits perfectly into its beautiful riverside setting. One south window is seventeenth century; it has a seventeenth-century font, and a cup of 1634 amongst its collection of plate. The churchyard contains a striking memorial to Tommy Dobson, Master of the Eskdale and Ennerdale Foxhounds for fifty-three years. The white headstone, with its finely carved effigy, is decorated with hunting symbols.

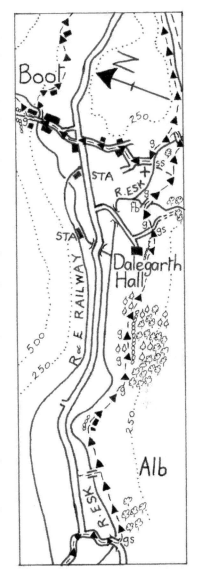

From the church follow the walled track, noting the course of the old mineral line after the first sharp bend. Walk on to meet the road opposite the Brook House Hotel. Cross over and go straight ahead up the lane, passing the Burnmoor Inn on the left, into the hamlet of Boot.

Boot is an attractive tiny settlement nestling at the foot of the fells. There are a number of colour-washed cottages including a shop cum post office. A narrow, picturesque eighteenth-century packhorse bridge is situated at the end of the road just before the water mill. Boot station, now abandoned, was the end of the line serving the iron ore mines above the village. There could be further tourist potential here by using the old track bed for a short extension of the line, and the establishment of a small mining museum. Visitors could combine a visit to the museum with inspecting the water mill, calling in at the Burnmoor Inn, and, if not too unsteady, wandering down the lane to the present rail terminus at Dalegarth.

The Eskdale Mill is believed to have operated hereabouts since the thirteenth century, but the earliest documentary evidence records a mill at Boot in 1578. It milled grain for the local farmers, mainly oats, barley and some wheat. Around the middle of the eighteenth century the building was extended to include a second waterwheel and an additional pair of millstones. The milling of corn ceased in 1920, but the waterwheel was kept working in order to generate electricity for the mill cottage. Cumbria County Council commenced restoration work in 1975, and the building and grounds were opened to the public in 1976. The mill is now powered by a 12ft 'overshot' wheel, using water from Whillan Beck, first through a ground-cut channel, and then along a wooden chute to the top of the wheel. Peat was used to fuel the drying kiln; it was cut on the fells, stored in small stone buildings until dry, and brought down to the mill by packhorse. Remains of these peat houses are still to be found on the fells above Boot.

Visitors with archaeological interests may climb the slopes of Boot Bank to the grassy plateau of Brat's Moss. This area contains a fascinating collection of Bronze Age cairns, standing stones, stone circles and clearance cairnfields. At GR NY173 012 there is a large stone circle which originally had 42 stones, only eight of which are now standing.

Alternative Route
Boot to Wasdale Head via Burnmoor
Maps A1b, p.31; A2a, p.33; A2b, p.27

Other explorers with their minds firmy fixed on the delights of Wasdale Head should proceed through the gate beyond the mill, and take the well-trodden path half right to a narrow gate in the wall on

Map	OS 1:25000 Outdoor Leisure, English Lakes (SW) 6
Highest elevation	Burnmoor Pass: 977ft (298m)
Height of ascent	840ft (256m)
Distance	5½ miles (8.8km)
Terrain	Grassy surroundings, easy gradients. A good low-level route

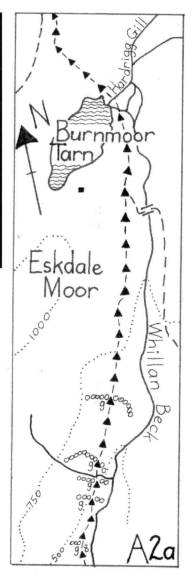

the right. Continue through walled enclosures and a series of gates to the open moorland beyond. This was the route of the old corpse way between Wasdale and Eskdale, by which bodies were brought for burial in St Catherine's churchyard. It is rumoured that the heathered acres of Burnmoor are haunted by a runaway horse carrying a dark object on its back. When the mist descends, keep your ears cocked for the sound of galloping hooves – don't linger!

In due course, the lovely expanse of Burnmoor Tarn comes into view. The path descends to cross the wide expanse of stone litter brought down by Hardrigg Gill, with the bulk of Scafell towering in the background. The gaunt remains of Burnmoor Lodge, a former hunting lodge, stand out starkly above the southern shoreline. There follows a gradual ascent to the wide grassy area of the Burnmoor Pass. Looking back, the gem of Burnmoor Tarn, nestling in its green trough, serves as a focusing point for the surrounding fells. In the distance is the attractive craggy pyramid of Harter Fell, and close by, the smooth slopes rise steeply to the ridge of Whin Rigg and Illgill Head.

The cairned path descends gradually, and given good visibility, there is an expanding view of Wast Water and the dominant peaks of Yewbarrow and Kirk Fell. From this point, the magnificent bulk of Great Gable is covered by Lingmell, but it will assume its familiar shape as one descends deeper into the dale.

Join the main route by the wall bordering Fence Wood, and continue as per main route (see p. 26).

A High-Level Route Option
Boot to Great Langdale
Via Three Tarns and the Band

Map	OS 1:25000 Outdoor Leisure, English Lakes (SW) 6
Highest elevation	Three Tarns 2,362ft (720m)
Height of ascent	2,247ft (685km)
Distance	9½ miles (15.2km)
Terrain	A walk through lovely riverside and wild upland scenery. Mountain walking over rough and stony ground

Walk by footpath via Hollins, Paddock Wray and Christcliff to the road. Bear left and proceed for a short distance before turning right to Doctor Bridge. Follow the track past Penny Hill, a former drovers' inn, along the riverside, and then turn left down through a wood to Whahouse Bridge. Go left over the bridge and take the path on the right to Birdhow and Taw House. Use the ladder stile to the right of the farmhouse, and continue on the path across the field to the footbridge over the River Esk. Brotherilkeld Farm lies on the opposite bank protected by a clump of trees.

Turn left and accompany the river upstream. Pass by imposing Heron Crag which lies on the other bank, and enjoy the lovely riverside attractions of deep pools and pretty waterfalls. Below Throstle Garth is the picturesque old packhorse bridge crossing Lingcove Beck. Don't cross it, but continue ahead, climbing steadily past more cascades. Take a breather for an opportunity to look back down this impressive valley. Taking a wider perspective, the mountain panorama is full of interest. Beyond, to the west of the upper reaches of the Esk, towers the Scafell Range; then, moving eastwards, appear the prominent outlines of Esk Pike and Bowfell bisected by Ore Gap. On the right, above Lingcove Beck, rise the formidable buttresses and serrated skyline of Crinkle Crags, separated from Bowfell by the Three Tarns Pass.

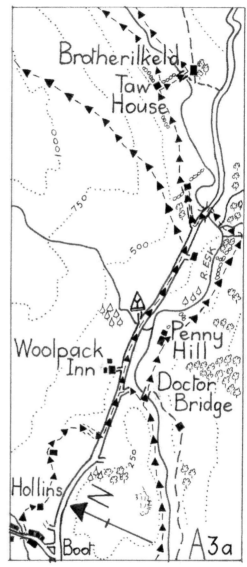

The route passes to the right of Churn How and ascends towards the grassy bowl of Green Hole. Cross the bed of Rest Gill, and follow the well-cairned route that climbs up through a rough section of stones and boulders to reach the depression occupied by the Three Tarns.

Heading for Great Langdale, a stony path descends, then slants left towards The Band. This is the long ridge separating the valleys of Oxendale and Mickleden. The route generally keeps to the Oxendale side of the ridge, providing a clearly formed way, with no difficulties. Lower down, at about a height of 1,200ft

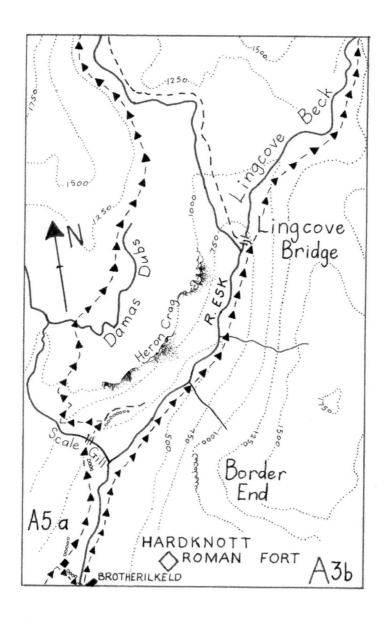

(366m), the walker is rewarded with an excellent view of Mickleden and the Langdale Pikes. Keep to the right-hand side of a craggy outcrop and descend to Stool End Farm; it is then only a short distance along the farm road to the welcoming bar of the Old Dungeon Ghyll Hotel.

If this establishment is not of immediate interest, the main route may be rejoined just behind the hotel.

Other High-Level Route Options
Route 1: Boot to Wasdale Head via Scafell
Maps A3a, p.35; A4a, A4b, p.39; (M5, p.27)

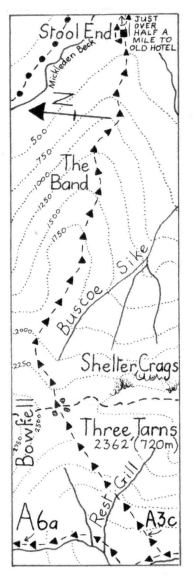

Map	OS 1:25000 Outdoor Leisure, English Lakes (SW) 6
Highest elevation	Scafell 3,162ft (964m)
Height of ascent	2,999ft (914km)
Distance	8¾ miles (14km)

Hollins, Paddock Wray, Bleabeck Bridge. Terrace route to Catcove Beck, Slight Side, Scafell, Green How, Fence Wood. Continue as per main route to Wasdale Head.

The terrace route ascends gradually through bracken and past rock outcrops. There is a steep climb to the rocky top of Slight Side, then a stony ridge walk to the summit of Scafell. This is a good way of descent to Fence Wood via Green How.

Route 2: Boot to Great Langdale via Esk Hause Col and Rossett Pass Maps A3a, p.35; A5b, p.40; (M7, M8, p.47)

Map	OS 1:25000 Outdoor Leisure, English Lakes (SW) 6
Highest elevation	Esk Hause col 2,490ft (759m)
Height of ascent	2,490ft (759m)
Distance	11½ miles (18.4km)

Along road passing Woolpack Inn and Eskdale Youth Hostel. Farm road to Birdhow and Taw House. Scale Bridge, Damas Dubs, Samson's Stones, Little Narrowcove Beck, Esk Hause Col, Esk Hause Shelter, Angle Tarn, Rossett Pass, Mickleden, Old Dungeon Ghytl Hotel.

Ascend from Scale Bridge via zig-zags to Damas Dubs. Walk half-right over marshy area avoiding the high ground of Rowantree Crags. Negotiate Sampson's Stones and continue up the narrowing valley of the Upper Esk. Continue over stony ground and up the rough, steep slope to the high grassy plateau of Esk Hause Col. Descend to the shelter and bear right for the descent to Angle Tarn. It is an easy climb to Rossett Pass. Take the old packhorse route to the right for a steady descent to lower Rossett Gill. It is level walking along Mickleden to Old Dungeon Ghyll Hotel.

Route 3: Boot to Great Langdale via Ore Gap and Rossett Pass Maps A3a, p.35; A6b, p.40; (M7, M8, p.47)

Map	OS 1:25000 Outdoor Leisure, English Lakes (SW) 6
Highest elevation	Ore Gap 2,543ft (775m)
Height of ascent	2,559ft (780km)
Distance	11 miles (17.6km)

Hollins, Paddock Wray, Doctor Bridge, Penny Hill, Whahouse Bridge, Birdhow, Taw House, along River Esk, Lingcove Bridge, Green Hole,

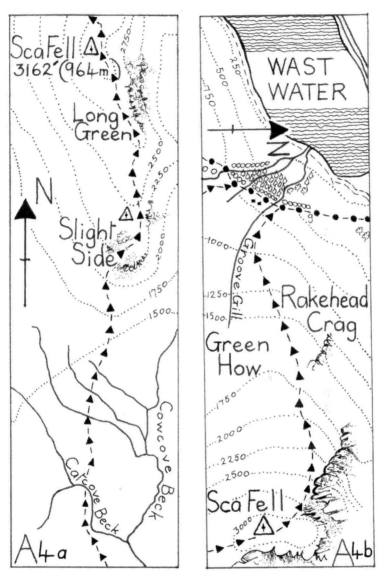

Yeastyrigg Gill, Ore Gap, Angle Tarn, Rossett Pass, Mickleden, Old Dungeon Ghyll Hotel.

This is splendid riverside walking, leafy at first, then open surroundings with a mountain view ahead. It is rougher underfoot after Lingcove Bridge. Lingcove Beck displays a series of waterfalls.

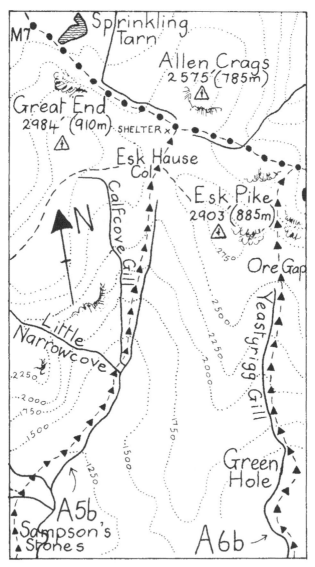

Enter the grassy basin of Green Hole. There follows a long, rough ascent of Yeastyrigg Gill, with better progress above to the right of the stream bed. Note the red subsoil at Ore Gap due to the present of haematite. Descend to Angle Tarn with an easy climb to Rossett Pass and continue as in Route 2.

2. Wasdale Head to Ambleside

Map	OS 1:25000 Outdoor Leisure, English Lakes (SW) 6
Highest elevation	Langdale to Wasdale Path below Esk Hause Shelter 2,379ft (725m)
Height of ascent	3,035ft (25.6m)
Distance	16 miles (25.6km)
Terrain	Clearly defined and well-graded paths amidst beautiful mountains, tarn and valley scenery

The Geological Picture

APART FROM THE OUTCROP OF GRANITE AROUND ESKDALE and the approaches to Wast Water, the underlying rocks in the Wasdale Head area, and indeed, the central mountain core of Lakeland, are predominantly those of the Borrowdale Volcanic Series. During a long period of volcanic activity in Ordovician times, a vast thickness of volcanic rocks – lavas and finegrained ashes – were poured out, largely under submarine conditions. This volcanic activity produced successive layers of hardened lava interspersed with beds of softer ash or tuff, which ultimately became fine-grained rocks.

The resulting scenery has come to be well known to visitors as typical of the Lake District. It is a marvellous landscape of bold ridges, rugged crags, rock terraces, gashed ravines, rock walls, buttresses and screes. Another feature of the region are the lakes. From the centre of this mountain complex, radiating ridges are separated by long valleys, diverging like spokes from the hub of a wheel. The sixteen major lakes lie on the floors of some, though not all, of the glacially eroded valleys. As the glaciers descended from the central dome, hollows were scooped from the valley floors forming a necklace of beautiful lakes, usually long and narrow. For example, Wast Water was gouged out to below sea level.

Sty Head Pass

The word Sty (or Stee) means a ladder, which may well refer to the zig-zags on the original valley route. The summit is a meeting place; the hub of a network of well-trodden routes between Wasdale and Borrowdale, and an important link to Great Langdale. The pass has been in use for many centuries by colonists, traders and dalespeople. Stone-Age people carried roughly-shaped stone axe heads from Langdale to the coast. When the poet Thomas Gray visited Borrowdale in 1769, he was discouraged from his attempt to travel by Sty Head. No doubt the local inhabitants did not want their smuggling activities to be interrupted.

Another mountain way in the area is Moses' Trod or Sledgate, which traverses the high ground from Honister to Wasdale Head. The route was supposedly named after a quarryman who illicitly made poteen using potatoes and bog water. This potent brew was smuggled out with his loads of slate along this well-graded packhorse trail.

In 1896, a route was surveyed to take a road from Wasdale Head round the head of Mosedale before it turned towards Sty Head. It was then planned to slant gently across the face of Kirk Fell and Great Gable to reach the top of the pass. From there it was proposed to descend into Borrowdale via Grains Gill. Baddeley's Guide Of 1902 noted the projected road, but thankfully it was never accomplished due to a tremendous public outcry.

FOR A DESCRIPTION OF THE HIGH-LEVEL ROUTE OPTION VIA GREAT GABLE; SEE PAGES 55-56

Main Route
Map M6, p.43

From the Wasdale Head Inn, bear left by the outdoor equipment shop to a small kissing gate on the right. A footpath sign indicates a route across the fields to St Olaf's Church. There, one gravestone in particular epitomizes the spirit of the place:

> *Here in the heart of the eternal hills*
> *Rises this shrine; the heritage of few*
> *Who made their way mid cotton grass and rills;*
> *Their footsteps marked in snow and summer dew.*

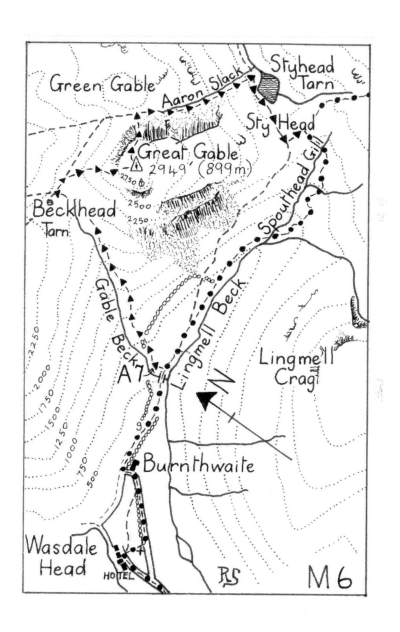

Turn left and proceed along the track noting large dumps of stone piled up in the corners of the small walled fields. Pass into the farmyard at Burnthwaite (accommodation is available here), and join the track coming up from the Wasdale Head Inn. Accompany the farm boundary wall, which is composed of rounded water-worn stones, to meet a farm gate and a kissing gate. Beyond, a wide pathway passes between walls to reach a long footbridge over Gable Beck. A cairn on the left indicates a path to Beck Head for an ascent of Great Gable (see pp. 55-56).

The direct route to Sty Head leaves the close proximity of the stream and begins to climb to a small gate in a wall. Many walkers take this route, which traverses the lower slopes of Great Gable to attain the summit of the pass. Apart from taking a little less time when compared with the valley route, it is useful in another respect, as chattering companions are often reduced to silence whilst negotiating this stony way.

However, if time is limited or the weather is foul, this route is clear and direct and presents no difficulties whatsoever.

Walk a short distance beyond the footbridge to a point where another path leads off to the right. Follow this to a gap in the wall, with an enormous boulder acting as a gatepost. Proceed through a bouldery area noting a lone larch tree to the left. Lingmell Beck has cut a mini-gorge on the right with a number of pools and waterfalls. Continue through another boulder-strewn tract to the watersmeet. Go a little way beyond and cross Spouthead Gill. The path traverses a tongue of land between the becks, and then zig-zags comfortably up the grassy slope.

Spare a moment or two to gaze at the superb mountain amphitheatre of Lingmell Crags, Broad Crag and Great End, and into the dark recesses of Piers Gill, Greta Gill and Skew Gill.

Also, look across to the far bank of Spouthead Gill for a lonely sheep fold, of which one side is composed of huge boulders. Spouthead Gill descends the long slope in a series of attractive cascades.

Cross a beck and continue to ascend another zig-zag section to reach easier ground in the upper combe. The path crosses the infant Skew Gill and then Spouthead Gill, and aims for two cairns on grass ahead. Bearing slightly left, climb the slope initially on a short stretch of paved path, and then head towards projecting outcrops and a small ravine. The way keeps to the right-hand edge of the ravine, and then levels out across grass to reach Sty Head. The stretcher box is situated at the foot of a huge boulder. Bear right.

From Sty Head the route crosses level ground, before commencing an undulating ascent on a clear path, to reach the western edge of Sprinkling Tarn. The area around this attractive irregularly-shaped stretch of shallow water was, centuries ago, the home of 'Branded Björn', a Norse highwayman who preyed on travellers.

To the right, the grassy slopes of the Band fringe the intimidating barrier of Great End, its craggy face seamed with dark gullies. Looking back, Great Gable has assumed another form; it only needs a covering of snow to look like a giant plum pudding with a garnishing of white sauce – a most appetising view.

The path crosses two watercourses and comes alongside the edge of Ruddy Gill, whilst another route goes left down Grains Gill into Borrowdale. A little further on a path slants off to the right and heads up to Esk Hause Col. Continue ahead on a gradual ascent to the upland plateau of Esk Hause. Situated to the right just above the Langdale/Wasdale Head path is a cross-shaped stone wall shelter, 2,379ft (725m). The area in the vicinity of the shelter and the col between Esk Pike and Great End, 2,490ft (759m), is commonly known as Esk Hause. For the purposes of route descriptions in this section of the Ravenber, the two locations will be called Esk Hause Shelter and Esk Hause Col respectively (see high level route 2: Boot to Great Langdale, p.38). This high sloping plateau is the hub in the radiating formation of ranges and intervening valleys. From the centre of this volcanic mass flow the valleys of Eskdale, Wasdale, Borrowdale and Great Langdale. During the Ice Age the mountain coves contained glacial ice, which, on descending, plucked out bowl-shaped hollows. The loose rock created a dam which held back the water, and so formed a lake or tarn. Angle Tarn is a typical mountain lake at a height of 1,870ft (570 m).

Ascend a short distance to Tongue Head where the route is joined by a cairned path on the right descending from Ore Gap (see high level route 3: Boot to Great Langdale, p.38).

Angle Tarn comes into view. Descend the hillside on a wide path to the shore of the tarn. The surroundings are a perfect example of a glaciated landscape, with the circular stretch of water set in a combe under Hanging Knotts. One can see the spread of hummocky moraines left by the retreating glacier marking its track down into Langstrath.

Here a path follows the tarn outlet for a little way, and then aims for Lining Crag and the Stake Pass, The main route continues ahead and climbs up to a large cairn at the summit of Rossett Pass, 2,001ft (610m). Walk forward to another large cairn for a better view of the Mickleden valley. Descend the stony path for a short distance, and as the main gill begins to fall away, look for a small cairn indicating a path slanting off to the right. This particular section of path was originally part of a well-graded packhorse route used for the transporting of goods from Langdale to the coast. No doubt smugglers also came this way with contraband landed secretly at Ravenglass. An interesting feature close by the gill is the lonely grave of a packwoman, with its rough cross of recumbent stones. She probably died on the mountainside and was buried here in the 1790s.

The descent from Rossett Pass using the zig-zag route is the preferred option. Nobody in their right mind should consider the dreadful stony penance alongside the gill. Much good stabilizing work has been completed on the zig-zag route, and the National Trust and conservation volunteers should be praised for their efforts. The zig-zags have another advantage, for the better surface enables the walker to enjoy the splendid view of Mickleden and the Langdale Pikes in relative comfort.

After a level section marked by cairns, descend through a small cutting with reddish coloured rock underfoot. Continue the traverse beneath crags to reach a point where the path swings sharp left.

Look for a rock cantilever like a huge gatepost on the right. Stop and listen for a moment to the sound of water gurgling close by. The way descends steeply over a paved section, and then slants right beneath rock outcrops. Bear left after shelving slabs and continue on a slabbed surface towards a small beck on the right. The way is loose and bouldery, but another paved section appears and descends to cross the gill on the left. The route is paved and stepped, and passes a cairn on the right by a huge boulder. Proceed to another cairn with a stone tablet indicating Stake Pass and Esk Hause. At the head of Mickleden alongside Rossett Gill and Green Tongue is an area of hummocky moraines, deposited there when the small glacier from Langdale Combe came to an end.

It is now level walking along the valley floor accompanied by the lively beck. Look out for a deep inviting pool close to the track. The beck then turns away with bracken and grass now on either side. On the left Langdale Fell rises steeply to the Pikes, with a tongue of scree funnelling out of a gully below Pike o'Stickle. The route now follows the Cumbria Way as far as Skelwith Bridge.

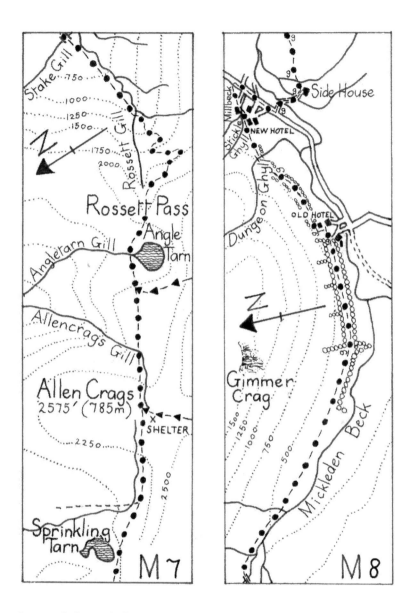

The Neolithic inhabitants of Lakeland found a seam of finegrained, grey-green volcanic tuff that emerged on the surface along a high-level contour around the head of the Langdale valley. This extremely hard stone was particularly useful, as it could be skilfully worked into a very sharp edge. The greatest activity was certainly centred on and about the wide gully which falls to the east of the summit of Pike o'Stickle, and extends to within a short distance of the Mickleden valley bottom. Abundant flakes and discarded axes have been discovered in the screes to the west of the south scree gully directly below the summit of Pike o'Stickle.

At a point some 1,800ft (549m) above sea level is a small, irregularly shaped but artificial cave, which may or may not have been connected with the stone axe manufacture. Another belief is that it was made during more recent times during the search for ores, especially haematite.

Completed axes have not been found in the screes or on the various chipping sites, and evidence indicates that the roughly shaped tools were transported to the coast to be polished with sandstone. From the coast the axes were taken by land or water to other parts of the British Isles.

A descent from the lip of the gully east of the summit of Pike o'Stickle is not recommended, as the passage of many feet has greatly eroded the surface making it very smooth and slippery.

Follow the track to a gate by a sheepfold and continue between walls towards Middle Fell Farm which lies below to the right. Proceed to a gate and kissing gate with a National Trust sign indicating Mickleden. If you don't require accommodation or refreshments at the Old Dungeon Ghyll Hotel, then aim left above to another gate and kissing gate in the wall. Walk behind Raven Crag House and proceed on a pleasant fellside terraced path alongside a wall. Pass a stone barn on the left with walls now on either side. Notice the huge blocks of stone in the tumbled wall. Descend to a small gate followed by a slight ascent, and continue on to cross a footbridge over Dungeon Ghyll Beck. Go forward to a gate with a kissing gate in a wall. Note a path coming in from the left from the direction of Dungeon Ghyll Force, which includes routes from Loft Crag, Harrison Stickle and Stickle Tarn. Descend and pass through gaps in fence and wall, and head for the New Dungeon Ghyll Lakeland Inn. The adjacent Sticklebarn Tavern offers bunkhouse accommodation.

There are two paths on opposite sides of Stickle Ghyll that climb up to Stickle Tarn for ascents of Harrison Stickle and Pavey Ark. According to Alfred Wainright, the highlight of the routes alongside Stickle Ghyll is the impressive view of Pavey Ark, which he considered to be one of the finest scenes in Lakeland.

Cross the footbridge over Stickle Ghyll, and then over another watercourse by means of a huge slab of green slate. Go through a small gate to Millbeck and continue down the farm lane to the valley road. Turn right and walk past the parking area to a footpath sign and gate on the left. Take the track across the field, and over the stone bridge crossing Great Langdale Beck towards Side House. Look back across the valley for a panoramic view of the Langdale Pikes, with an impressive perspective of Harrison Stickle.

Stickle Tarn lies in a hanging combe beneath the ice-scratched rocks of Pavey Ark. As the glaciers ground out the main valley floor, the water from the becks of the side valleys was often left hanging, and tumbled down to the floor of the dale in a series of waterfalls such as Dungeon Ghyll and Stickle Ghyll,

Bear left through a gate and kissing gate and cross a small footbridge. Keeping left, pass through a gap in a wall, and continue along a wide path to a gate and kissing gate. Ascend to a paved section, through a small gate and into a sheepfold. Cross a watercourse and follow a wall to a gate and kissing gate. Note a rock escarpment above on the right capped with a copse of trees.

The path climbs up to a marker post and continues between walls. Pass another marker and then a barn to reach Oak Howe cottage which is situated on a knoll. Bear left and walk along the track towards Great Langdale Beck, but do not cross over the bridge. The route now aims towards a gate and keeps alongside the beck. It is level going, passing over a cattle grid and then though a number of gates and kissing gates with a camping field to the right. Cross over stone arched New Bridge and proceed on the track, bearing right at a fork. Here it becomes a metalled surface for a short distance before the way bears right behind the village school. After passing beneath a canopy of fine beech trees the path joins the road at Chapel Stile.

At this point there is an attractive stone-built pillared shelter amongst the trees, access to which is through a small metal gate. This is a Grade I listed 'butty stop' – shelter, a seat, a litter bin, a well-stocked village store across the way, a convenient telephone box and Wainwright's Bar round the corner.

The route now turns right on to a bridleway below the Langdale Hotel, crosses over the bridge, and leads through a wooded area along the river bank. There are quarry workings to the right, and across the river the land is now part of the Langdale Timeshare Estate. This area, now landscaped, was formerly the site of a gunpowder works. At one time many waterwheels provided power, and now many of the old watercourses and some of the buildings have been incorporated into the leisure complex.

The way proceeds along a metalled road and descends into Elterwater village.

Chapel Stile and Elterwater were busy places when the slate quarries and gunpowder works were in full production. Lake District slate has been used in roofing and flooring for a very long time. The slate obtained from local quarries, such as Elterwater, and from Spoutcrag on the flanks of Lingmoor Fell, has always been renowned for its beautiful markings. The green colour of the volcanic slate is due to the presence of the mineral chlorite, and the markings the result of ripple marks and current bedding. The beautiful colours range from the pale green of the Elterwater quarry through to the silver grey and green of Spoutcrag.

There was a growing demand for gunpowder in the late eighteenth and nineteenth centuries, particularly for the growing Lake District industries of slate quarries, lead, iron and coal mines, A gunpowder mill was established in Elterwater in 1824 and worked until 1930 using water piped from Stickle Tam. The raw materials of sulphur and saltpetre were transported up Coniston Water or along Windermere. Charcoal was obtained locally using coppiced oak and hazel. High-quality charcoal was obtained from juniper bushes which grew abundantly on the lower fellside slopes.

The various stages in the manufacture of gunpowder were both complicated and dangerous, and there were numerous accidents during the milling and packing processes. There were some safety measures including special boots without nails and copper horseshoes.

During the Second World War Kurt Schwitters, a refugee from Nazi Germany and a pioneer of abstract art, used a barn at Elterwater in which to assemble a collage (or Merzbau, as he called it) from discarded materials. This collage, the last one he made, was never completed, and is now held by the University of Newcastle-upon-Tyne.

Elterwater, set in a lush green pastoral landscape, is now largely a tourist centre, with an attractive cluster of houses and cottages around the village green. It has the popular Britannia Inn and a Youth Hostel.

Cross over the arched bridge and turn right through a parking area to a footpath sign by a small kissing gate. Continue along the river

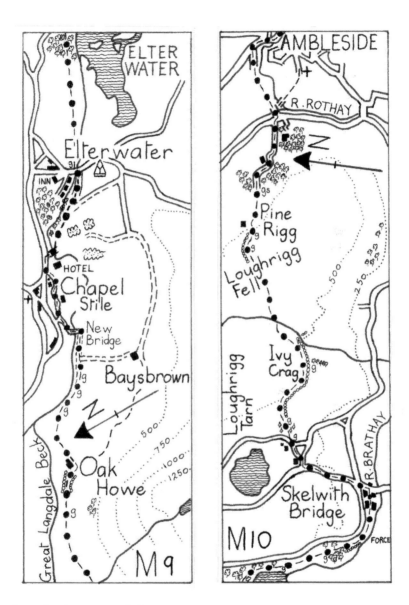

bank with glimpses of the lake to the right. Pass through a section of mature woodland to a kissing gate near to the edge of the lake. There is a fine view across the water to the Langdale Pikes beyond. The lake, set in sylvan surroundings, is noted for roach, pike, rudd and eels.

The name Elterwater is an adaptation of the old Norse word *elptarvatn*, 'lake of the swans'. Proceed across the meadows to a gate and kissing gate. Enter a wooded area and walk alongside a wall. Cross a footbridge to view the waterfall of Skelwith Force. In glacial times the ice failed to remove the harder rock, and the River Brathay has cut a deep gorge to pour over the rock step.

Continue through the works yard of the Kirkstone Galleries. Here green Lakeland slate is sawn and made up into a wide range of objects. There is also a shop and a tearoom.

On reaching the road, walk past the Skelwith Bridge Hotel, and proceed straight ahead at the junction up the minor road – gradient 1:4.

Turn right at the next road junction and walk along for a few paces to bear left towards Tarn Foot. Follow the track to the right past a National Trust farm, and continue straight ahead at the next track junction. Beyond the gate the track begins to ascend and climbs up through a grove of conifers to a gate. This is a well-marked route with the names of places written on tablets of slate. A wall accompanies you on the right, with rough fellside on the left rising to Ivy Crag. Pass through a gate, and a little further on, past a line of five trees, is an admirable prospect of Lake Windermere. Keep straight on when the wall veers off to the right, and continue over grassy and bracken-covered terrain. Bear right and descend to cross a small stream. Walk up the slope and descend gently to a gate with good views to Rydal and the Fairfield Horseshoe.

Loughrigg is the name given to this area of undulating rough ground; it is a colourful canvas of bracken and rocky outcrops crossed by a network of footpaths. The fell's modest height and position makes it an excellent vantage point for the higher hills beyond the surrounding valleys.

The way follows a wall and descends to a gate and kissing gate. Pass a dwelling on the left, Pine Rigg, a former golf clubhouse, and descend to another gate and step stile to enter a wooded area. The track, which is now metalled, swings round Miller Brow and passes Brow Head Farm. Continue to descend steeply through the trees to a cattle grid and a public bridleway sign. Bear right on the road to a gate and cattle grid, and turn left over the hump-backed Miller Bridge spanning the River Rothay. At this point there is a choice between two short routes into Ambleside: either straight on or to the right through Rothay Park. Taking the former, continue on a good path into a small housing development, along Stoney Lane, and join the main A591. Turn right into the centre of town.

Ambleside

Ambleside (the name derives from 'Amelsate', *saetr*, meaning 'on a sandbank by a river'), with its dark grey Lakeland stone houses, is set against a backcloth of colourful fells. It lies on the east side of the River Rothay with its northern part astride Stock Ghyll. The town is a major tourist centre with ample accommodation, including a youth hostel, gift shops, bookshops, cafes and outdoor pursuit emporiums.

The Romans built a fort, Galava, at the head of Windermere. The first structure was of turf and timber, and later rebuilt of stone on an artificial mound during the reign of Trajan (AD 98-117). The fort, sited in Borrans Field (Norse for 'heap of stones'), has long since been robbed of stones, but the foundations can still be seen, NY 373 034. There is evidence that the fort was attacked and burned, probably on two occasions. A road was constructed westwards from Galava to Hardknott, and on to the Roman supply port of Ravenglass; it is assumed a road ran from the fort at Watercrook (Alauna) near Kendal to Galava. A spectacular road ran south-west from Brocavum (Brougham) across high upland culminating in a stretch over Loadpot Hill and High Street, down to Troutbeck Park and then probably to Ings and Watercrook.

The oldest part of Ambleside is centred around Smithy Brow, which has a number of old cottages and a network of narrow lanes. This locality lay on the packhorse route over the Kirkstone Pass. A market charter was granted in 1650, and as the settlement prospered, the focus of the village moved down to the area of the market cross; it became a centre for wool and yarn.

A few of Ambleside's old buildings remain, in particular the quaint Bridge House that straddles Stock Ghyll. It was probably built by a man who wished to avoid paying land tax. This popular tourist attraction now serves as a National Trust Information Centre.

Towards the end of the eighteenth century Ambleside became a famous tourist resort. The beauty of the scenery and the area's association with the Romantics attracted wealthy business people, artists, poets and writers. Artists who visited and lived in Ambleside included JMW Turner and JC lbbetson. Harriet Martineau, author, social reformer and fell walker settled there in 1845. The parish

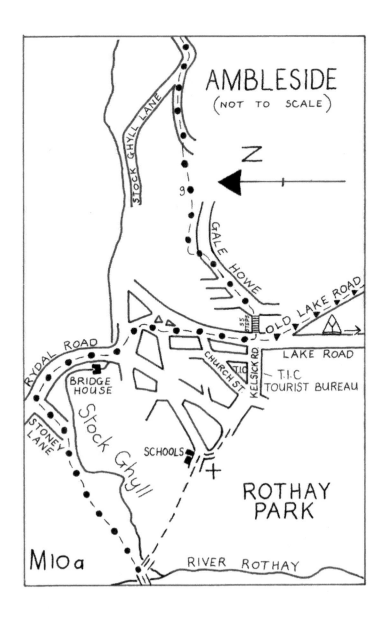

church of St Mary, with its tall spire, was built in the early 1850s, designed by Sir Giles Gilbert Scott. Inside the church, a mural depicts the Annual Rushbearing Ceremony. This ancient custom, which dates from medieval times, is usually held on the first Saturday in July.

Harriet Martineau, a close friend of Wordsworth, did not share his (and other writers') opposition to the extension of railways into the Lake District. Today, this should give much food for thought, when one experiences the traffic-congested streets of Ambleside and other Lakeland towns and villages.

A High-Level Route Option:
Wasdale Head to Sty Head via Great Gable
Map A7, M6, p.43

Map	OS 1:25000 Outdoor Leisure, English Lakes (SW) 6
Highest elevation	2,949ft (899m)
Height of ascent	2,687ft (819m)
Distance	4 miles (6.4 km)
Terrain	A magnificent mountain, rough and stony, with precipices on NE and SW faces. It is a mountain to savour and easily accessible to fell walkers

Ravenber walkers with enough energy and time to spare may decide to include an ascent of Great Gable. However, it would be prudent to consider one's capabilities; plus the added factors of the day's mileage, a full pack and the location of pre-booked accommodation.

Leave the main route just beyond the footbridge over Gable Beck, bearing left at a cairn. Ascend to a gate in a wall, and climb up the steep grassy rib of Gavel Neese to a point where the screes begin. Continue to traverse left on a stony path high above Gable Beck to reach the col at Beck Head. This section of path is part of Moses' Trod, an ancient packhorse route, used for the transportation of slate and illegally made whisky.

From the marshy depression at Beck Head, bear right towards the NE ridge of Great Gable. The route climbs roughly and steeply up the angle of the ridge, to follow a line of cairns leading to the summit. Set into the rocks that surround the summit cairn is a bronze plaque, a war memorial, which also records the gift of the fell to the National Trust by the Fell and Rock Climbing Club.

This grand exposed top with a commanding panorama of Lakeland is still a great favourite, and remains a very special objective for all lovers of the hills.

A short walk in a south westerly direction leads to the Westmorland Cairn. This well-built pile of stones is perched on the lip of the steep crags of Great Gable's southern face. From this vantage point the visitor is rewarded with an impressive view of Wasdale and Wast Water. Return to the summit cairn and follow a line of cairns in NNE direction. Then proceed on an easterly bearing to negotiate a section of rocky slabs. Resume a NNE line and continue to the col at Windy Gap. Bear right for a steady descent on a stony path down the screes of Aaron Slack. The stream bed is choked with boulders, but the water may be heard trickling under the stones. Continue down to Styhead Tarn, whose grassy surroundings are a popular high-level camping site. Bear right and follow the path to Sty Head. Walkers not interested in, or requiring, the contents of the stretcher box may take a short cut slanting left to rejoin the main route to Great Langdale.

3. Ambleside to Askham

Map	OS 1:25000 Outdoor Leisure, English Lakes (SE) 7 (NE) 5
Highest elevation	High Street Summit 2,717ft (828m)
Height of ascent	4,199ft (1,280m). (4,295ft (1,309m) including Thornthwaite Crag)
Distance	17¾ miles (28.4 km). (18½ miles (29.6 km) including Thornthwaite Crag)
Terrain	A long high-level walk over mainly grassy fells, on good well-defined paths, with impressive wide-ranging views. A classic walk

Main Route:
Ambleside to Troutbeck

Highest elevation	1,588ft (484m) Wansfell Pike
Height of ascent	1,424ft (434m)
Distance	2½ miles (4 km)

CONTINUE ALONG RYDAL ROAD into Market Place and along Lake Road passing Church Street on the right. On the opposite side of the next road junction, Kelsick Road and Lake Road, is a flight of 55 steps. Climb up to emerge on Lower Gale, and walk up Gale Howe passing the entrance to High Gale. Turn left at a footpath sign. The path bears to the right round a bungalow, and continues rising gently past attractive gardens of houses to a metal kissing gate and a footpath sign. Proceed between tall beech hedging and along a small drive to reach Stock Ghyll Lane. Bear right and walk up the lane past Charlotte Mason College. Pass over a cattle grid, and continue for a short distance to a metal ladder and step stile on the right. Walk up on grass to a ladder stile. Ahead the slope steepens. Eventually the route negotiates some rock slabs to reach a ladder stile over a fence. just beyond is a loose cairn marking the summit of Wansfell Pike, 1,588ft (484m).

There are extensive views circling round from west to north, including Wetherlam, the Scafells, Bowfell, Harrison Stickle, Great Gable, Fairfield, Red Screes, Froswick, Ill Bell and Yoke. Looking southwards, Lake Windermere stretches and curves away.

Given clear conditions the view towards Morecambe Bay continues to be in sight on the descent towards Troutbeck.

Follow a clear path down easier slopes to reach a gate, with a sign exhorting visitors to keep to the designated way. Continue for a few paces to a gate, stile and footpath sign. Bear right down the track, Nanny Lane, to reach a gate and step stile. Proceed with pleasant grass verges and a forward view of the impressive undulating Froswick, Ill Bell and Yoke ridge. After a sharp bend, the track is bordered on the right by hawthorn, holly and sycamore. The stony way descends to a small gate; it swings between farm buildings, with a warm welcome from friendly dogs.

Turn left, and walk along the road for a little way to the lane turning down to the Mortal Man Hotel.

Alternative Route:
Ambleside to Troutbeck

Highest elevation	804ft (245m)
Height of ascent	738ft (225m)
Distance	3½ miles (5.6 km)

Continue along Lake Road and then slant left on Old Lake Road. Pass Blue Hill Road and Fisherbeck Park Lane, bearing left up Skelghyll Lane with a bridleway pointing to Jenkin Crag, Skelghyll and Troutbeck. The way overlooks Hayes Garden Centre with views to the head of Windermere. The immediate area of Skelghyll Woods, carpeted with bluebells in springtime, is a fine fellside tract of mature beech, sycamore and ash. Pass a footpath sign and follow the track as it swings round and crosses Stencher Brook.

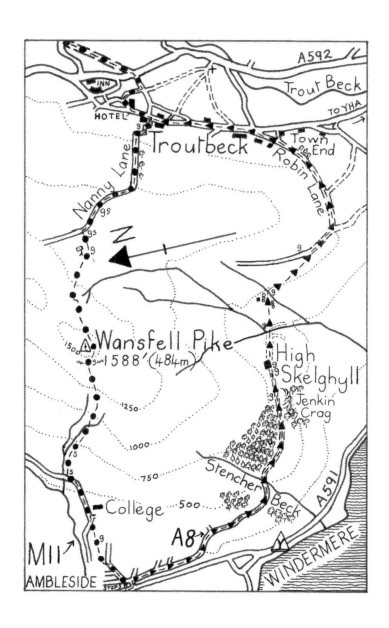

The track continues to climb through lovely woodland of oak, beech, pine and birch. It is well worth deviating for a few yards to the right to Jenkin Crag. The platform of volcanic rock is a splendid vantage point looking out across the lake to the surrounding fells. This is a joyous wild rock garden, with soft grass, ferns, mosses, bluebells, wood anemones, violets and sweet bird song; a very suitable place for a *lozzick* (translation: a snooze or a rest). This is an excellent idea if you are only going as far as Troutbeck.

Regain the path and proceed to a gate at the edge of the wood. The track continues through close-cropped grassy pastures, very reminiscent of alpine meadows. The low, whitewashed farm of High Skelghyll fits perfectly into its surroundings as though grown up with nature herself. Walk through a gate into an outer yard, then pass through another gate and out onto a metalled lane. Cross the bridge and turn left through a wicket gate signposted Troutbeck. The way climbs up gradually, passing a ruined barn, and enters a short walled section. Cross a stream to a kissing gate and climb gently to another gate. A track, the Hundreds Road, comes in from the left, and the way continues to pass some stone steps leading up to a viewpoint – Pillar indicated on OS map. Pass a track going off to the right, and on to a second track turning off in the same direction.*

Accommodation Note

Walkers bound for Windermere Youth Hostel, Bridge Lane, Troutbeck, should bear right at this point. Descend steeply to a lane. Turn left and then a right fork to join the road, Bridge Lane. Turn right.

Continue ahead along Robin Lane, which becomes a leafy shaded track, passing Rose Cottage and two other cottages. The dwellings are fine examples of local vernacular architecture. Bear left on joining the road by Troutbeck Post Office. Refreshments are available here, such as ice cream, minerals and cups of tea. For those requiring stronger beverages, continue for a short distance along the road to the Mortal Man Hotel.

Main Route:
Troutbeck to Askham

The journey from Ambleside to Askham can be shortened by using accommodation at Troutbeck. The village lies on the old packhorse trail from Ambleside to Kentmere. It is little more than a series of

Highest elevation	High Street Summit 2,717ft (828m)
Height of ascent	2,775ft (845m)
Distance	15¼ miles (24.4 km)

small settlements and farms lining a mile of narrow road, from Town Head at the northern end to Town End in the south. A number of wells were built by the Dawson family, with each one serving a particular hamlet. For example, just below the junction of Nanny Lane and Bridge Lane is a well dedicated to St Margaret. There are some fine examples of local domestic architecture, houses, bank barns and a well-preserved spinning gallery. The village is a pleasing mixture of slate, stone and white-painted exteriors.

A historical building such as Townend is an exceptional example of Lake District life of past centuries. Townend was originally a wealthy yeoman's house built about 1626. It contains hand-made carved oak furniture and panelling, books, oil lamps, papers, pictures, and fascinating domestic implements accumulated by the Browne family. The house was lived in by members of the family until 1943; it is now under the guardianship of the National Trust and is open to the public.

The Mortal Man Hotel, on the site of a seventeenth-century inn, is renowned for fine views over the valley and for its unusual sign board:

> *O mortal man that lives by bread,*
> *What is it makes thy nose so red?*
> *Thou silly fool that looks so pale.*
> *'Tis drinking Sally Birkett's ale.*

Try it to the tune of 'Tannenbaum' (or 'The Red Flag'!)

From the Mortal Man descend the little lane that swings round behind the hotel, bear left at the bottom of the slope and continue to the main road. Go straight across and follow the bridleway; it is a verdant wild-flowered snicket, the way bordered by lush hedges of blackthorn and hazel, and perfumed by the odour of wild garlic. Join the metalled lane, Ing Lane, and walk along this level stretch to cross Ing Bridge. Pass a barn on the left, and through a metal gate across the lane. Beyond Hagg Bridge a footpath sign on the right indicates

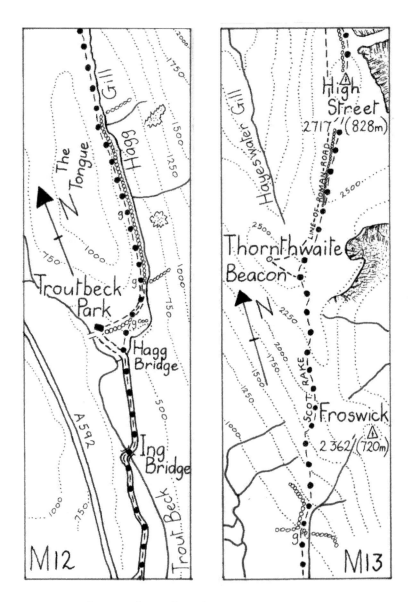

the way across the meadow. The whitewashed farm of Troutbeck Park lies slightly to the left in front, as the path climbs gradually to a footpath sign and a kissing gate.

Follow the track to the right along a pleasant open route above the beck Hagg Gill. Two more gates are encountered with old quarry workings on the right, before a metal gate is reached by the side of a small shattered ash tree. The accompanying wall on the right now veers away with a clear view up to the head of the valley and the steepening hillsides. There are several thorn trees dotted about in the vicinity. Cross a small watercourse, and aim for the left-hand comer of a wall in front to a gate by the beck. Proceed ahead up the slope, reaching a groove in the fellside. This is Scot Rake, which is the line of the Roman road over High Street.

Looking back, there are fine views to Wansfell, Lake Windermere and the Coniston Fells. Continue the gradual climb amidst grassy surroundings to reach the Froswick, Ill Bell ridge. If time is available, the ascent of Thornthwaite Crag is a further option. Bear left along the ridge to a wall, and then follow it along to the distinctive tall column of stones marking the summit. From this point it is necessary to walk east and then in a north-east direction to rejoin the main route.

Otherwise, on attaining the ridge above Scot Rake, walk north-north-east followed by a bearing of north-east. The clear path traces the line of the Roman road and bypasses the summit of High Street; it commands a beautiful aspect westwards to Hayeswater and beyond to Place Fell and Ullswater.

However, the main route keeps in step with the wall directly to the summit of High Street, 2717ft (828m). Its top is marked by an OS survey column.

High Street
Before the coming of the Romans, early Britons had travelled across the long upland ridge of the High Street range to avoid the thickly forested, swampy valleys. They also attached great importance to the moors at the northern end of the ridge, for this area is noted for its burial cairns, stone circles and standing stones. Roman surveyors utilized this route as it stood on the direct line from the fort at Brocavum (Brougham) towards Troutbeck Park, probably with connections to Alauna (Watercrook) and Galava (Ambleside). Roman engineers laid down this unusual road across wild countryside for the movement of infantry and pack ponies, not, as it is often thought, for wheeled traffic. The road varies in character at some points from a distinct agger, or embankment, through terraceways to hollow ways.

Much later in time, the breezy top of High Street rang with the

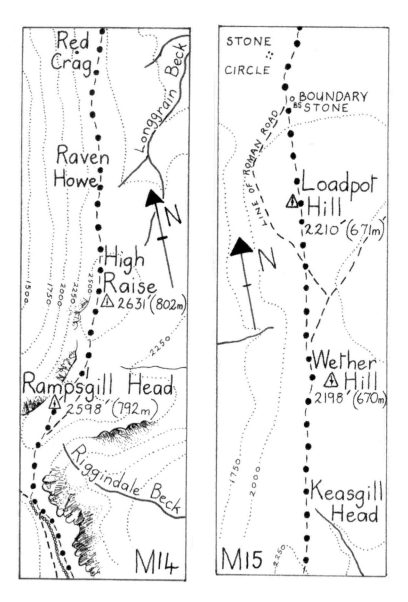

laughter, shouts and cries of local shepherds, who assembled there
to identify stray sheep. This gathering developed into wrestling,
jumping and horse-racing contests. Barrels of ale were taken up there
to fortify the contestants and spectators. The summit area of High

Street is still marked as Racecourse Hill on the 1:25000 OS maps.

High Street's summit is wide and grassy, but its eastern flank falls away in severe crags, which encompass the Lake District's deepest tarn, Blea Water. On clear days the views are exceptional, from the Eden Valley to the high line of the distant Pennines and the Howgill Fells, round to the full extent of the Helvellyn Range. It is an easy matter to follow the wall along the escarpment down to the col at the Straits of Riggindale. There is an impressive view down deserted Riggindale towards Haweswater. This long, narrow valley is bordered by the precipitous Long Stile, Rough Crag ridge and the steep scree slopes of Kidsty Pike. Golden eagles are once again nesting in the valley crags, and are carefully watched over by protective wardens.

The lower path following the line of the Roman road meets the wall at a gateway. Accompany the wall for a few paces to a point where the path diverges. Bear right, walk to the top of the fell, and proceed on a northerly bearing to reach the small cairn marking the summit of Rampsgill Head, 2,598ft (792m). A more prominent pile of stones stands on the lip of the north-west crags. (NOTE: In misty conditions walk on a north-north-east bearing from Rampsgill Head to High Raise. Then follow a bearing of north-north-east to Wether Hill, and head in the same direction to Loadpot Hill.)

The route continues on grass to High Raise, where the steep western slopes fall abruptly to Ramps Gill. This lonely valley lies within the confines of Martindale Deer Forest, where there are no public rights of way.

The summit of High Raise, 2,631ft (802m), is crowned with a large number of stones, and furnished with a sizeable cairn and wind shelter. The subsidiary top of Low Raise lies half a mile slightly north of east capped by a burial cairn. Proceed to a section between a wall on the right and a fence on the left. Some parts are deeply eroded, other areas mushy with ill-drained peat. East of Raven Howe, a network of streams gradually coalesce to form the lively Measand Beck which flows into Haweswater. The wall and fence now widen apart and the small Redcrag Tam comes into sight.

It is now lovely grassy walking underfoot with a distant view of Ullswater. The fence on the left slants further away down the slope, and a wall appears, only to slink away in the same direction. The way descends a little to Keasgill Head; then climbs gradually to a rounded grassy mound followed by a little depression, and continues on to another grassy mound sporting a small cairn. This is the summit of

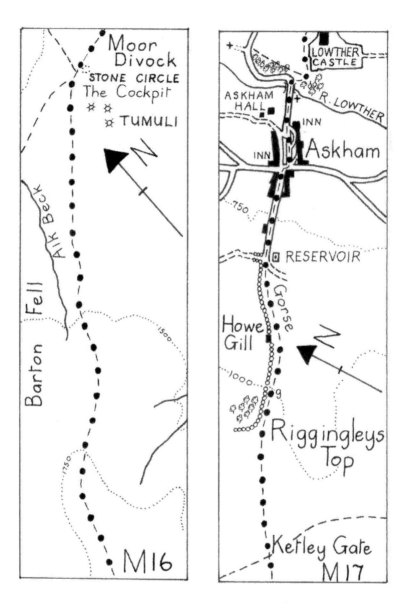

Wether Hill, 2,198 ft (670 m). From this point the view takes in the firm outline of the Pennines and the prominent Helvellyn and Fairfield fells. Looking north-west there is a two-part aspect of Ullswater. Descend a little, and then climb steadily to pass the scant remains of a chimney belonging to Lowther House, a former shooting lodge. There is nothing else of the building to be seen; a great pity, for it would have made an excellent location for a mountain bothy on the Ravenber route. Proceed to a boundary stone cum cairn and an OS survey column, No. 10789, marking the summit of Loadpot Hill, 2,201ft (671m). Again, the eye is drawn to the splendid crests of the Helvellyn range, and across the Eden Valley to the bulk of Cross Fell and other Pennine tops.

Friends of Roman roads should bear in mind that in the vicinity of Loadpot Hill the line of the old route terraces round the western slope before resuming its north-north-east course.

Proceed directly ahead over grass, passing a cairn, and descend to regain the line of the Roman road at Lambert Lad (BS). The hill slopes are now falling away with a wide open vista of grassy fells. Here and there are shaggy black ponies to keep you company. A standing stone with several recumbent stones is passed on the way. At GR 462 200, ignore the path to Arthur's Pike, and continue to descend gradually with several fenced-off plots to the right. Further on to the left is a larger fenced-off mound – a reservoir.

Village of Askham

The going is now delightful over soft springy turf. Bear right to a stone circle marked on the OS map as the Cockpit.

On the wide exposed plateau of Moor Divock is a complex of five small stone circles, ring cairns, avenues and barrows. The whole group is spread out along a stretch of moorland, and was used as a family cemetery over several generations in the Mid Bronze Age. Parallel lines of stones connect the small circles. None of the stone circles is more than 25ft (7.6m) in diameter, and one excavated in 1866 contained a Yorkshire food vessel.

Walk ahead for a short distance to meet a boggy section. Don't give up now, but you have a choice – go through it or through it! Pass an area of shake holes, back on the limestone, to reach an important track junction at Ketley Gate. Note the small standing stone to the left. The signpost carries the following information: PB Askham, PB Pooley Bridge, PB Howtown, PB Helton. Follow the clear grassy track ahead for a short distance, then slant to the right on a north-north-east bearing, and aim for Riggingleys Top.

Walk towards a small, almost square copse of trees, on lovely close-cropped turf in an area of limestone pavement. Descend slightly to a gate in a wall, and continue down the meadow. Go past the barn, Howe Gill, and an extensive patch of gorse to join a clear track. After passing a farm and a cattle grid, descend on a tarmac surface between wide grass verges into the village of Askham.

4. Askham to Dufton

Map	OS 1:25000 Outdoor Leisure, English Lakes (NE) 5; OS 1:25000 Outdoor Leisure, Howgill Fells and Upper Eden Valley, Sheet 19
Highest elevation	Highcross Wood, Newtown 787ft (240m)
Height of ascent	1,050ft (320m)
Distance	16¾ miles (26.8 km)
Terrain	A walk through farming country of the Eden Valley; an undulating landscape of pastures, streams, hedgerows and woodland. Quiet villages with ancient churches

ASKHAM, 'the settlement of the ash trees', is a well-appointed place and very appealing to look at; it has long laid claim to be the prettiest village in the district. There are a fine number of attractive stone dwellings of the seventeenth and eighteenth centuries. These houses and cottages, set at interesting angles, are white and colour-washed, with differently coloured door and window mouldings. Spreading out before them are mature tree-bordered wide grass verges, splashed with the colour of snowdrops, crocuses and daffodils during springtime. The village has two inns, and accommodation may be obtained at the Queen's Head and at the Punchbowl.

Askham Hall is the ancient manor house of the Lowther Estate. The Hall belonged to the Sandford family from 1375 until 1680, and the massive pele tower and other adjoining parts are of the fourteenth century. The Hall, which has been the seat of the Earl of Lonsdale since the dismantling of Lowther Castle, was converted in the late seventeenth or early eighteenth century; it is a spacious house with three irregular wings round an oblong courtyard. As with many border peles, the Hall still retains its feature of tunnel vaulting at ground level.

Close by Askham Bridge is the village church of St Peter, built in 1832 on the site of an older building. Its plain simple interior contains no stained glass, but it has a much older south transept, which for a long time was the chapel of the Sandfords. The building houses an Elizabethan tomb chest and a round-headed plain font, dated 1661.

The church of St Michael is set back from the road in a magnificent situation high above the river; its monuments to the Lowther family and the Earls of Lonsdale are of much interest. In the churchyard is the Lowther Mausoleum, circa 1857. This strange looking structure contains the monument to William, Earl of Lonsdale. The seated white figure is a picture of loneliness, and rather sad. Perhaps he would have preferred to gaze out across the lovely estate parkland.

As you descend the main street and pass the Punchbowl Inn, look to the left through the gateway to Askham Hall. Beyond its high stone wall there are fine examples of topiary to be seen in front of the house, and in February the borders are carpeted with drifts of snowdrops.

Beyond the Hall, the road dips down to the gracefully arched Askham Bridge spanning the wide rocky bed of the River Lowther. St Peter's Church, on the right, lies in a sylvan setting on the banks of the river. As the road swings left beneath a steep wooded bank, head for the right-hand end of the bridge, and take the path which climbs up through the trees overlooking the river.

NOTE: There is no recorded right of way along this short length of path, although it looks an obvious link into the rights of way network, ie: FP 34200 and RP 342008, and is marked FP on the 1916 OS map. There is a possibility that this link may be dedicated as a public footpath, or at least a permitted route.

If permission is not granted, the alternative is to walk up the road, and take the right of way, FP 342006, opposite the drive to St Michael's Church. Walk through Castlesteads Plantation to meet the route in question at the top of the wooded slope. This will add a good half a mile on to the distance from Askham to Dufton.

Bear left and walk to meet the high wall surrounding Lowther Castle. Look for an almost secret doorway on the right, all be-creepered and wreathed in ivy. Fluted columns line the entrance which is headed by a decorated pediment. What tales could that doorway tell? Perhaps it was an entrance to a secret garden, a location for trysts and assignations.

A view opens up across the parkland. Walk alongside the railings and soon the facade of Lowther Castle comes into sight. Now a hollow shell, this mighty Gothic-style building was begun in 1806 and completed in 1811. The original building stood on an adjacent site; it was occupied by the Lowthers from the reign of Henry II, pulled down in 1685, rebuilt, and burned down in 1720. From 1880 to 1944, the title 'Earl of Lonsdale' was held by Hugh; a great sportsman who left the famous Lonsdale belts for boxing. His favourite colour was yellow – which he used for servants' livery, cars, and also as the colour of the Automobile Association of which he was the first president. The present dilapidated building exhibits a wonderfully varied skyline, an array of symmetrical, turreted and embattled shapes. As you stand in front of the massive gatehouse, it is no use expecting a liveried footman to appear with a silver tea service. Forget it; you should have a vacuum flask to sustain your needs.

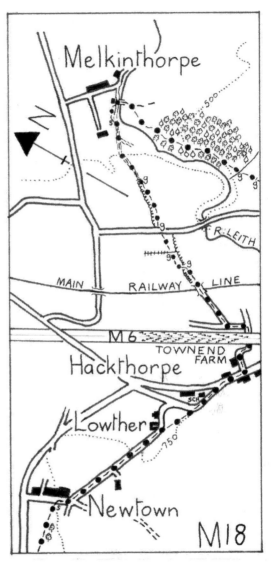

From the gatehouse an avenue of fine trees stretches away across the park. All is not quiet, as the constant drone of traffic from the nearby M6 is easily detected. Walk ahead to a gate and follow a line of trees that lead up to a row of dwellings called Newtown. The right of way arrives at a ladder stile, and goes between two rather forlorn looking stone gateposts to reach the road. Newtown was an early effort at town planning, when John Lowther decided to replace the existing Lowther village.

Turn right, passing the entrance to the estate sawmill, as the road swings sharp left. There is about three quarters of a mile to walk along this quiet road, but take heart, a welcoming sign appears – TEA ROOM and LAKELAND BIRD GARDEN. As the tarmac strip gently descends, a distant view of the Pennines will, no doubt, put a spring in your step. Lowther village, on the left, is an attractive design of two closes, plus water pump and trough; it was built in 1765-73 by James Adam. Directly in front, on the angle of the sharp bend, is a step stile in the wall followed by a short stretch of footpath. Pass an entrance to the Lowther Adventure Park on the right. On the opposite side of the road is a primary school football pitch, so tiny that the goalkeepers are probably the top scorers.

Hackthorpe (from Old Norse, Haki's Thorp, meaning Haki's settlement or farm), a village divided by the A6, lies in undoubted Lowther country. Even the inn is named after the famous family, while the village school has the Lowther shield cut into the sandstone. At the south end of the village stands Hackthorpe Hall, an attractive white-washed Jacobean farmhouse with mullioned windows. The artist Jacob Thompson lived in the village, in a cottage called 'The Hermitage', during the latter years of his life.

Cross the main road, and just past the post office turn left down a farm track. Pass under the motorway bearing left to walk parallel with it, before, thankfully, turning away to the right down to a sandstone bridge crossing the main railway line. At this point the track ends, so proceed ahead along the right-hand side of the hedge. The line of the path is not clear on the ground, but where the hedge bends slightly go through a gate to the other side, and aim for a gate in front. Now walk down the field to a gate at the bottom with power lines crossing overhead. Turn left along Waterfalls Road for a few yards to a gate on the right. Follow the hedge to a gate, and continue down a sunken grassy way meeting some waterlogged sections. Some farm buildings appear on the left, and at a small fenced-off area of the track, go left through a gate and follow the hedgerow down the field. Turn right by the first dwelling on the edge of Melkinthorpe, and cross the footbridge directly ahead over the River Leith. Continue for a short distance and bear right at a track junction. The PB leads through Melkinthorpe Wood, which is a pleasant tract of mixed woodland

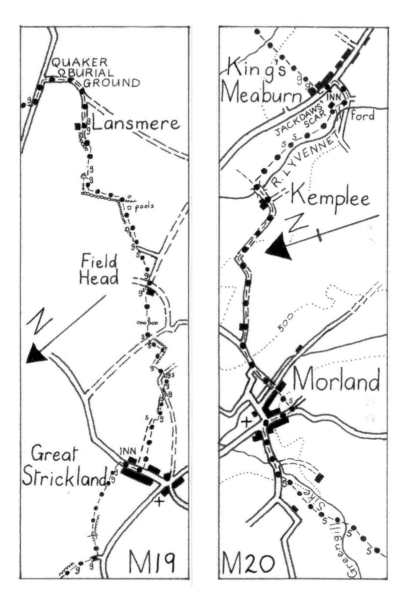

containing oak, willow, birch and conifer. The bridleway reaches an area of rhododendrons by a gate. Proceed straight ahead to a gate, and continue with a hedge on the left to another gate. The track then passes through another gate beyond to meet a minor road. On the left, an FP sign indicates the direction of the route to Great Strickland. The land has recently been felled of timber, and the path proceeds diagonally across the cleared area to accompany the left-hand side of a fence to a stile. Enter a field and go on for a few paces to a stile in the hedge on the left. Walk through the fields to a gate before the farm. Pass a barn on the right to another gate, and continue ahead to the road at Great Strickland. Turn right, and walk towards the centre of the village.

Great Strickland (Magna Stirkeland or Styrkeland, from Old English, *styrc*, land or pasture for young bullocks or heifers) is situated in a pleasant, green, entirely agricultural landscape, between the A6 and the River Eden. The villages, hamlets and farmsteads are quiet places served by a network of country lanes, such as Priestclose, Airygill and Maudy. The nature of the countryside is in great contrast to the rough fells and dark crags of central Lakeland. Great Strickland is served by a church, a chapel and a post office; the Strickland Arms provides bed and breakfast accommodation and bar meals. In the recent past, the community won the trophy for Cumbria's (or should it be Westmorland's?) best kept small village. This is a mid-Westmorland haven, where some footpath journeys become voyages of discovery (readers of this guide book will appreciate this statement in the next few pages).

Just a short distance along the road, the existing path, 325001, is indicated by an FP sign, but is subject to a diversion order. The proposed new route will start a little further up the road on the left, and will join with the current route at the far end of a long thin field. The existing route proceeds through a farmyard, continues across a large field to a stile in the right-hand corner, and then bears sharp right round the end of a long thin field. This is the point where the proposed diversion route will link up. Walk to a gate, then left through a stone stile, and along a fence to a stile into Maudy Lane. The lane is actually a track at this point.

Go through a gate and across to another gate on the right. Keep on a diagonal route to another gate and a flimsy stile. Bear left, and follow the semblance of a green track to a gate. Head to the right alongside a fence, then turn left at a wall and accompany it to a stile.

Cross the farm lane, through a couple of wall stiles and up the meadow to Field Head, where the farmyard is entered and exited via three metal gates. Take the right-hand gate on the left beyond the farm, and go diagonally across the field to a stile leading into a lane. Go through a gate, and follow the fence boundary with a few trees and thorn bushes; this in turn becomes a stone wall to a gate near ponds. Turn left and accompany the wall, climbing steadily; then head right and keep alongside the fence to a lone ash tree and a gate. Proceed across a small field to a gate and keep by the fence which is succeeded by a wall.

The route heads towards Lansmere Farm and continues through the farmyard and two gates, to become a wide clear track. Off to the right, a stile gives access to the site of a Quaker Burial Ground. The tree-girt and walled enclosure is a secluded, well cared-for spot, and contains a number of ancient gravestones. Of particular interest is a stone with an inscription in Latin. This is supported by a tablet carrying an English translation, with both stones sheltered under a canopy.

When the track meets the road, turn left, and walk for a few yards to a gate on the right, with a FP sign to Morland. Descend gently towards a gate on the left, across to a stile, and down to the corner of the field near a stream gully. From the stile cross Greengill Sike, climb up the opposite bank to follow a hedge to a couple of stiles. Bear right round a depression, which is being used as a tip, to cross a wire fence, with a yellow marker arrow on a nearby tree. Morland village now comes into view. There is a deep gully on the right with newly-planted trees, but beyond the stream is another tip, with concrete, tins, blue plastic bags and old tyres. Descend to an FP sign and a large slab of stone through a stone wall. Walk up the road into Morland village.

If there is time to spare, the great attraction here is the ancient parish church of St Laurence. This eleventh-century church, which has a number of Saxon features, is an attractive building with a red sandstone tower capped by a pretty lead spire. The village is situated in the Vale of Lyvennet, and the surrounding area consists of pleasant pastures sheltered by copses of woodland. The village stream, Morland Beck, accompanies the appropriately named Water Street; its tranquil unspoiled appearance is enhanced by a long, white-painted footbridge and its quota of contented ducks. For refreshment and relaxation, the Crown Inn is located in the village square.

Proceed past Hill Top House to a FP sign on the left. Descend behind houses, over a small ladder stile, between hedges to stone steps, and into a cobbled yard alongside the former King's Arms Inn. Cross over the footbridge, and walk straight ahead up the road to a PB sign on the right. This is a good wide track, suitable for a fast pace, between hedges and trees through pleasant open countryside. At Kemplee Farm, a PF sign indicates the way to Bolton. Cross Chapel

Bridge over the River Lyvennet and bear right along the river bank. The leafy banks harbour a covering of primroses, celandines, daisies, violets and forget-me-nots. Proceed through the meadow by a strip of newly planted trees. Small rock outcrops appear to the left as the path approaches a stile, quickly followed by another one. Enter Barnholme Wood to the sound of the river tumbling over its rocky bed; here and there celandines and bluebells carpet the woodland ground. Negotiate a stile, and continue through a delightful meadow with the impressive Jackdaws' Scar, complete with real jackdaws, rising vertically from the valley floor. Walk along the track, passing a white-painted cottage and two stone gate pillars. To the right the lane fords the river which is also crossed by a long footbridge.

Turn left and walk up the road, bearing left at the top into Kings Meaburn. The cottages of this small rural community line the single street, which also includes a chapel and the White Horse Inn. The settlement gets its name from an early ownership by the Crown, which was taken from the Lord of the Manor, Sir Hugh Morville, for his part in the murder of Thomas á Becket.

Just beyond the inn, by Smith House, an FP sign on the right indicates the way to Bolton. Go through two gates, one at the rear of the building, and another that leads into a long narrow field. Descend gently to some wooden planking across a stream and walk up to a gate. Follow the fence and hedge on the right-hand side, go through a gate and then keep to the left-hand side of a plantation. Proceed through the patch of woodland, bearing slightly left to a fence. During my initial wanderings, there was no stile at this point, only a primitive cover over barbed wire and a wobbly stone to stand on.

Continue along the right-hand side of a hedge to a gate, and accompany the hedge beyond to a stile in a stone wall. Follow the hedge to a corner, and a stone gap stile with a wooden fence in front. At this point, the village of Bolton comes into view. Walk diagonally across to a step stile near a metal water trough, and head down the fence to a gate. Cross a stream by means of two large stones, marked FB on the map, and aim slightly left to a hedge gap with a stone step. Proceed up the hedgeside to a corner exit through a small gate, and go on up the track ahead to a metal gate. Continue past the farm to another gate, and on to meet the road. An FP sign points towards Kings Meaburn.

The village of Bolton lies high on the west bank of the River Eden. An important link road from the A66 crosses the river by means of

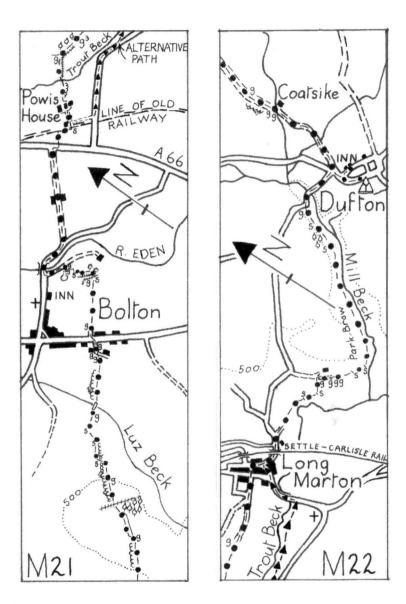

the fine red-sandstone Bolton Bridge. All Saints Church contains many Norman features, such as the base of the tower, two doorways, the nave and chancel. The bell turret dates from the seventeenth century. There is an effigy of a praying woman outside the church near to the porch, and an ancient sixteenth-century wooden chest inside the building. Great credit is due to the local people who devote such loving care on their beautiful parish church.

Just across the road from the entrance to the churchyard is the New Crown Inn. Return to GR NY 6395 2290.

Cross the road to an FP sign indicating Bolton Mill, FP 308005. Enter a small trackway to a gate, and then on for a few paces to a stile. Walk down the field towards a simple step stile which lies down-fence from the gate. Bear up left through a small area of young trees, and continue to follow the hedgerow to the left with an elevated view across the valley. A faint path descends alongside a fence, past gorse bushes, to a stile. Proceed for a few yards to a stile on the right, go on for a few paces in the field, and then bear left around the sewage works perimeter fence to a gate.

NOTE: There has been building work on the sewage site, and the line of the path from the gate does not seem clear. The right of way should follow the hedgerow straight ahead, but there is an unstiled fence across the route. This can be climbed, but an alternative is to turn down the works track to a gate, turn left and walk along the metalled lane to Bolton Bridge. There, the FP sign is *in situ*, pointing the way beyond a fastened-up gate along the line of the hedgerow.

Walk over the fine twin-arched Bolton Bridge, dated 1870, then along the road for a short distance, and turn left on the BW to Redlands Bank Farm. The track climbs gently and in a straight line to meet the A66. Bear right and walk a few paces along the verge; it's time to gather yourself together for a quick dash across to the other side of this busy main road. An FP sign indicates the way to Long Marton. The path through the field actually crosses the corner edge of a Roman camp. A concrete ladder stile leads on to the old railway track bed. Turn right and walk for a few steps to a bungalow.

Take the stile on the left and walk down the farm drive to Powis House.

Approach the farm, and continue round the building on the right, to meet the corner of the hedge on the far side. Walk along the left-hand side of the hedge, then descend left to the side of Trout Beck. Cross over the beck on a splendid new footbridge, and continue up the field on the left-hand side of the fence to a gate. Turn right passing a conifer plantation to a gate. The way continues through two more metal gates and below a copse of pines and oaks, to a point where the track swings off to the left. Keep slightly to the right, and walk along the right-hand side of the fence in front to a wooden gate. A track now leads to a lane which continues as a metalled surface, passing a small housing development and on into the centre of Long Marton. Turn right at the road junction, and walk towards the stone building at the fork in the road.

There is an alternative which involves some road walking. After leaving the old railway track bed near to Powis House, walk down the farm drive to the road. Turn left and proceed to a FB sign situated just beyond the bend in the road. Follow the path, which also had obstructions and where new stiles have now been installed, along the top of the stream bank. Continue along the beckside to the road. Turn left and walk up the road into Long Marton.

Long Marton (from Old English, Mere-tun or Maer-tun, 'tun by a lake', or 'the farmstead with a pool') has a quiet main street with buildings on both sides of the road, and is set in the heart of farming country. The parish of Long Marton stretches up to the moorland heights of the Pennines, which dominate the background, and are a strong influence in the landscape.

A good number of houses are built of the local red sandstone, as is the parish church of St Margaret and St James, which is situated a little distance to the south of the village. This lovely, interesting building has an impressive twelfth-century tower; and among its treasures are two sets of ancient carved stones, probably Saxon in origin. The one above the south doorway is a tympanum depicting a winged ox in a boat, a dragon, and a winged shield charged with a cross. The other tympanum, over the original west doorway, is carved with a dragon, merman, club and cross. The north-east corner of the graveyard contains several graves of gypsies who died whilst attending the Appleby Horse Fair. This well-known event is still held every June.

The spectacular Settle-Carlisle railway runs through the village. It was the last of the great main lines to Scotland, and built due to the unfriendly rivalry between the Midland Railway Company and the London and North West Railway Company. The former decided to construct its own route north, and engineers surveyed the line, taking a straight course following the Ribble and Eden rivers. It was difficult terrain, and the engineers had great problems with cuttings, bridges and tunnels. Conditions were poor, and accidents, disease, drunkenness and misery were facts of life in the construction camps. The 72 miles (115km) between Settle and Carlisle is, without doubt, the most scenic railway journey in England. A battle by railway enthusiasts prevented the closure of this magnificently engineered line, which now serves as a good tourist attraction in the Eden Valley. However, I would ask the question, 'Why were Long Marton's station platforms taken away?' The village is very useful as a base for good walking in the Eden Valley and on the nearby Pennines.

Bear left along the Dufton road, noting the fine stone building on the corner. This is the Parish Institute, built in 1893 with the facilities of a games room, reading room and assembly room. Pass under the railway bridge, and descend to a row of railway cottages with a fine view of Dufton Pike ahead. Head to the right at an FP sign down a grassy lane to a gate. Cross the meadow to another gate, aim for the bend in the stream and on to a stile.

Continue across a small field to a stile, bear left and walk up the boundary hedge to reach a gate. Turn right along a track, and pass below Park Farm, through two gates, into a walled enclosure and on to a gate. Proceed along a track between thorn bushes to another gate. Cross a narrow meadow and another intake field to reach a stile. Aim ahead for the left-hand comer of the pasture to a stile close to the beck. The bank away to the left is a pleasant sight when covered in bluebells and primroses. Walk along this charming little valley of Mill Beck under the slopes of Park Brow; there is the soft gurgling of clear water in idyllic surroundings. This section of the Ravenber route is in great contrast to the bare Pennine slopes to be met on the next stage of the journey. Head for the corner of the hedge by the beck, which looks a good trout stream, to a stile and an old plank. Proceed to a gate in front, but do not cross the beck on the rickety bridge.

The valley narrows to a path on the bankside above the beck, and heads for a step stile in a wall and a small conifer plantation. Continue high above the beck to a stile, and go between a stream and a stagnant pond. Follow a wall to a gate and FP sign; turn right, walk over Mill Bridge and up the road to Dufton.

5. Dufton to Garrigill

Map	OS 1:25000 Outdoor Leisure, Howgill Fells and Upper Eden Valley, Sheet 19; OS 1:25000 Outdoor Leisure, North Pennines, Teesdale and Weardale, Sheet 31
Highest elevation	Knock Fell 2,605ft (794m)
Height of ascent	2,415ft (736m)
Distance	15 miles (24km)
Terrain	Well defined route, grassy, some peat and boulders. Remote moorland, faint path initially but soon clear on ground. Good waymarked route through pleasant valley pasture

DUFTON (Dove Farm) is a pleasantly situated village at the foot of the eastern fellsides in the Eden Valley. The tree-fringed green is bordered by an attractive collection of houses, many built in the local red sandstone, and dating from the seventeenth to the nineteenth centuries. For many Pennine Way walkers on the long-distance trek from Edale to Kirk Yetholm, the sight of this quiet peaceful place is a welcome relief after the bleak moorland crossing from Teesdale.

The village contains the Stag Inn, a post office cum shop, the village hall built in 1911, and a youth hostel. This is a large stone house on the green. The former Wesleyan chapel, now a private house, has a niche on an external wall with the broken-nosed figure of John Wesley.

One of the objects of attention, a magnet particularly for photographers, is the splendid sandstone fountain which stands on the green. The London Lead Mining Company, which commenced mining operations in the Dufton area in the nineteenth century, benefited the village. There were typhus epidemics in Teesdale in 1818 and 1830, and at the outbreak of cholera in 1849 the company decided to overhaul all water supplies; considerable sums of money were spent on providing reservoirs and piped water supplies. The company's aim was to maintain a healthy, well-housed and sober labour force.

The church of St Cuthbert, a plain building with a gallery, is set a short distance out of the village; it was rebuilt in 1784, and restored in 1853, but has records that go back to 1292. Tradition relates that it was one of the places where monks from Lindisfarne rested with the body of St Cuthbert, as they fled from the depredations of the Vikings.

It is interesting to note the arrangement of houses in the fellside villages. Most of them have their backs to the fell, and only a few farms lie on the eastern slopes. This is due to the Helm Wind, a peculiarly parochial blast that operates in these parts. The wind relies on a certain set of circumstances for its operation, and is likely to occur in winter and spring. An easterly airstream ascends the gradual slope of the Pennines to Cross Fell and its neighbouring summits, where it is cooled and becomes quite dense. The clouds, called the Helm Cap, build up above the heights, and because the air in the valley below is warmer, the cold wind rushes violently down the western escarpment with a weird moaning noise. Fellside villages feel the full force of its turbulence; it can uproot trees, destroy crops and remove roofing tiles.

Although the village itself is so small Dufton parish covers an extensive area, and is one of the largest in England. It stretches over the Pennine watershed to the River Tees, from lush pastures, woods and farmland to the vast inhospitable heather and peaty moorlands.

Pennine Geology

The geology of an area ultimately determines the landscape features. In the north of England the Pennine uplands are formed almost entirely from rocks classified by geologists as belonging to the Carboniferous Period. Back in earliest prehistory, even before recognizable life-forms had evolved, rocks were formed in ancient oceans and seas. These early rocks, called Pre-Cambrian, were successively squeezed and folded into mountain ranges, then worn down again over a period of many millions of years. This is the bedrock, the ancient worn-down land surface on which the sediments of the Carboniferous Period were deposited. Great quantities of these sediments were brought down by rivers and streams, to accumulate on the newly-submerged sea bed some 250 to 330 million years ago.

Further south, the sediments were laid down in clearer waters, which led to the formation of the Great Scar limestone, as is found in the Craven area of Yorkshire. Deposits of muds and sands also collected in the shallower lagoons and river estuaries to form alternate bands of shale, sandstone and limestone, such as in the Wensleydale district of Yorkshire. Later, vast quantities of sands and muds from great northern rivers were deposited to become millstone grit; these coarse grits are the rocks which form most of the high ridges and hill summits between the dales.

At the end of the Carboniferous Period, great earth movements resulted in mountain building, and the pushing up of the Pennine chain. During this activity, vast quantities of molten rock entered the joints and fissures of the existing strata. This solidified as a hard, distinctive quartz dolerite rock, found in places such as High Cup Nick, Cauldron Snout, Peel Crags on the Roman Wall and the Farne Islands. The faults in the strata were also infilled by minerals, some of which have been at various times of high economic value: ores of lead with silver, zinc and iron, accompanied by gangue, or non-metallic minerals of quartz, calcite, barytes and fluorspar.

Main Route

From the north-west corner of the village descend on the road, and follow the hedged track on the right to Coatsike Farm, with a fine view of Dufton Pike. Proceed through a gate into the farmyard and across to another gate. The track, Hurning Lane, continues between tall hedges to a gate, and on to two sets of step stiles across field access tracks. A watercourse running down the centre creates a boggy section just before two more step stiles. Go through a gate, and the track narrows with a wall to the left and a hedge to the right; it continues between walls to the derelict, although characterful, farm building of Halsteads.

The ground now opens out, with meadows on either side of the track, then descends to cross the tree-fringed Great Rundale Beck. Pass through a wall stile and cross the stream on stone slabs, with a view of the giant white sphere on Great Dun Fell. Climb gradually to a gate and a stone step stile in lovely grassy surroundings. The track swings left across a tiny stream, Small Burn, and climbs up the open fell to become a pathway. Go through a wall stile, then on for a few paces to a step stile over another wall, and cross the footbridge over Swindale Beck.

NOTE: In bad weather conditions, avoiding the summit of Knock Fell, follow the wall northwards. Then continue on a path north-east to meet the service road to Great Dun Fell.

The scene is now a wild one, with the stream flowing rapidly over its bed littered with boulders. Climb up the steep slope, slanting to the right, and follow a cairned path along the rock-covered hillside, gradually becoming a grassy way. From twin cairns, cross the stream issuing from Knock Hush, and aim for the substantial cairn in front with some peaty sections to negotiate. The cairn called Knock Old Man is a well-built squarish structure, with good views to Great Dun Fell and across the Eden Valley. Walk easily to the large pointed summit cairn of Knock Fell, 2,605ft (794m).

The views westward on a clear day from the escarpment edge are supremely expansive. In the farmlands below and beyond the skirts of the hill slopes, there is a patchwork quilt of colours, dark green, emerald, brown, sage and yellow; all shades gradually merging away to the far horizon of purpled Lakeland peaks. Distance gives these familiar and much-loved mountains a touch of unreality, as they stand out in sharp relief in the crisp light of the early morning sun. Drifting clouds occasionally obscure the backcloth of slopes, peaks and ridges, as though to tantalize the watcher, who patiently waits for the mists to pass on and once more reveal the well-known mountain forms. A sudden sharp breeze momentarily jerks the wisps of tough moorland grass into life; it is time to go.

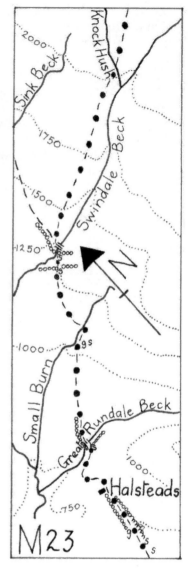

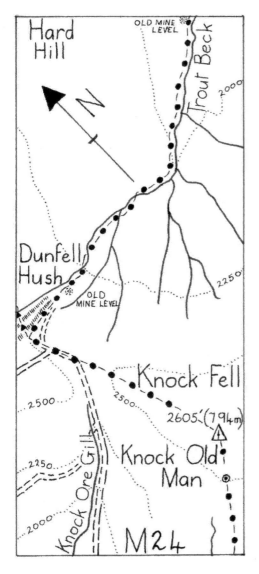

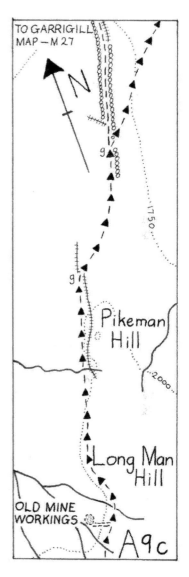

From the summit cairn continue on a northerly bearing along the plateau with peaty and stony sections. Descend slightly across an angular boulder field, and then through a peaty section to another cairn. Follow the line of metal posts in an area of shake holes to meet the Great Dun Fell service road.

Walk ahead on the road for a short distance to a PW sign, and continue climbing, more or less straight on, up to the lip of Dunfell Hush. (Departure point for Alternative Route: Dunfell Hush to Garrigill via Cross Fell; see p.91).

On the lip of Dunfell Hush turn right at a cairn, and notice a view of Cow Green Reservoir in the distance.

Early exploration of ground for mineral veins, particularly lead, meant that the method of hushing was used. On a steep hillside a dam was made to hold back water, and when everything was ready the water was released. The powerful flow tore away the ground material of soil, peat, vegetation and rock. The debris was examined for signs of ore at the foot of the slope as well as in the sides of the hush. These hushes can often be seen in the former lead mining areas of the northern Pennines.

Follow the direction of this impressive-looking trench, through an area of old spoil heaps, to reach a clear grassy track. As the infant tributaries of Trout Beck gradually appear, walk on the left-hand side of the watercourse, then cross over to the right-hand side. The surrounding moorland stretches away as far as the eye can see – a wide landscape and a wide skyscape. From Dunfell Hush the initial mile of descent is on an easterly bearing, and then the beck is followed on a northeasterly bearing. In the beginning the path is a little indistinct on the ground, but it becomes clearer as the beck gets bigger; this is a good example of how quickly a moorland watercourse gathers strength within a short distance.

There are one or two deep pools now. Cross to the left-hand side of the beck at a convenient spot and follow a lovely grassy section. The way continues with some boulder hopping, then on grass again, to become a rough path clinging to the stream bank in an area of mine workings. Just after an elongated spoil heap, look for an almost hidden entrance to a mine adit. The path follows the north bank of Trout Beck, and meets a track going off to the right across a bridge to Moor House. A little further on, the mature stream joins the River Tees at Troutbeck Foot.

The Moor House National Nature Reserve covers nearly 4,000 hectares of moorland; a vast area of blanket peat mosses, heather, bilberry, rough grasses and countless rivulets and watercourses, extending from the Dun Fells towards the River Tees. The leached acid soils give rise to the mat grass, *Nardus*; areas where water is unable to drain away and becomes stagnant produce the vivid green *sphagnum* moss, which creates dangerous patches of bog; the purple moor grass, *Molinia*, flourishes where springs or seepages appear.

This immense peaty tract has many little corners where specialized moorland plants can survive, such as the starry saxifrage, bird's eye primrose, tormentil, grass of Parnassus, cloudberry and cranberry. Shy clumps of mountain pansy mark the sites of overgrown spoil heaps. The peaty, ill-drained moorland covering contains many species of mosses, liverworts and lichens.

Moor House Nature Reserve was the main UK site for the International Biological Programme (1966-71), and became the first British Biosphere Reserve in 1975. Research has been directed to the study of peat, its growth and erosion, moorland management, the effects of sheep grazing, biology of plants and animals, tree establishment and climate.

The track crosses over the River Tees, bearing left with a fine view of its wide bouldery bed, and ascends to an area of mine workings. The tiny stream coming in from the right is the infant river South Tyne, and it is interesting to think that the area is the birthplace of two famous rivers. The stream now follows the track on the left hand side, which varies from tarmac to a gravelly covering. However, a fast pace can be achieved, and the wild surroundings help one to forget the unyielding surface.

The valley gradually deepens and various tracks lead off to old mine workings. The way passes rock outcrops, and descends on a concrete surface to cross a stream with a small gorge on the left. The small collection of farm buildings on the right are important storage areas for animal fodder. Ascend a little and continue along the track to a cattle grid, with the sight of greener pastures beyond a line of wind blasted conifers. There is a cattle grid followed by the derelict building of Dorthgill, and then an old lime kiln, before you meet the country lane that continues into Garrigill. Various notices proclaim a 'Public Bridleway'; 'No Unauthorised Motor Vehicles Beyond This Point to Teeshead'.

Turn right, and descend the hillside on a track which has both metalled and loose sections. Go through two gates and pass the ruined building of Dorthgillfoot on a rough surface. Cross the bouldery river bed on a wooden bridge, with derelict mine buildings upstream along the river bank. Ahead on rising ground lies Tynehead Farm.

Cross over the cattle grid to an FP sign on the left, indicating a public byroad to Yad Moss and its ski tows, and a route down the valley to Ashgill. So, bear left. Walk across the field to a gap in a wall with an arrow marker. Proceed on to a gate, noting the small gorge that has been cut by the river; its bed a mixture of small boulders and bare rock.

About a quarter of a mile downstream from Tynehead is a raised

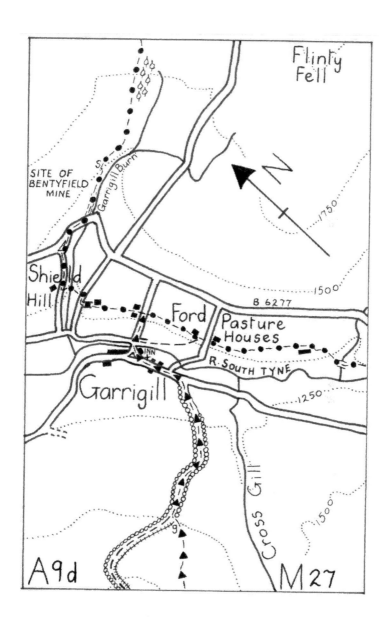

rectangular area believed to be a Roman camp, Chesters. The right of way passes through the site, with the old shafts and debris from the washing process lying between the path and the river; it is thought that the Romans and their slave labour worked the alluvial gravel for lead ore which had a high silver content. In fact, the silver-rich ore was probably washed down the burn from the Clargill Head veins. These veins were later worked by the London Lead Company, and yielded upwards of 43oz of silver per ton of lead.

Keep to the right of Hole House Farm, and proceed through a gap in a fence, passing more mine tips on the right. Walk across a very pleasant riverside pasture to a stile, and descend to cross a stream to a step stile in a wall. Just beyond, a footbridge on the left carries a path to Over Lee House. The track along the river bank passes through delightful surroundings, almost parkland in quality, to reach the FB over Ash Gill. An important looking signpost directs visitors to all major points of the compass. Even though it may be towards the end of the day, and comfortable accommodation awaits the walker, a short detour to view Ashgill Force is recommended. A path leads to a wooded ravine where the water tumbles and cascades over rock steps.

Return from the waterfall on the path that ascends the slope, and accompany the wall to Ashgillside Farm. From here a clear, well-marked route with good stiles continues through pastures, and by the farmsteads of Pasture Houses, Ford and Loaning Head. Ravenber walkers who have booked accommodation in Garrigill village have a choice of short paths, from Ford or Windy Hall or from Loaning Head, for short descents to Garrigill Bridge. The small community of Garrigill, tucked away in the upper part of the South Tyne Valley, is a charming place with stone-built houses grouped round the village green.

There was one charity school in the eighteenth century founded by a legacy in 1685, which specified 'Twenty Shillings a Year to a Schoolmaster at Garrygill, towards his Maintenance; and forty shillings a Year to the said Schoolmaster for teaching six poor Children of the poorest Inhabitants in Garrygill, gratis, till they can read the Bible through, and then others to be put in their stead.'

St John's Church, built in 1790, contains a holy water stoop and an old font. The Redwing Congregational Chapel dates from 1757.

The village is a very welcome sight after the long tramp by Trout Beck and Tynehead, or over the Dun Fells and Cross Fell. NOTE: Return via the lane to Loaning Head on the next day to rejoin the main route.

Otherwise, continue straight ahead through meadows to the derelict farm at Dodbury and beyond to the road. Turn right for a short distance to an FP sign on the left, and descend the steep valley slopes of Garrigill Burn. The route, which has good stiles and waymarkers, crosses the stream on stone slabs, and then ascends the steep slopes on the far side to a step stile and FP sign.

Alternative Route:
Dunfell Hush to Garrigill via Cross Fell
Map A9c, p.85; A9d, p.89

Map	OS 1:25000 Outdoor Leisure, North Pennines, Teesdale and Weardale, Sheet 31
Highest elevation	Cross Fell 2,930ft (893m)
Height of ascent	From Dufton 3,251ft (991m)
Distance	To Garrigill village 14¾ miles (23.6km). To Garrigill Loaning Head; main route 15 miles (24km)

The walk lies over exposed summits and escarpment slopes, with Cross Fell the highest point on the long-distance route. Its austere bleak top is rimmed by a collar of boulders and scree. Originally named Fiends' Fell, it has a nasty trick up its sleeve, being long known as the mixing cauldron for the Helm Wind.

Cross Dunfell Hush, bear left and ascend on grass to the summit of Great Dun Fell, keeping on the eastern side of the 'great golf ball'. Descend to a col and climb grassy slopes to Little Dun Fell.

Descend to Tees Head, where there is a pathway of rock slabs. Ascend to a tall cairn, and continue along the wide grassy plateau to the summit of Cross Fell; with a cross-wall shelter, OS survey column and a litter of cairns.

On a clear day the effort is well worthwhile, for this high watershed commands excellent views, ranging from the superb panorama of Lakeland mountains to the hills of southern Scotland.

Descend stony slopes on a bearing just west of north, becoming north-north-west, to reach a cairned path. Turn right and pass Greg's

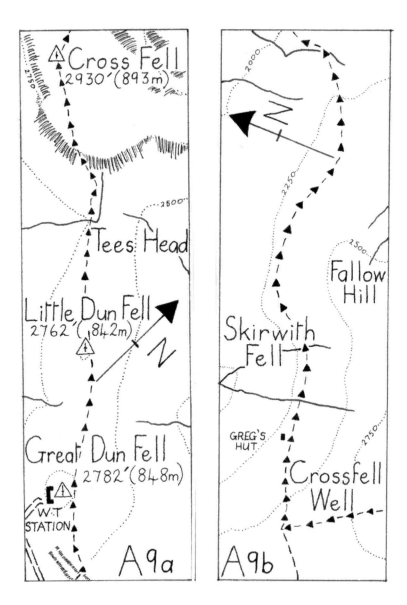

Hut, once a lodging shop at the lead mine, and follow the clear track down to the village of Garrigill.

In order to rejoin the main route, walk over Garrigill Bridge, and up the lane to Loaning Head.

6. Garrigill to Allenheads

Map	OS 1:25000 Outdoor Leisure, North Pennines, Teesdale and Weardale, Sheet 31
Highest elevation	Co. boundary, Coalcleugh 1,913ft (583m)
Height of ascent	1,512ft (4612m)
Distance	11¼ miles (18km) calculated from Garrigill Shield Hill
Terrain	Valley, moorland and high fellside scenery. Some defined and well marked routes. There are some grassy sections underfoot and other conditions of rough moorland vegetation and soft peaty ground

Lead Mining in the Northern Pennines

LEAD MINING FLOURISHED in the eighteenth and nineteenth centuries amongst the most northerly and highest part of the Pennine Hills. The main centre of operations was roughly the area where the counties of Cumbria, Northumberland and Durham meet, drained by the main rivers, the Tees, the South Tyne, the West and East Allen, the Wear and the Derwent. This wild and beautiful expanse of moorland lies mostly between 1,000ft (305m) and over 2,000ft (610m), with the settlements in the dales all more than 700ft (213m) above sea level. The valleys and high fellsides were scattered with shafts, levels, tips, mine buildings, processing plants and smelt mills. The three main mining concerns, the London Lead Company, the Blackett/Beaumonts and the Greenwich Hospital, were the major employers of men, women and boys until the end of the nineteenth century. Today, the remains of these mining enterprises are an obvious reminder of this once great industry; but the paths, tracks and packhorse ways linking mines with settlements are a valuable part of our heritage, and now followed by hill walkers and ramblers.

Lead has been formed in the earth under entirely different conditions from those which created coal. Earth movements way back in the earth's history created faults in the strata, which were intruded by molten rock from deep within the earth's crust. As the magma cooled, mineral-bearing liquids travelled along the fissures of the carboniferous limestone and the minerals crystallized. The mineralized faults or fissures are known as veins, and usually lie vertically in limestones and sandstones, or as horizontal deposits in limestone, known as flats. The lead ore, galena, a sulphide of lead, with associated ores of silver and zinc, is found with non-metallic minerals such as quartz, fluorspar, calcite and barytes.

Once the presence of veins had been established, initially by hushing, the ore was extracted by vertical shafts and horizontal levels; the latter used as waggonways and for the purpose of draining the mines. The famous Nent Force Level between Alston and Nenthead was driven for nearly five miles by the engineering surveyor John Smeaton, of Eddystone Lighthouse fame. The first 2½ miles (4km) was conceived as an underground canal to drain the mines, and barges were employed to carry materials and ore. For many years it was a regular tourist trip as far as the Lady Shield Falls.

Although water was the constant enemy of the lead miner, the greatest threat to health lay in the atmosphere of the mine. The miners' tools consisted of hammers, picks, wedges, spikes, shovels, crowbars and gunpowder – no pneumatic drills. The constant drilling and blasting made the air heavy with fumes and minute particles of rock; it is recorded that most lead miners died at an abnormally early age, owing to respiratory diseases. Ventilation was gradually improved using water wheels and the hydraulic water blast engine; the latter sucked foul air from the working face, replacing it with fresh air along the level.

The crushing and washing of the ore was originally a wasteful process; the technology was gradually improved, and much less galena was lost through being washed away down the streams. All the smelting operations were carried out in furnaces, in specially built smelt mills sited near water, which supplied the power for blowing the bellows. The smelters and refiners needed a high degree of skill to carry out these operations successfully.

Towards the end of the nineteenth century, the price of lead fell sharply due to imports of cheaper foreign ore. On Alston Moor, this change of fortune, together with the gradual exhaustion of local veins, led to a collapse of the industry and a decline in population. The two major companies surrendered their leases in the 1880s. By 1891, the population of the Alston Moor area had fallen to just under 4,000, as many families left to seek work, particularly in coal-mining districts.

Main Route
Map M27, p.89

Walk up the rough lane from Shieldhill to meet the B6277, Alston to Langdon Beck road; bear right and proceed for a short distance to a sharp bend over Garrigill Burn. Turn left at an FP sign and follow the stream running through the old workings of the Bentyfield Mine. Pass a conical walled shaft, vertical bays and a horizontal level to reach a step stile and marker. There are some Scots pines, and a ruinous mine building with a masoned culvert for a stream, inscribed GS Co. 1849. Continue to a step stile over a fence, and slant up left on a paved way to a marker. Accompany a tumbled wall, cross a watercourse and strike uphill by a conifer plantation. Head slightly left to meet a mine boundary stone, an oblong stone pillar with the inscription GS Co. 1849 on the south side and BF Co. 1849 on the opposite face. Looking back across the South Tyne Valley, there is a fine view of Great Dun Fell and the dark bulk of Cross Fell.

Take an east-north-east bearing, rising gradually over upland pasture, to reach a wall with a through stile and marker post. Aim slightly right towards a wall and walk alongside it to a marker post. Go through the wall stile and cross tussocky ground with drainage ditches, keeping an eye on a tall marker post in the wall beyond. In front, the greener valley pastures of the River Nent come into view. Head towards the corner of the conifer plantation, and descend gently to a marker post and stile. Bear left, and follow the fence and wall to another marker post and stile.

From this point, the right of way continues to descend on a bearing just north of east, crossing three fields with clear stiles and markers to meet a path junction.

Proceed across the next field to a corner stile and marker; notice the yellow pansies growing in the corner of the pasture. Follow the wall initially, and then head for a gate and marker. Pass a house and

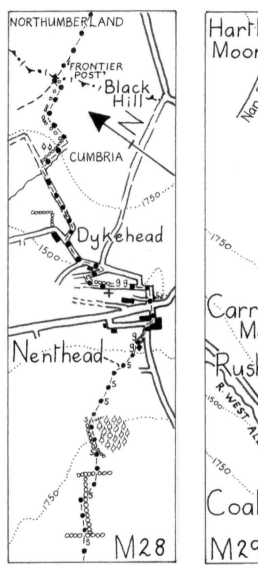

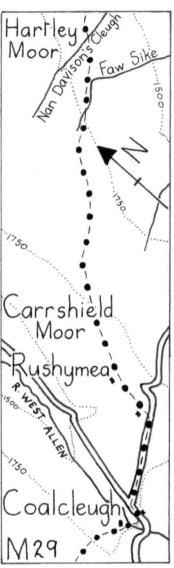

continue down the track to another gate, and beyond to the minor road. Turn left and walk downhill to a junction; turn right and swing left towards the centre of Nenthead opposite the Miners' Arms.

The village of Nenthead was created by the London Lead Company in the eighteenth century as their base of operations on Alston Moor. Originally, it was little more than a collection of mining offices, a smelt mill and a school, plus a few houses. Early in the nineteenth century, the Company planned a new settlement near the smelt mill. More cottages were built with land and gardens, and the plots were often worked by the women to provide food to supplement the miners' wages. The miners cum smallholders could also run sheep on the upland pastures. The Company provided facilities for its workers, including a chapel, miners' reading room and library, an inn, a market hall, a clock tower and a new school; it also showed an admirable concern for the welfare of the workpeople, providing disablement funds and medical care.

In 1895, a Belgian company took over the mines, and the village took in many foreign workers and engineers, who helped to preserve the industrial and domestic buildings in the neighbourhood. It is interesting to note that Nenthead was the second village in the area to have electric street lighting, and had one of the earliest Cooperative stores. Today, a heritage centre has been established from the dereliction of the old smelt mill site, but the village still tends to look careworn and neglected. Much has been achieved to revitalize this historic community, but more could be done to make Nenthead an important base for touring this lovely area of the high Pennines.

Cross the main road to the black-and-yellow painted, cast-iron drinking fountain. Visitors to Middleton-in-Teesdale may have noticed its twin. At Nenthead, the fountain was erected by RW Bainbridge Esq. of Middleton House, in commemoration of a testimonial presented to him and Mrs Bainbridge by the employees of the London Lead Company and other friends, on 28th September, 1877. RW Bainbridge was the London Lead Company's chief agent. Just across the way from the fountain is the Lead Company's Workmen's Reading Room – now the Nenthead Over 60s Rest Room.

Walk past the fountain, follow the road with a steep bank of stone setts and head straight on where the road turns sharp right. The building in front resembles a church, but is in fact the village hall; an FP sign indicates the route to Wellgill. Proceed to a metal gate, and pass into a walled, grassy area to a wooden gate; there is a church on the left. Continue between walls to a junction, turn right uphill, and swing to the right past derelict buildings. Look for the ornate metal standpipe, made in Kilmarnock, with a lion's head motif; this was part of the Lead Company's policy for the improvement of water supplies to its employees. Swing to the right to reach the minor road to Greenends. Turn left, passing a cottage with a large painted clock face in the wall: Old Peter Cottage.

Continue along the road passing a turning to the left, and just before the farm buildings at Dykeheads turn right up the wide track. This wide moorland way gradually climbs, with the grassed-over mounds of former mine workings much in evidence. Cross a stream and turn right at a gap in the wall. Negotiate the posts and wire cluttering the gap, and proceed up the hillside alongside the wall, with no sign of a path on the ground. Away to the left are two or three woebegone pines on ground disturbed by old workings. The going is hard, over rough tussocky grass following a tumbled wall and fence. Keep a sharp look-out for a broken wall coming in from the left near the crest of the slope. Turn left, walk along the top side of the wall round the pasture to reach the moor ridge, 1,913ft (58 m). There is a wall and fence ahead, but slant left through the tumbled wall to meet a stile and a marker post.

This is the frontier between Cumbria and Northumberland. You won't find a customs post, you don't have to show your passport; but on a day of thick mist and rain, you may just wonder why the hell you are here at all!

Proceed on an easterly bearing across the moor for a short distance to a grassy trench; follow the right-hand side to a watercourse, where a faint trod appears. The route winds its way through broken ground, with the sight of a white cottage in front. Continue along a broad track, cross a stream with a rocky bed and a little waterfall to reach a gate. The track passes a cottage, crosses a stream and climbs up to the road at Coalcleugh.

The mining field was situated high on the moors at a height of 1,821ft (555m); it is still an isolated and dreary place, with just a handful of dwellings remaining. One is tempted to think of the employees, particularly women and young boys, working on the washing floor with no protection against the bitterly cold Pennine weather, and enduring constant exposure to wind and rain.

Records reveal some interesting insights into the life and working day at Coalcleugh. In 1703, Sir William Blackett started making annual payments to a schoolmaster at Coalcleugh – £5 a year, in addition to the quarterly or monthly payments by parents of pupils. The school continued into the nineteenth century. In the early1760s the water pressure engine was invented by William Westgarth, the resident mine agent. By 1765 a level at Coalcleugh contained a horse-drawn waggonway a mile in length. In 1813 explorations for ore were hindered by the necessity of carrying large quantities of deads (waste material) from the mine. Of the miners who left Coalcleugh in 1824 owing money, five had gone to other lead mining areas, three to collieries and two to America. In the survey of 1861 in the Coalcleugh area, of the 19 houses without smallholdings, only five had gardens.

Turn left and walk to a road junction, where, in good visibility, there is a chance of a quick peep at distant green pastures in West Allendale. Bear right, and continue for a short distance along the moor road to a PB sign on the left indicating the route along the Black Way to East Allendale. This is the beginning of the walk over Carrshield Moor, immediately evocative and inviting: rough grasses of varying hues, two lonely weather-beaten trees, black-faced sheep, and a roofless stone building.

Descend to an FB and approach the ruined building of Rushymea. The route is well marked and climbs gently on soft grass – a joy to be on, it puts a spring in your step. There is a stone cairn pillar away to the left as the path reaches the moorland crest. Heather and shooting butts appear, with stone cairns and marker posts indicating the way through some peaty patches. The way descends with a cairn above on the rim of Blackway Head; it now becomes rougher underfoot, with moor grass, rush and boggy peat. In the distance, varied green patches stand out clearly on the slopes of East Allendale. Pass through to a firmer grassy area, but only for a short distance. Unfortunately, horse traffic is making a fair job of churning up the soft ground – watch for the Swin Hope Light Horse on manoeuvres!

The path continues to descend to a marker post, then on to a section of exposed rock, and descends to cross the romantically named Nan Davison's Cleugh; or perhaps it was named in honour of her for falling off her horse.

The way ascends steadily to pass numbered shooting butts, with mixed sections of hard and soft ground. After passing a marker post the ground levels out, and the path heads towards another waymarker. Just beyond lies a stone-walled sheep enclosure, shown on the OS map as Phillipson's Fold, GR NY 8310 4845 (NOTE: see for other route options from this location pp. 102-107).

It's time to rest and reflect on one's surroundings.

There was the sound of a dog barking in the valley, and then silence. It was a brilliantly clear day in late October, with bright sun and a few fleecy pads of clouds. There was no wind or air movement whatsoever; the moorland grasses had to be studied very intently to see if they did move. A glorious panorama stretched and receded into the distance. There were shades of varying hues, the dark outlines of stone walls, warm-coloured stone farms and barns dotted here and there; some in places huddled together for companionship, others isolated and aloof. But whatever their form, they all seemed to fit neatly and uniformly into a pattern on the lower fellsides. Dark masses of conifers, and copses, clumps and solitary broadleaved trees, their leaves changing colour, stood out sharp and clear amidst the surrounding duller greens.

Sweeping down from the heights of Stangend Rigg, Killhope Law and Green Hill, the moorland slopes were patterned with patches of bilberry, heather, moor-grass and heath rush. At the far end of the dale, the village of Allenheads nestled at the fell foot, well protected by a girdle of trees; its plumes of chimney smoke rose vertically in the still air.

The crisp light sharply picked out the human impact on the landscape: the humps and hollows, tips and scars of old lead mine workings; the drainage channels, quarries and reservoirs, and the lines of old tracks and packhorse ways making their journeys along valley and fellside. The older field boundaries and intakes curved this way and that almost with a will of their own; whilst the disciplined rows of enclosure walls were straight and regular. Set out in these sheltered pastures, the sheep appeared as motionless pieces on a scenic chessboard.

No buzzing or droning of insects disturbed one's concentration; all around was silence, a silence one could hear and feel. Sitting at this spot, seemingly folded into the hills, was a lovely experience to savour in this busy sophisticated world.

Leave the Black Way just prior to the marker post at Phillipson's Fold, and slant to the right on a bearing just north of east. Descend the moorland slope through grass, rush and heather, aiming for the far corner of walled pastures. Bear right at the angle of the wall, and walk down the track to a gate and a minor road. Turn left, pass a cottage and an old quarry and descend to a track on the right-hand side of the road. Proceed towards Swinhope Mill, cross over the footbridge on the left, and ascend the field to a step stile and marker post. Continue on to a ladder stile and across a small walled paddock to another ladder stile. Bear left, and walk up the pasture, passing White Ridge, to reach a ladder stile at the top. Continue straight on along the track to a gateway. Cross the road to an FP sign at GR NY 8433 4765. (NOTE: this is the point of departure for route options 4 and 5; see p. 105).

Slant to the right down the field towards a metal gate, as there does not appear to be a stile across the fence in the spot shown on the OS map. Walk to the other side of the field to a single plank step stile, and continue along the same bearing to a stone step stile. Pass depressions of disused quarry workings to reach a FP sign. Cross the minor road at Hammer Shields and walk to a stile at the left-hand side of a black hut.

Proceed to a gate in a boundary wall which is lined with mature sycamore trees. The path ahead crosses the sloping field and makes for metal hurdles in a wall gap, then descends to a stile of sorts. Keep to the right-hand side of a small stone building, bear right, cross a stone footbridge, and proceed along the track to a metal gate. Just beyond, slant left through an area of long grass and heather to join the road.

On the opposite side of the road is an area of waste land which was the site of the Allenheads Smelt Mill. The mill was built by the Blacketts in the early eighteenth century, and by 1821 contained three ore hearths, a slag hearth and a roasting furnace. Cross over Old Smelt Mill Bridge (1926) spanning the River East Allen, turn right, and walk on the quiet road that accompanies the river towards Allenheads.

At the end of the day, this is a leisurely one-mile stroll in interesting surroundings: there are rows of old cottages, a circular walled mine shaft with a rowan tree growing out of it, one of several on a straight alignment along the east side of the road; attractive cast-iron water standpipes with a lion's head motif, a Wesleyan Methodist Chapel built in 1900; a stepped weir on the river, where the water was led away along a mill race to power the bellows at the smelt mill; and Beaumont House, built in the early part of the nineteenth century for a land agent.

The road reaches a small irregular square in the centre of the village, with the Allenheads Inn on the right, and the Post Office and Heritage Centre on the far side of the square.

Alternative Route
Options from Phillipson's Fold

1. To Allendale Town
Maps A10a. A10b, p. 103

Map	OS 1:25000 Outdoor Leisure, North Pennines, Teesdale and Weardale, Sheet 31. OS 1:25000 Outdoor Leisure, Hadrian's Wall, Haltwhisle and Hexham, Sheet 43
Highest elevation	Co. boundary, Coalcleugh 1,913ft (583m)
Height of ascent	1,568ft (478m)
Distance	13½ miles (21.6km) from Garrigill

As main route from Garrigill to Phillipson's Fold: then continue along the Black Way to Knock Shield, Rowantree Stob, Pry Hill, Acton Burn; East of Crowberry Hall, Park Farm, Peckriding, Allendale Town (main route, see pp. 93-99).

2. To Hexham
Maps A11a, A11b, p.104

Map	OS 1:25000 Outdoor Leisure, North Pennines, Teesdale and Weardale, Sheet 31. OS 1:25000 Outdoor Leisure, Hadrian's Wall, Haltwhisle and Hexham, Sheet 43
Highest elevation	Crawberry Hill 1,197ft (365m)
Height of ascent	1,040ft (317m)
Distance	12½ miles (20km) from Allendale Town

As Route 1 to Allendale Town, then Shilburn, Struthers, High Struthers, Burntridge Moor, Rowley Wood, Crabtree Ford, Rowley Head, Rye Hill. Then continue as per main route (see pp. 116-120).

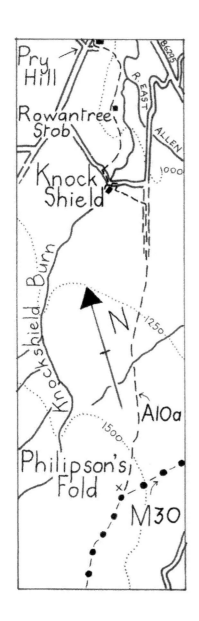

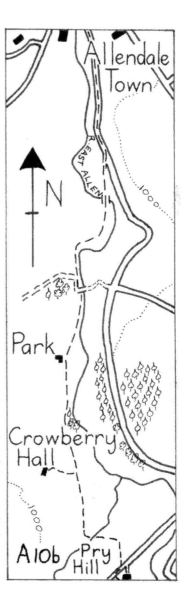

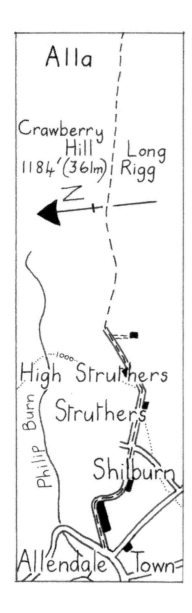

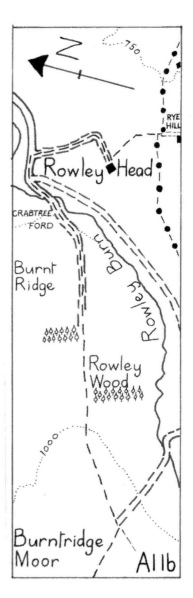

3. To Blanchland
Maps A12a, A12b, p.106

Map	OS 1:25000 Outdoor Leisure, North Pennines, Teesdale and Weardale, Sheet 31. OS 1:25000 Outdoor Leisure, Hadrian's Wall, Haltwhisle and Hexham, Sheet 43
Highest elevation	Hangman Hill 1,352ft (412m)
Height of ascent	1,204ft (367m)
Distance	10¼ miles (16.4km) from Allendale Town

As Route 1 to Allendale Town, then Finney Hill, Stobb Cross, Blaeberry Cleugh,Westburnhope Moor, Hangman Hill. Proceed as per alternative route to Blanchland (see pp.120-122).

4. To Valley of Devil's Water, Omitting Allenheads
Map A13 (M32, 33, 34)

As main route from Garrigill to Swin Hope, GR NY 8433 4765, then descend to Low Huntwell and River East Allen. Continue to Fell View, ascend Green Hill on main route, proceed along Broad Way to Hangman Hill and straight ahead to the Valley of Devil's Water. Distance 18½ miles (29.6km) Garrigill to Stotsfold Hall, Devil's Water (see pp. 93-101, 107, 111-116).

5. To Blanchland, omitting Allenheads

As Route 4 to Hangman Hill, GR NY 886 521, then turn right and continue as per alternative route to Blanchland. Distance 20 miles (32km) from Garrigill (see pp. 93-101. 107, 120-122. Maps A13 [M32, 33, A12b, A12c, A12d]).

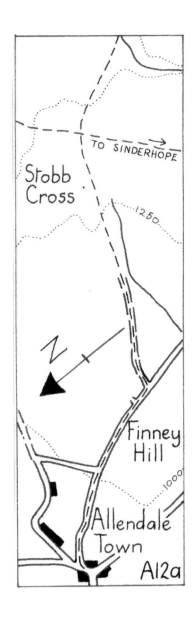

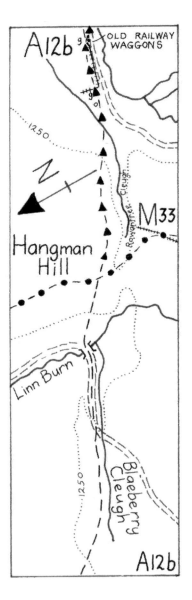

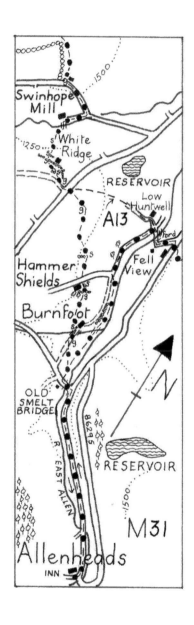

7. Allenheads to Hexham

Map	OS 1:25000 Outdoor Leisure, North Pennines, Teesdale and Weardale, Sheet 31. OS 1:25000 Outdoor Leisure, Hadrian's Wall, Haltwhistle and Hexham, Sheet 43
Highest elevation	Green Hill 1,726ft (526m)
Height of ascent	1,079ft (329m)
Distance	16½ miles (26.4 km)
Terrain	A walk of scenic contrasts. From an upper dale, over expansive heather-clad moorlands, along a river valley of verdant loveliness, to undulating pastures. Easy walking on good tracks and on mainly well-marked paths

ALLENHEADS IS TUCKED AWAY at the far end of the East Allen valley, and records reveal that a settlement existed here from around 1670. People came into this remote and barren part of Northumberland to seek and work the rich veins of silverbearing lead ore, involving processing and smelting. The Allenheads lead mines produced a seventh of all lead mined in Great Britain.

Estates were sold around the area to the Blackett family, and fortunes were increased by the mines, making the dale a busy place during the eighteenth and nineteenth centuries. The Blackett and Beaumont families were later joined by marriage, and mining continued into the 1880s.

Mention has previously been made of water as the greatest enemy of the lead miner; but it was also successfully employed as the main source of power. Water power, through the medium of waterwheels, became the major feature of nineteenth-century mining; but the use of hydraulic (water-pressure engines) produced a much more efficient and cost-effective way of working the mines.

Allenheads

The principle of the hydraulic engine was the use of the weight of a column of water upon a piston moving in a cylinder. The hydraulic engine could be placed on a level at the foot of a shaft, down which a water feed pipe could descend 150ft or more. The used water could

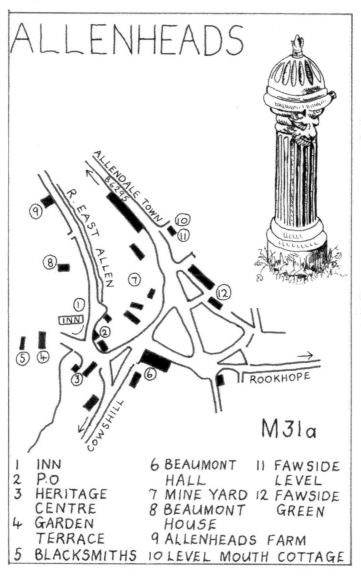

ALLENHEADS

ALLENDALE TOWN B6295

R. EAST ALLEN

INN

ROOKHOPE

COWSHILL

M 31a

1	INN	6	BEAUMONT HALL	11	FAWSIDE LEVEL
2	P.O	7	MINE YARD	12	FAWSIDE GREEN
3	HERITAGE CENTRE	8	BEAUMONT HOUSE		
4	GARDEN TERRACE	9	ALLENHEADS FARM		
5	BLACKSMITHS	10	LEVEL MOUTH COTTAGE		

be released into the level and out to the surface river or stream, where it subsequently powered more water wheels in the valley. Two of the nine hydraulic engines were installed in the Fawside Level at Allenheads by Thomas Sopwith for pumping, and other hydraulic engines were used on the dressing floor at Allenheads, and in the construction of the 4¾ mile Blackett Level.

As in other lead mining areas, the miners were encouraged by their employers to pursue a dual role, as mine workers and smallholders. In 1861, a survey was carried out of the Beaumont estates. In Allenheads, 81 houses out of 123 had a piece of enclosed meadow or pasture land in connection with the house. Most miners had at least one cow for milk, butter and cheese; they also had geese, and kept ponies for transport. Although the miners' agricultural activities helped to supplement their food supplies, cereals could not be grown, and had to be brought in from outside the area. Rye provided the basic cereal for bread, and oatmeal was used for 'crowdy', a form of porridge eaten with milk or treacle.

In the eighteenth century the education of the miners' children was a hit-and-miss affair, with limited facilities provided by generous individuals, or through parental efforts. The masters were poorly paid, receiving less than the miners, and as incomes fluctuated with the price of lead, so paying pupils were withdrawn. In the mid nineteenth century, education in the areas controlled by the Beaumonts was reorganized by Thomas Sopwith; and monies were obtained from the Company to construct new school buildings in Allendale and in neighbouring Weardale.

With regard to religion, it was due to the lack of interest taken in these isolated northern dales by the Church of England that Methodism came in to fill the vacuum. Its teaching was conveyed in such a lively and homely way that the new faith instantly appealed to the miners and their families.

In 1987, an Allenheads Trust was formed with the aim of revitalizing the village. A derelict seventeenth-century inn, which had become a coach house and latterly a bus garage, was transformed into a heritage centre, providing a social amenity for the local community, tourist information facilities and a display area. Close by is the Engine House, designed to accommodate the Armstrong Hydraulic Engine. Built in 1852, this 9hp engine powered a saw mill and serviced lead mines on the Allendale estate; it is the sole survivor, above ground, of many similar water-powered engines used for pumping and winding duties underground. The engine, with two large flywheels, is a twin-cylinder double-acting machine, and worked until the 1940s, powered by water supplied from reservoirs high above the village.

Situated behind the Engine House, a former byre has been converted into a cafe and coffee shop. Higher up, past the present inn, the old blacksmith's shop has been refurbished and now displays the original tools of the craftsman and many items concerned with village life.

The Allenheads Inn was formerly the residence of Sir Thomas Wentworth, Fifth Baronet, who succeeded to the Blackett Estates in 1777. The house, built between 1770 and 1790, became the inn in 1860, replacing the old hostelry across the road. The building, which is full of character and interest, provides a warm welcome and comfortable accommodation. A few years ago, the interior was rather like a museum, due to the interest of the landlord. The building contained a multifarious collection of articles and relics of bygone years. The public bar was a sight to behold, with walls, ceiling and floor festooned with fascinating objects, including animal heads, an aeroplane propeller, tools, old bottles, chamber pots, panama hats, a brace and bit, a gas mask, goggles and ladies shoes.

Main Route
Map M31 p.107

From the centre of Allenheads retrace one's steps along the quiet riverside road to the Old Smelt Mill Bridge. Turn left for a few paces to where the path begins opposite an old stone building. Continue through patches of heather and long grass down to the river bank and alongside a wall. Note the mouth of the Haugh Level in the earth bank on the opposite side of the river. This was driven more than two centuries ago to drain the Allenheads Mine.

Cross the footbridge over Middlehope Burn. The farm to the left, Burnfoot, was an inn at one period in its history, and there are remains of an old cock-fighting pit nearby – a popular pastime in the 1850s. At the point where the Middlehope Burn meets the main river, there is a chance to admire the fine masonry weir and headworks constructed to provide hydraulic power for the Breckon Hill Mine. Follow the wall overhung with sycamores where the river flows into a deep pool; the land rises steeply on the opposite bank, forming a very attractive mini-valley. Ignore the footbridge crossing over to Peasmeadow, and continue along the river bank on the river side of the wall. Join a tarmac lane with an FP sign and a copse of trees beyond the wall, and proceed to a ford across the river. A notice reminds you to try your brakes, but if you feel a need for more paddling practice, then here's an opportunity, because there are more watercourses to cross further on. However, in this case there is a convenient footbridge close by.

Climb up the minor road from the ford. Half-way up on the right is a sturdy stone building now used as a barn; this was the mine shop of the Breckon Hill Mine. A 'mine shop' usually comprised the smithy and office on the ground floor level, with lodging accommodation on the floor above.

Cross over the main road at Fell View to an FP sign, which indicates a bridleway to Hexhamshire. Climb up round the site of an old quarry, and continue to ascend the grassy slopes following a series of blue-topped waymarkers. Looking back there is a fine view of East Allendale to Coatenhill Reservoir and Coalcleugh Moor. There are the fresh-looking valley pastures of Swin Hope and Middle Hope backed by a rolling coverlet of moorland.

Bear left on reaching a track, with the OS survey column on Green Hill, 1,736ft (529m), now clearly visible. Breast the rise rejoicing in the name of High Haddock Stones, and admire the magnificent moorland panorama: acres of heather-clad slopes forming a rich carpet of brown, green and purple. One can see the valley of Beldon Burn pointing to Blanchland and a teasing glimpse of the high heathland south of the Tyne Valley.

The good track enables the walker to put in a fast pace to reach two black corrugated iron huts, not open, probably used for moor-management purposes. However, they do provide a barrier, a momentary respite, from a howling gale. Imagine the teams of packhorses, 'galloways', journeying along this lonely Broad Way, each horse carrying two pokes of ore weighing 2 cwt from East Allendale to Hexhamshire.

Proceed through a gate in the fence and continue on a surface that alternates from stones to soft grass. On the left there is a cairn or currick situated on higher ground with craggy outcrops. Pass through another gate in a fence, noting a boundary stone, and walk on ahead following the fence. The track, which has now become a thin path through the heather, aims for a gate with a waymarker in the fence to the left, and descends to the lip of Rowantree Cleugh. These cleughs are a common, often surprising feature of these local moors, with the sudden appearance of a steep-sided valley.

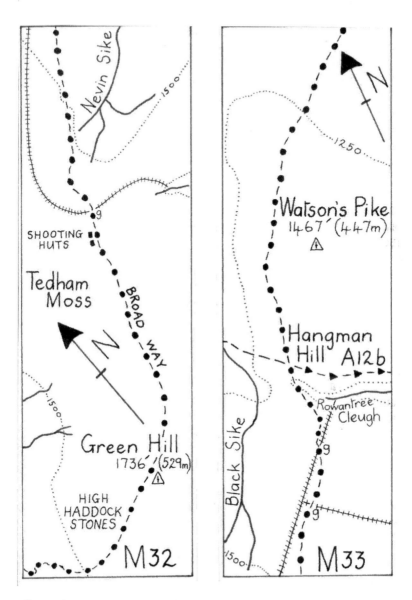

Follow the rim of the cleugh, descend to what could be a wet section and up to a marker post. This point, GR NY 886 521, is a crossroads of routes: left to Allendale Town via Westburnhope Moor (see Alternative Route 3, p.105), or right via the alternative route to

Blanchland (see pp.120-122). This intersection of routes lies on Hangman Hill, where no doubt many legends and not a few ghosts abound – not the most comfortable place to eat your sandwiches.

The route continues in a north-easterly direction, climbing gradually across the slopes of Watson's Pike. A few stones lie on the surface of the moor, some with strips of yellow tape indicating the way. There is not much to see, only a wide tract of open land and heather: but wait, look again, to the north is the escarpment holding the line of the Roman Wall, and in the far distance the purpled outline of the Cheviot Hills. This is enough to raise the spirits, but it may be better to move away from Hangman Hill.

The path winds gently down the moor slopes, passing a double arrow marker and an area of disturbed ground, to reach a minor road at Kingslaw Plantation.

If time is short, bear left, walk along the road to the north end of the plantation, and turn right at an old railway waggon; it will reduce the distance by half a mile (0.8 km). Ravenber purists not wishing to dodge out on any section of the route should ignore that advice, and pass over the cattle grid straight ahead. Use the step stile on the left behind the wall, and proceed alongside the fence heading in a straight line towards a dwelling on the skyline. The ground is rough and reedy, with long grass and hidden wet patches. Aim for an electricity pole, cross a watercourse and walk to a stone step stile over a wall. Proceed towards the right-hand side of the house through more long grass to a wooden gate; there may just be a couple of horses here very interested in the contents of your rucksack.

Go through a gate on the left, pass the house, Gair Shield, and walk across a paddock to a gate. Pass a haybarn to a gate, continue down the track to another gate and through the plantation to meet the minor road. Turn right and walk for a few paces to reach the old railway waggon.

NOTE: Although the road route will save half a mile on the distance and the footpath route is rougher underfoot, the line of this right of way needs to be walked – *en avant!*

Walk through a gap and continue alongside the wall, passing a gate and possible access up to Gair Shield House, although this is not marked as a right of way. Keep on straight ahead, keeping an eye out for a scrubby line of thorns along a fence on the right. There is a sort of stone step stile over the wall, then a wooden hurdle; it may be easier going through the gate several yards beyond this point. Follow the

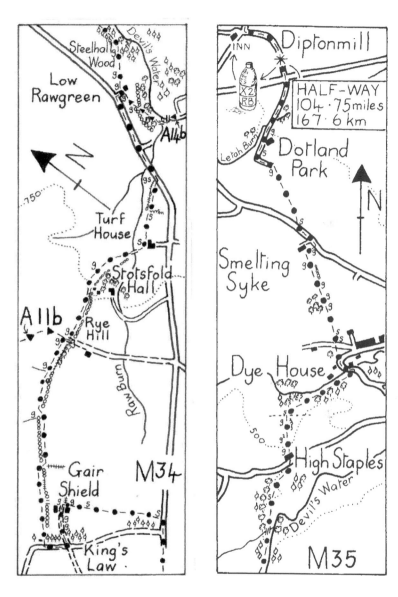

wall on the right-hand side now, through some reedy grass, and continue down the field to a gate on the right. Accompany the wall with a cleared area, Stotsfold Plantation, on the right, passing a drinking trough (for animals) built into the masonry. Along this section there is an inner fence leaving a gap of 3ft or so. This could be the line of the path, since it has an easily climbed hurdle at the far end. However, there is no access made at the top end in order to use this way. Go through a metal gate and walk along the left-hand side of the fence lined with trees. Pass through the gate in the far right-hand corner and turn right on to a track at Rye Hill. NOTE: This is the point at which alternative Route 2 rejoins the main route (see p.102).

Proceed for a few paces to a metal gate marked with yellow tape, then bear left through a gate, also waymarked, and follow the track alongside the wall. This is a very pleasant tree-lined section complete with a small stream. Note a stone slab crossing the stream leading to a small gate, where a path leads into the grounds of Stotsfold Hall.

There is a collection of buildings on the right, as the path keeps to the left of a white-painted hut with a tin roof, it has the appearance of a defunct cricket pavilion. Continue to a waymarked gate in a wall, and follow the high stone wall and electricity supply poles. Aim to the right and cross a single strand of barbed wire into a rough tussocky area. When you think all is lost, a tall pole with yellow tape pin-points the position of a footbridge almost hidden in bushes and trees. If you don't spot the tall waymarker, the bridge lies just beyond a vertically challenged telegraph pole. Walk up the field pasture towards Turf House Farm and to a yellow-topped marker pole and stile on the left. Aim slightly left across the next field and descend to a step stile in the hedge. Accompany the fence and wall, lined with large bushes and trees, through a meadow to a gate and step stile. Bear left along the road and walk for half a mile (0.8 km), then turn right down the track to Low Rawgreen, GR NY 9267 5655. NOTE: This is the point where the alternative route from Blanchland rejoins the main route (see pp.123-126).

Turn left, pass through a yard to a gate, then along the hedge and fence to another gate. Continue to follow the fence and wall, and then bear right through a gate just past a spring into Steelhall Wood. Proceed through an area of conifers and broadleaved trees, then on a narrow way between conifers and into more open woodland. The Devil's Water now runs through a gorge to the immediate right; do not cross the footbridge, but walk straight ahead on a delightful path along the river bank. Cross over a small footbridge and accompany the river for a little way, then keep to the left on approaching an amphitheatre-like pasture surrounded by a bank of trees. Cross a plank footbridge, climb the slope to a step stile and walk diagonally across the field to meet the road. If there is a growing crop it would be considerate to walk around the hedge side.

Turn left through High Staples and proceed to a gate. The route lies ahead across a yard, through gates and a small pasture, to follow the left-hand side of a hedge to another gate and on to a path crossroads. Continue straight on after a step stile, and walk into the wood, now on a track, that swings to the right following Rowley Burn to Dye House Bridge. Note the detached house on the far bank, which has an attractively laid-out garden with variegated conifers.

Turn left, cross the bridge, and at the second corner take the arrowed path on the left by a wall up to a small kissing gate. Proceed to a wicket gate, passing a magnificent beech tree. In fact, the immediate surroundings are just like beautiful parkland – a superb contrast to the austere Hexhamshire moors. Cross the drive to a stone step stile opposite, and forward to another in the fence. Continue up the field alongside a wall to a kissing gate just inside the wood, and walk along a narrow pathway to a similar gate. Follow the tree-lined fence to a gate, and then accompany a wall and fence to a small gate in a wall. Aim for a gate in front, then follow the arrow to the right along the fence opposite the house called Smelting Syke; an interesting name, one of many found in this part of Northumberland. There is a welcoming notice on the gate that gives access to the lane; too long to quote, but it ends like this:

> *Welcome to Hexhamshire.*
> *But please close and fasten all gates.*
> *Enjoy it as I do.*
> *Many thanks, have a nice walk.*

Bear left, and walk a short distance to a step stile in a wall on the right. Head across the large meadow on a north-north-west bearing to a gate in the far corner. Note the pleasing sign: SHLH take note!

Follow the track as it swings round to the right to a ladder stile in a wall. Proceed past Dotland Park Farm to another gate, and bear left down a

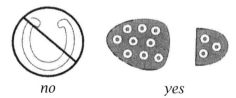

no   *yes*

metalled drive. On the left is the attractive wooded dell of the Letah Burn, its banks dotted with numerous wild flowers. As the dell swings away to the right, its course bordered with mature trees, the farm lane continues ahead to join a minor road. Cross over and walk down a sunken grassy way lined with a lush variety of hedging and trees. NOTE: You have reached the half-way mark – open that bottle of brown ale! The route descends steeply into the valley of the West Dipton Burn and the peaceful sequestered hamlet of Diptonmill. The pub at Diptonmill has a seat outside with 'Outpatients' written on it, and a sign above the door indicating 'Duck or Grouse'.

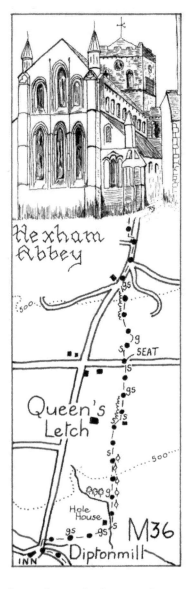

During the Wars of the Roses, Northumberland was strongly for the house of Lancaster. At the Battle of Hexham in 1464, the forces of Margaret of Anjou, queen of Henry VI, were heavily defeated.

Many stragglers from the Lancastrian army fled for their lives through the surrounding wellwooded country of the Rowley Burn, Dipton Burn and the Devil's Water. There is the legend of Margaret being befriended by a notorious local outlaw in the Queen's Cave; this is situated a short distance away in an isolated spot above the Dipton Burn.

Walk over the bridge turn right at the FP sign to Hole House, and head along the track to a gate and step stile. Continue across the pasture to another gate and step stile; pass in front of the house to a stile and turn left along the wall. Cross the stream at the far end, climb up through the wood to a small gate and go forward to a step stile. The way maintains a gradual ascent to a marshy section in the corner of the field and a dilapidated step stile. Bear right to another stile by a ruined building, and proceed along the right-hand side of the hedge in a northerly direction. The complex of buildings away to the west goes by the interesting name of Queen's Letch; a name meaning a slip, which commemorates an accident to Queen Margaret's horse.

Walk up to a gate and a broken stile, and continue on to meet the road with a stile and FP sign. This point is the crest of the long slope that rises from the valley of the West Dipton Burn. A short distance westwards is the site of Hexham Racecourse, surely the most beautiful steeple-chase course in the country, with panoramic views to the Pennines and Cheviots.

Cross over the road to a welcoming seat for the weary. This is a bonus spot at the end of the day for the following reasons: firstly, there's only 1¼ miles (2 km) to go; secondly, it's downhill all the way; thirdly, this high ridge of Yarridge provides an excellent viewpoint for Hexham and the country beyond the Tyne Valley.

So, continue with a spring in your step and a song in your heart; even though it means recycling the songs, tunes, hymns, anthems and choruses that you have hummed, warbled, whistled or murdered during the day.

Descend to a step stile, then more steeply slanting right to a gate,

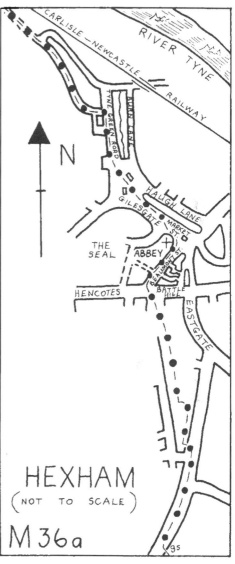

and across left to the hedge line. Continue the descent to the road with an FP sign, stile and gate. Turn right down the road, pass a road junction on the right, then forward for a short distance to a junction on the left. Immediately below is a little walled entry – watch out, you could miss it! There are gardens and houses on the left and allotments to the right. Turn left at the bottom, and then proceed down St Wilfrid's Road. There is a Post Office just along on the right, and on the wall corner is a plaque to Wilfred Wilson Gibson, 1878-1962, Poet.

Go straight across the main road at Battle Hill, by the War Memorial, then walk along Beaumont Street past the Abbey Grounds to the centre of Hexham.

Alternative Route
Allenheads to Blanchland
Maps: M31, p.107; 32, 33, p.113; A12b, pp.106, 113; A12c, A12d, p.121

Map	OS 1:25000 Outdoor Leisure, North Pennines, Teesdale and Weardale, Sheet 31. OS 1:25000 Outdoor Leisure, Hadrian's Wall, Haltwhisle and Hexham, Sheet 43
Highest elevation	Green Hill 1,726ft (526m)
Height of ascent	938ft (286m)
Distance	12½ miles (20 km)

As main route to Hangman Hill (see pp. 111-113). Turn right at the marker post at the western end of Rowantree Cleugh, GR NY 886 521. Take the path through the heather to a cairn on the crest of the slope overlooking the cleugh. Keep straight on through the heather to a cairn on the side of the track. A clearer path continues to a marker post, then it strikes off to the right. Aim for a cairn on rising ground in front, proceed along the lip of the cleugh to another cairn and slant left to a track. Bear right, descend the slope, passing two cairns, cross the stream and make for a gate beyond a small grassy rise. Walk slightly right, passing a circular sheepfold, called a stell, to a gate in the corner of the fence. In fact, after reaching the small grassy rise, a clear well-used trackway follows the right-hand side of the fence, quickly reaching two old railway goods waggons, GR NY 9005S138.

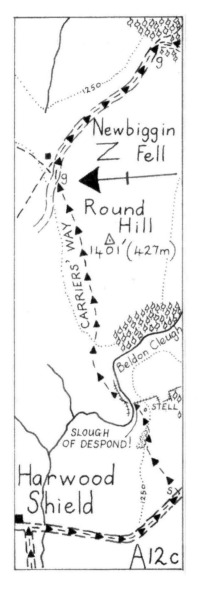
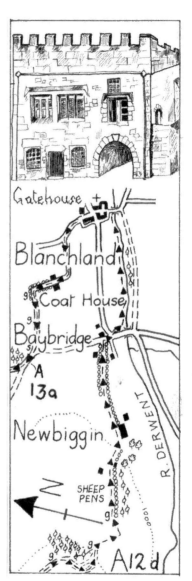

This is a good lunch spot; the old vans provide shelter from the wind, making a sun trap, and there is soft grass on which to enjoy forty winks. You may receive a visitation from local moorland residents, but if you have mutton butties, don't feed them! On my last visit, there was also a venerable agricultural roller, Stalker by name; any cricket club would be thrilled to have this piece of equipment.

Walk along the track towards Harwood Shield, a solid, impressive-looking farmhouse with a walled garden and shelter belt of trees. Turn right down the track, cross over the bridge and ascend the hillside on tarmac for a short distance, until reaching a rough surfaced way once more. At the top of the slope turn left at a stile and waymarker.

NOTE: THERE IS ANOTHER OPTION FROM THIS POINT OF THE ALLENHEADS TO BLANCHLAND ROUTE:

Continue on the track past this point for a short distance to reach a gateway on the left leading to Riddlehamhope Farm. Follow the track along Beldon Side to Newbiggin and Baybridge. There is a choice of routes on either side of the River Derwent into Blanchland.

OTHERWISE CONTINUE OF THE PREVIOUS ROUTE:

Cross over the heather moor, slanting slightly left, to reach the edge of a small escarpment with shaly outcrops. Keep to the left of a stell below and aim for a yellow-topped marker post – although what you are looking at is just the top portion of the post, the rest of it having sunk in a boggy area. If you make it to the fence, slant thankfully up the rough heathery slope to escape from Beldon Cleugh.

Walk on an easterly bearing, keeping to the north of Beldon End Plantation, and north of the rising ground of Round Hill. This route, the Carriers' Way, becomes more evident on the ground, and continues to a wooden gate with waymarker. There is a stout stone barn to the left with a metal lean-to structure. Turn right on to a good track across Newbiggin Fell leading to a gate. Approach a gate on the plantation track and continue to descend bearing left to another gate. Proceed down the slope on the left-hand side of the boundary at first, then on the opposite side to meet a track at the bottom. Turn left, with a wall and plantation on the right. Go through a gate, past sheep pens and the walled garden of a house. Head left down a wide track with magnificent purple beech trees in front, and a colourful heather garden to the right in the grounds of Newbiggin Hall. Walk along the metalled surface to an FP sign at Baybridge. Keep right at the road junction, pass a picnic site on the right, and immediately before the bridge, take the footpath on the left along the north bank of the River Derwent. On reaching the bridge turn left into the village of Blanchland. There is also a right of way through woodland on the south bank of the river leading to Blanchland.

The name 'Blanchland' derives from *Alba Landa*, Norman French *Blanchelande*, meaning 'untilled land'; Wainwright suggests:

'Your imagination is indeed impoverished if you can enter this picturesque village for the first time and not thrill at the spectacle it affords'
(A Wainwright, *A Pennine Journey*)

Blanchland lies embowered among fine trees in the deep glen of the upper Derwent, and is approached by moorland roads, tracks and pathways. Its beautiful setting and physical composition attract artists and photographers, who wish to draw, paint and record a range of fine interesting features. The lines of neat warm-coloured stone cottages form terraces, round the square, the heart of the place; with the pant or covered pump a distinctive object. The whole scene is overlooked by a handsome gateway.

The abbey was founded in 1165 by Premonstratensian monks; Blanche refers to the white habits of the monks, similar to those worn by the brothers of the Cistercian order. The monks cleared the riverside woodlands, and created glades or haughs that are a landscape feature today.

Blanchland suffered many depredations from the Scots. A local story says that in 1327 some Scottish raiders failed to detect the abbey's location because of its remoteness; to celebrate their deliverance the monks rang a peal of bells, but unfortunately the retreating Scots heard the sound, retraced their steps and sacked the place.

In the sixteenth century, the domestic buildings of the abbey were purchased by the Forsters of Bamburgh for use as their home, and were later bought by Nathaniel, Lord Crewe, Bishop of Durham. When Lord Crewe died, the estate was left in trust for charitable purposes.

Of the former monastic buildings, only the imposing gateway and

Map	OS 1:25000 Outdoor Leisure, Hadrian's Wall, Haltwhistle and Hexham, Sheet 43
Highest elevation	Birkside Fell 1,293ft (394m)
Height of ascent	1,283ft (391m)
Distance	11½ miles (18.4 km)

parts of the abbey refectory and the guest house remain, now
incorporated into the Lord Crewe Arms. The abbey church became
ruinous after the dissolution of the monasteries, but the choir was
restored in 1752 and converted into the parish church.

Alternative Route
Blanchland to Hexham
Map A13a, p.121

From the centre of Blanchland walk up the metalled land following
the Shildon Burn. Turn left at a PB sign to Coat House, pass a small
copse and follow the track up to the house. Pass through the farmyard
into a walled track. Swing left through a gate, proceed alongside a wall
with thorn bushes, and then by a fence, with a grassy surface
underfoot. Go through the left-hand gate, then through a wide gap
and arrive at a ladder stile with a PB sign.

Enter a tarmac lane, and continue ahead past the entrance to
Birkside Farm. Opposite Stothill Plantation take the right of way on
the left and walk along the track, lined with posts at intervals, to a
step stile and gate in the fence. Proceed across Birkside Fell. Keep on
a north-west bearing to another post, with the path becoming
indistinct at times. Join a track coming in from the left and continue
to a wall and wooden gate with FP signs. Follow the direction of the
arrow, slanting left, and descend the heather moor via a series of well-
positioned waymarkers to cross a small watercourse. Head down a
grassy groove to the left of a stell, to a marker post with three arrows
on it, and descend to another marker post meeting a track coming in
from the right.

This is the valley of the Devil's Water, and the lovely tree-fringed
stream will now be followed for the next five miles. Descend to a gate,
bear right at barns near Burntshield Haugh to another gate, and keep
on the gradually ascending track. Follow the bank of an old thorn
hedge to a gate, and continue past a mixed boundary line of fence and
trees. Proceed through a pasture to a gate and step stile, and cross a
sloping meadow, bearing slightly left to a step stile at the bottom
corner of the fence. Descend left round a shattered silver birch tree
to a gate, and bear right to a gate in the fence.

The immediate area is very attractive. The stream, with little
waterfalls, enters a depression. A gate gives access to a woody glade;
the path follows along the bank of the Devil's Water, past old mine

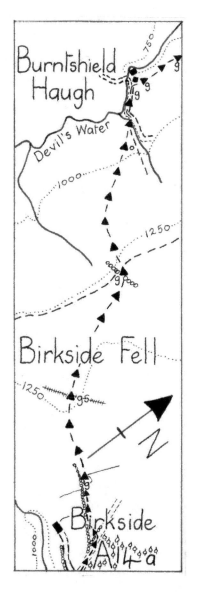

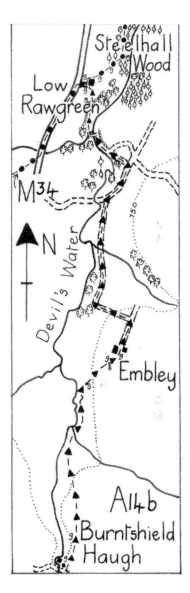

workings on the left bank to a point where the track bifurcates, with the left-hand section leading down to a ford. Keep straight on, and then strike up some stone steps to a stile. Climb up, slanting right, to some trees, aim for a track through gorse bushes and on to a gate in a wall. Bear left, passing a duck pond, and through a metal gate into the farmyard at Embley.

Carry on straight ahead, then bear left downhill, passing a sharp pointed stone pillar on the right, as the track bends into an area of broadleaf woodland with wild flowers in abundance. Pass through a metal gate, and follow the track that swings to the right, which now has a metalled surface. Keep to the right at a junction and walk along a tree-fringed lane, which then climbs gently past gorse bushes. Leave the lane, and head left down the track lined with tall conifers and birch trees. The way descends steeply in a sunken groove, and continues down a rather damp section to meet the Devil's Water once more. Walk alongside a wall by the river bank; cross over two footbridges, and immediately after the second bridge, bear right and strike up into the wood. The path is a little indeterminate here, but walk through the wood containing fine beech trees, its floor carpeted with primroses, violets and daises. In order to fix your bearings, just walk to the left a little and follow the boundary wall to a metal gate. Cross a meadow and aim for another metal gate at Low Rawgreen, GR NY 9267 5655. NOTE: At this point the main route is rejoined (see p.116).

I must admit that I have more than a sneaking regard for the alternative route via Blanchland; but that's just my opinion.

Riddlehamhope, near Blanchland

8. Hexham to Wark

Map	OS 1:25000 Outdoor Leisure, Hadrian's Wall, Haltwhistle and Hexham, Sheet 43
Highest elevation	Roman Wall, Carrawbrough 781ft (238m)
Height of ascent	With Route 1, 1,056ft (322m) With Route 2, 1,178ft (359m)
Distance	13½ miles (21.6 km)
Terrain	A fine riverside walk to an attractive village; an ascent to the line of the Roman Wall and a temple. A journey over wide upland pastures and 'One more river to cross'

THE SETTLEMENT OF HEXHAM grew up on the banks of two small streams flowing down the hillsides into the valley of the Tyne. It is one of the oldest and most picturesque of Northumbrian towns, and it stands on a terrace on the south bank of the Tyne, near to the meeting of the waters – the North Tyne and the South Tyne. It was known by the Saxon name of *Hagustaldes hām*, which became Hextoldesham, and which is the origin of the present name. Many routes met at or near the place, the settlement prospered and gradually it expanded southwards up the rising ground.

Viewed from the bridge over the Tyne, there is a fine skyline of medieval buildings that immediately attracts the attention – Hexham Abbey, the Moot Hall or Gate Tower and the Manor Office. However, the scene is interrupted by a few intrusive and unsympathetic modern buildings.

The steeply sloping street of Hall Stile Bank leads to the Market Place, where many of the fine old buildings are situated; and here, the narrow streets radiate out from this the historic centre of the town.

The imposing building of the Manor Office, constructed in 1330, served as a prison and as the administrative centre of the Regality of

Hexhamshire. Nowadays, it houses the Middle March Museum. The Moot Hall or Gate Tower, a late fourteenth-century or early fifteenth-century tower house, lies between the Manor Office and the Market Place. It was formerly the residence of the Archbishop of York's representatives. Courts of justice were held here until 1838.

Hexham was an important trading centre from early times, with permission to hold two fairs established in 1239. The Market Place contains the covered shambles provided by the Lord of the Manor, Sir Walter Blackett, in 1766, and currently houses a twice-weekly market (Tuesdays and Saturdays). The famous and flourishing livestock market is situated on the eastern side of town.

Market Street is the old route into the heart of the town and is lined with a good mixture of interesting buildings, some Georgian structures, now shops, and older dwellings with tell-tale doorheads. Another interesting street is St Mary's Chare or Back Street, which preserves the spirit of old Hexham; here is found the former 'George and Dragon', no longer an inn, but with an unchanged exterior. Fore Street is the main shopping street, which allows shoppers to move about unhindered by traffic; it joins two other main thoroughfares with the fascinating names of Priestpopple and Battle Hill. Beaumont Street is a pleasant highway built about 1860, with one side bordering Abbey Grounds Park, and the opposite side a treelined row of buildings that includes the Queen's Hall and the offices of the town's newspaper, the *Hexham Courant* – which sounds a very lively sort of paper.

There are no signs or records to indicate that Hexham was at any time a Roman site, but Wilfred chose it as the place for his magnificent church in honour of St Andrew. The workmen were able to use the readily accessible masoned stone from the former Roman fort and supply base at nearby Corstopitum (Corbridge). In Saxon times it was easier to take the stones from some existing and perhaps ruinous building than to quarry them.

Hexham had a troubled history: attacked by the Danes in 875, it was pillaged and destroyed. The church was not reconstituted until 1113 when the Augustinian priory was founded, although the building is of two periods, 1180-1250 and 1850-1910. Very difficult times occurred in the north after the Norman Conquest, and Hexham, close to the border, was for centuries subjected to incursions by the Scots. In April 1297, the Scots attacked and plundered the priory, including the herding of children into Hexham school, blocking the doors and setting fire to the building. Hexham never fully recovered from these misfortunes, with the priory and convent becoming impoverished.

Now beautifully restored, the Abbey church claims to be the finest Early English church in Great Britain, and stands proudly in the centre of this historic town. The Abbey has a number of historical objects worthy of note. From Wilfrid's time there is the bishop's seat or Frith-Stool; it was later used as the seat of sanctuary. This round stone chair is now in the chancel of the priory church. Steps lead down from the centre of the nave into the fine Anglo Saxon crypt, which consists of a barrel-vaulted chapel and ante-chapel. This was constructed of Roman masonry from Corstopitum. Other wonderful items of abbey furniture are the painted oak choir screen, the magnificent rood screen, and the font, made from the base of a Roman pillar.

Hexham's great glory are the Early English transepts; the south transept, built in 1220, contains the unusual Night Stair and the richly arcaded upper walls. The stone stairway, which formerly led to the dormitory, was used by the canons when they came into the church for matins. The small room at the top was probably used as a look-out for people fleeing to the church for sanctuary. Today, it is the choristers' robing room.

Of the stone crosses, the finest once stood at the head of Acca's grave – Acca became a bishop after Wilfrid. The shaft is superbly carved, with vinescroll ornament, and dates from c. 740; a tribute to the 'Golden Age' of Northumbria.

One famous Roman relic is the gravestone of a Roman soldier with the rank of standard bearer, who was killed at the age of 25 and buried at Corstopitum. The grave represents a mounted soldier riding over a prostrate Briton. The soldier is well armed, wearing a helmet with high crest and plume and carrying a sheathed sword. The native is naked, carrying a large oval shield and grasping a short sword. Below the sculpture is an inscribed panel:

> *To the gods the shades Flavinius*
> *standard bearer of the cavalry of Petriana*
> *of the white troop twenty-five years of age*
> *and seven years' service is laid here.*

An equally interesting stone with a Roman inscription is the slab which forms the headway in one of the passages in the crypt.

Bridging such a major obstacle as the River Tyne proved a difficult undertaking for the Hexham authorities. Between 1767 and 1782, two bridges were completed and one started, but a mixture of floods, storms and blizzards proved disastrous to the bridges. However, Robert Mylne, architect and engineer, completed the fourth bridge in 1793, and this handsome structure still stands today.

Main Route
Map M36a, p.119

From the Market Place walk along Market Street and Gilesgate, and descend to the main road. Cross over, and proceed along Tyne Green Road with the stream on the right-hand side. Turn left before a bus depot, to where the lane quickly narrows and enters a caravan site. Continue past East Lodge, where the way opens out into a wide grassy area. Proceed ahead on a grass track to meet another track, and on to a railway crossing. Cross the railway into Tyne Green Country Park, and walk along the track between the railway and the River Tyne. This is the site of the Border Counties junction where the line from Redesmouth crossed the Tyne and joined the Carlisle to Newcastle line. Bear right further on, and follow the red arrow marker along the river bank to cross a plank footbridge. Walk slightly right towards the wide concrete span of the A69(T) road bridge. It is possible to walk straight ahead and under the bridge, but the path bears left alongside the embankment, passes under the road by the railway, and continues back down towards the river. Follow the red arrow markers along the river bank, past the point where the two Tynes meet, and through a gate before the railway bridge. This area is called Kingshaw Haugh. The FP emerges on to a minor road with an instructive notice board advertising the delights of the Tyne Green Trail. Turn right to the toll cottage, cross the bridge, turn left, and walk along the road to Fourstones Paper Mill. Bear left just before the railway crossing at an FP sign, ¼ miles to Fourstones, 2½ miles to Allerwash.

The path continues along a concrete way, then becomes narrow with nettles, emerging on the river bank. This is a delightful section with numerous wild flowers, colourful gorse, a grand river and the rising hill slopes in the distance. Leave the river bank, with a waymarker pointing to the right to a kissing gate. Aim for a similar gate to bring you back on the river bank once more. Walk past a house with a neatly mown right of way, then by another cottage, and

continue along by the riverside. There is
undergrowth on either side of the path,
and hedges, then the way becomes tree-
bordered with silver birches, sycamore
and alder. This section of the path needs
a little attention as it is sliding into the
river. NOTE: If the worst comes to the
worst, there is an escape route back at
the last cottage. Walk to Butt Bank and
along the road to Newbrough.

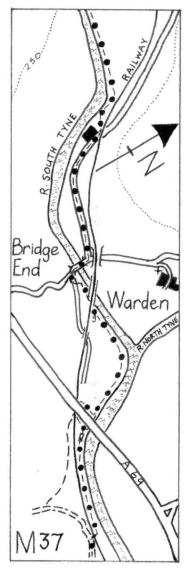

Turn right under the railway bridge
alongside a stream and climb up some
steps. Bear left at an arrow marker, and
proceed up the track to a minor road
and FP sign. Turn right for a short
distance, then left along the next road,
and keep walking smartly past Sewage
Wood into the village of Newbrough.
There are public toilets on the left just
before the road junction, with a metal
water fountain and a licensed restaurant
on the opposite side of the road.

Newbrough lies on the line of the
Roman Stanegate, which was the first
Roman road in Northumberland; a
strategic route between their fort and
supply base at Corstopitum (Corbridge)
and Carlisle. The forts on the Stanegate
were at first set on a day's march apart
(11-13 miles), then other forts were
added in between. With the building of
the Wall, the Stanegate's military use
was superseded and the forts acted as
supply depots.

In 1217 Newbrough was granted a
royal charter by Henry III, and became a
borough town, hence the name 'new market town'.

Turn left into the main street and a most attractive aspect is
revealed. The impressive warm-coloured stone buildings include the
Town Hall, complete with clock; it was built in 1878 and presented to

the local people by Miss Jane Todd. Next door, near the war memorial, which is pleasantly set back with seats, is the Mechanics' Institute, erected by public subscription in 1854 and presented to the Women's Institute in 1948; the WI members must be extremely proud of their meeting place. The Red Lion Inn is a hostelry dating back to 1190, which takes its name from the Scottish royal lion; it is a most welcoming establishment and provides excellent refreshments.

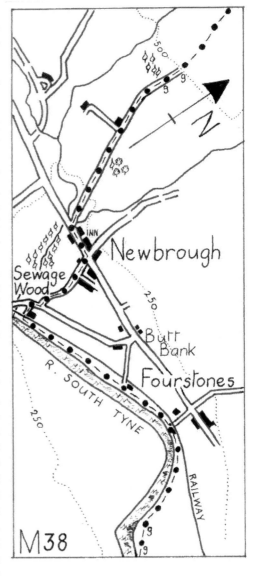

Continue along the road, turn right before the bridge and climb gradually up a long straight lane. Pass a wooden bungalow and the entrance drive to Newbrough Lodge, and proceed ahead, still climbing, on a pleasant tree-fringed grassy way. Meet a gate and an FP sign and ascend on grass alongside a wall. Looking back there are wide-ranging views across the Tyne Valley to the Hexhamshire hills. Pass beneath electricity pylons to a gate with arrow marker, and head on a north-north-west bearing across wide open spaces to a gate with the ubiquitous bull sign. Descend to cross the infant Meggie's Dene Burn.

The village of Newbrough has a legend of Old Meg the witch. She was burned at the stake, and buried in the dene with a stake through her heart after being refused Christian burial.

This information is just what you need, so glance furtively in all directions and hasten uphill alongside a fence to a gate. An arrow now directs you to the left-hand side of the fence, up to a metal gate before the B6318 road at GR NY 8640 7134. Do NOT go through it. Bear left, follow the wall to a stile, and on towards the car park at Brocolitia Roman Fort. Note: the right of way follows the perimeter of the Roman Fort round to the Temple of Mithras. (For a hundred yards or so on either side of the car park, the route is shared with that of *A Pennine Journey*. A guidebook produced by the Wainwright Society is published by Frances Lincoln; this is a revised route tracing Alfred Wainwright's 1938 journey from Settle back to Settle – a distance of 247 miles).

There is nothing to be seen of the Roman Wall at this point, as the more interesting sites lie further along to the west. The road, which follows the line of the ditch and the Wall, passes the site of Milecastle 31 and the fort (GR NY 8720 7145) of Brocolitia. However, if time permits, there is an excellent section of the vallum just a short distance east of Carrawbrough Farm.

The only visible part of the early second-century fort of Brocolitia is an earthen rampart, but just outside the south-west corner of the fort are the interesting and visible remains of a small mithraic temple GR NY 8588 7105. Originally founded at the beginning of the third century, it was extended to its present size later in the same century before being destroyed. At the northern end stand three altars dedicated to Mithras. In all probability, there would have been a relief illustrating the bull-slaying ceremony in the recess behind the altars. Today, the three altars are copies; the originals are in the University Museum, Newcastle upon Tyne. The central aisle of the temple, now represented by concrete posts, was originally flanked by raised platforms where the worshippers waited. Just inside the entrance of the building was a small ante-room which was equipped with a sunken pit used for initiation ceremonies. Also down the central aisle stand four small altars, and the desecrated statues of the two torch-bearing acolytes, Cautes and Cautophates, who represent light and life, and darkness and death, respectively. Just to the north of the temple lies the well and shrine of the nymph Covetina, where votive offerings of coins, brooches and bronze pins were made.

The Roman Wall
Emperor Hadrian visited Britain in AD 122 and decided to deal effectively with this part of northern Britain. He planned to create a

definite frontier by the construction of a wall from sea to sea; a demarcation line that would divide the Roman Empire from the barbarians.

The Wall was intended to be 80 Roman miles or 73½ English miles (117km) long. It was to be a stone wall 10ft (3m) wide and about 20ft (6m) high, from Wallsend-on-Tyne to the River Irthing. West of the latter point, the Wall was to be of turf, with a base width of 20ft and a height of about 17ft (5.1m) topped by a timber defence work.

The Wall was accompanied by a ditch on the northern side, except where cliffs made it unnecessary. Spaced at intervals of about one Roman mile (1,260 yards) were small forts or milecastles which contained living quarters for a small number of soldiers. Between each milecastle were two turrets built of stone measuring about 14ft (4.2m) square internally. Although the Wall itself ended at Bowness on Solway, a number of milecastles and towers have been traced further along the Cumbrian Coast.

The Wall was constructed by various detachments from Legions II Augusta, VI Victrix and XX Valeria Victrix. The Wall is not of uniform construction throughout its length, due to the different work rates of the squads involved.

The strategy behind the idea of the vallum was to create a barrier to the south, protecting the area from surprise attack. The vallum consisted of a large ditch protected by linear banks. The main purpose of the ditch, Wall and vallum was to form a frontier against hostile northern tribes, while still allowing the peaceful movement of people, and the growth of civilian settlements outside the military forts.

Today, there are substantial remains of this remarkable monument. The central section, cresting the dramatic outcrops of the Whin Sill, affords views second to none in the northern Pennines; it is a memorable experience to stand on these dolerite crags, and follow the Wall as it snakes over a succession of rises and dips.

From the temple, take the flagged path to a ladder stile, then across more slabs through the marshy area of Meggie's Dene Burn to reach a stile. Take care and quickly cross the road to a track and a footpath sign; Public Bridleway to Greenhaugh. Walk along the track to a gate and ladder stile, and then cross a footbridge over the infant Crook Burn. Climb up the gentle slope in front to a step stile in a fence, and proceed along a semi-avenue of trees to another gate and step stile. There is an odd-looking building to the right, with each gable end

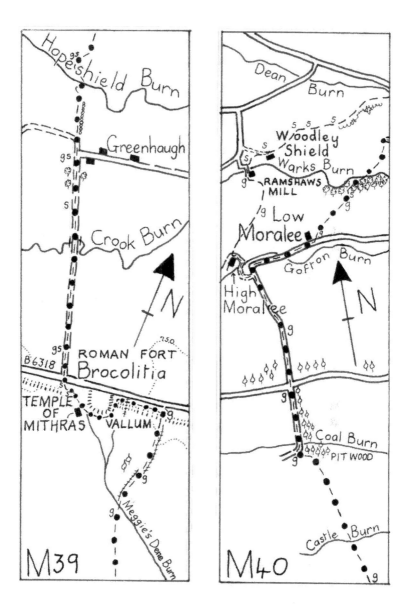

decorated with three raised stone projections, the middle ones higher
than the outside ones. Go straight ahead over a cattle grid, then
alongside a wall and ignore the track that heads left to Stooprigg
Farm. Descend to cross Hopeshield Burn and climb the slope to a step

stile in a fence by a metal gate. Follow an earth boundary with several wind-blasted hawthorns to a gate. Continue on the same line and cross Castle Burn to meet a wooden gate. Keep on uphill, and descend an area of wide cow-dotted rough pasture land; stride over a watercourse, and aim for the left-hand corner of Pit Wood. Walk to a gate with a bull notice, and on up the tarmac farm lane to meet another gate. Generally, there are a lack of waymarkers along this section of the route from the B6318.

Head straight across the road, with a glimpse of the village of Wark away to the right. Walk down the road to a metal gate, and forward to a farm track entering in from the left to High Moralee, GR NY 8435 7595.

This is the moment of decision, because there is a choice of routes, of roughly the same distance, from this point to the village of Wark:

Route 1: The Ravenber route via Warksburn Wood
Route 2: The alternative route via Ramshaws Mill

Route 1

Continue to descend on the road and cross the stream to a gate. Ascend the slope to Low Moralee; there is no FP sign, only the often-encountered bull notice. The footpath route is supposed to cross the field diagonally to the bottom right-hand corner; if the field is under crops it would be considerate to walk round the edge. You meet a conglomeration of gates forming a small paddock; go through the far metal gate, past an ash tree, and bear round an emerging spring, to reach a barbed wire fence at the edge of the wood. Beyond is a steep bank with lush ground cover. There is no clear way down this difficult slope over fallen branches, roots and vegetative litter.

One can genuinely utter a sigh of relief on reaching the banks of the Warks Burn. Cross over and ascend the slope, aiming slightly right to meet the end of a track. Bear right and follow this way down to meet the B6320. Turn left and walk into the centre of Wark.

I came this way, but from the opposite direction, during a previous long-distance walk from Cape Wrath to Land's End. There had been a spell of dry weather and only a little water was flowing in the burn. However, during my Ravenber reconnaissance, there had been periods of heavy rain, and on reaching the burn along the route as previously described, there was a different story. The Warks Burn was in flood; an

impassable obstacle, swift-flowing, too wide and too deep to ford. There
was no other way than to retreat up the slope back to GR NY 8435 7595.

Route 2

Bear left down the farm road that descends steeply to cross the bridge
over the Gofton Burn. Walk past High Moralee to a point where the
track bends. Head to the right up the pasture slope to barbed wire at
GR NY 843 763; follow the fence to an unopenable gate at GR NY 844
764, and turn right along the wall to a point where a fence joins it.
Turn left, and descend the slope, following a slight earthen bank, to a
gate with a bull sign. Pass Ramshaws Mill, cross the bridge, and
forward to a two-plank palisade on the right that hides a set of stone
steps. Slant up the pasture to the right to join a track and on to a
ladder stile. Proceed along the north side of the farm, Woodley Shield,
and ascend to the top right-hand corner of the field and a step stile.
Bear right, continue to a large gap and step stile, and then along the
fence to a step stile in the corner with an arrow marker. Follow the
fence and hedge on the right with a waymarker, and walk down the
field to cross a culverted stream to a kissing gate. Turn right, walk

Wark

down the road for a short distance to a junction, and go straight ahead into the centre of Wark.

NOTE: Representations were made to the Northumberland County Council, Rural Area Management, about difficulties on both Routes 1 and 2. Those outlined on Route 2 have been investigated and the problems resolved.

STOP PRESS: Splendid news concerning Route 1. The footpath between Low Moralee and Wark Village is now much improved. Volunteers have spent a considerable amount of time and energy clearing a footpath through Warksburn Wood and have constructed a good set of steps. All gates can now also be opened or have stiles next to them.

The crossing of the Warks Burn remains a ford which is easy to cross in most circumstances. Otherwise in flood conditions take Route 2.

9. Wark to Elsdon

Map	OS 1:25000 Outdoor Leisure, Hadrian's Wall, Haltwhistle and Hexham, Sheet 43. OS 1:25000 Outdoor Leisure, Kielder Water and Forest, Sheet 42
Highest elevation	Scald Law 1,010ft (308m)
Height of ascent	1,467ft (447m)
Distance	16 miles (25.6 km)
Terrain	Sparsely populated area, spacious pastoral upland, grass and heather moorland. Isolated outcrops of fell sandstone. Sections of afforestation

AFTER THE NORMAN INVASION IN 1066, it was only a short time before the unsettled north of England had risen in revolt. During William's bloody 'Harrying of the North', great areas were ravaged and put to the fire and sword; although it seems that Northumberland escaped the worst of the atrocities. The upper parts of Tynedale and Redesdale were probably free from Norman domination until the reign of Henry I in the early twelfth century.

Further north, the kings of Scotland trod a fine line between their own expansive aims and their relationship with the Normans. The Scots held extensive possessions in the north of England, and were permitted to retain hold on their English territories as vassals of the English king. The Scottish kings were to hold Tynedale continuously from 1150 to 1296, and their centre of operations was at Wark, which had a motte and bailey fortification overlooking an important river crossing. The settlement included a forge, a brewery, a bakehouse and a corn mill. The Scottish kings held court here, as, effectively, the area was part of Scotland.

By the Treaty of York in 1237, Henry III had reached an agreement with Alexander II of Scotland over the position of the border between the two countries. In order to impose some control over the area, the post of Warden of the Marches was created, with the Scots having a similar arrangement on their side of the frontier. The Liberty of Tynedale was brought under the supervision of the Warden in 1362, but as lawlessness worsened, the border area was divided into East and West Marches. In 1381, a Middle March was added which was to include the Liberties of Tynedale and Redesdale.

The conflict between the two nations through the fourteenth, fifteenth and sixteenth centuries meant that the border people had to decide which Crown to support, and in such an isolated area, it was often a question of 'every man for himself'. With no administrative control, acts of violence increased, with local people on both sides of the frontier allying themselves with the most powerful families. There were blood feuds between rival families which resulted in the sacking and spoiling of property, the stealing of animals, the taking of hostages and the inevitable reprisals. The reivers were well-mounted on sturdy hill ponies, and equipped with steel helmets, padded jackets and hand weapons. The raiders knew the countryside well, particularly the many different ways through the hills. The remote valleys and hillsides often echoed to the cries of battle, the smell of burning and the sounds of destruction.

The lives and property of the poor people of the northern valleys, Coquetdale, Tynedale and Redesdale, were continually at risk from the 'moss-troopers'. However, the wealthier yeoman farmers and small landowners were determined to resist the incursions, and built small strong refuges, called peles and bastle-houses, into which they and their families could retreat when danger threatened.

Bastles were defensible farmhouses of the fifteenth and sixteenth centuries, and are often confused with peles. Peles were usually squarish defensive towers, on to which farmhouses or dwellings were attached at a later date. Bastles were normally rectangular in shape, but several features indicate differences from peles on the one hand, and more conventional buildings on the other. With a few possible exceptions, bastles were the only farmhouses in the British Isles which accommodated livestock on the ground floor, and the farmer and his family on the upper floor. It is an interesting exercise to study OS maps of the border country and to detect the considerable number of peles and bastles that are spread throughout the area.

The name 'Wark' derives from Old English *(ge) weorc*, a fort. Perhaps it sounds a little odd when you say, 'I'm going to walk to

Wark,' but the local inhabitants pronounce it to rhyme with 'ark'. The resulting effect is particularly musical in the neighbourhood dialect, but probably just as confusing.

Many visitors pass through the village on the way to Bellingham, Kielder Water and the Border Forest Park. The centre of the village is the small green, dominated by a magnificent chestnut tree, planted in 1887; it is beautiful at all times of the year, especially when covered with its raiment of autumn leaves. A number of cherry trees were planted around the periphery of the green to commemorate the Queen's Silver Jubilee in 1977. The whole area is bordered by some interesting two-storey grey stone houses, and opposite is the imposing Wark Town Hall, built in 1874 as the Mechanics' Institute, a base for adult education in Victorian times. Abel Chapman, the famous sportsman-naturalist, is buried in the churchyard. He lived just outside Wark, and the beautiful avenue of lime trees on the Bellingham road were planted by him. The single-lane iron bridge spanning the wide North Tyne was built in 1878, and was a toll bridge at one time; it is interesting to note that the charges were a penny per person and two pence for a horse and cart.

Main Route

Cross over the bridge and turn left along the road to Birtley; there is a mile of road to do but the lane is quiet. As you climb out of the valley the view begins to extend up Tynedale to the forests and distant hills. The road passes over the track bed of the former Border Counties Railway; there is nothing quite so sad as a defunct railway line. An Act of Parliament was granted in 1854, and the line was opened to Belling Burn in 1856, a distance of 26¼ miles (42km). From the beginning the BCR intended to extend into Scotland, and the line was opened from Belling Burn to Riccarton junction in July 1862. Part of this former track bed is now submerged by the Kielder Water Reservoir. Passenger services between Hexham and Riccarton were withdrawn in October 1956, although goods trains continued to use the route until September 1958.

The road continues to climb and passes over two small streams to a wooden gate on the left at GR NY 873 775. Walk up the pasture and aim for the left-hand comer of a conifer plantation. Descend to a stream and a dilapidated ladder stile, cross the stream by means of a plank and proceed up the grassy slope with a fence and thorn bushes on the left. There is a stone with the letter M on it, and others in a line, all with a blue stripe on them. Continue to climb, crossing a number of humps and hollows, and head for the left-hand corner of the fence. There are the remains of several British camps encircling the village, and these provide proof that the area was inhabited at the time of the Bronze Age. The OS map indicates the site of Birtley Castle. Other evidence of the human impact on the landscape can be seen in the form of settlement patterns and cultivation terraces or lynchets.

Proceed along a narrow path and emerge on to a road opposite the church. The church is said to be Norman but was extensively refurbished in 1884. A pre-conquest stone slab found on the site, with the letters ORPE inscribed on it, probably represents a grave marker from a previous Saxon church, with the letters standing for [OR] ATE [P]RO [E]. 'E' would indicate the name of the person, such as Edmund, Eadric, Eadwald or some other Saxon name.

Bear left to pass a telephone box just before a playing field.

Birtley, (whose name derives from the Old English *Beorhte Leah*, meaning a bright clearing) is a peaceful village, proud of its well tended gardens, and previously a recipient of the Best Kept Village Award.

The area between Birtley and Elsdon is a sparsely populated, upland pastoral tract of countryside. The landscape is punctuated with isolated craggy outcrops of fell sandstone, and stretches of heather moorland and sections of afforestation; all these features are a precursor of things to come. Given misty weather conditions the walk becomes a journey through a Chinese watercolour scene.

Beyond the village, bear left and pass an old railway waggon on the right; note the cowslips growing in the opposite hedgerow. Take the ladder stile on the right, and walk on a north-east bearing across the fields, aiming for the farm of Pittland Hills. Pass through a low wooden fence in lieu of a stile in an area of humps and hollows. The way is not clear, but it could be through a gate just above; which is in direct line with a gap in the wall on to the road. The main route section from Wark to Elsdon is almost devoid of waymarkers, and mainly noted for its lack of stiles.

Go through the farmyard to a gate, through a small paddock, then to a gate on the right. Follow along the fence, then bear slightly right, aiming for a lone house, and on to a gate on the right-hand side. The house, Bog Shield, has a lean-to roof at the near end. Walk along to the right of the fence, and note the small door on the left of the

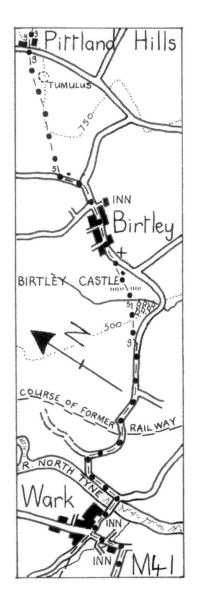

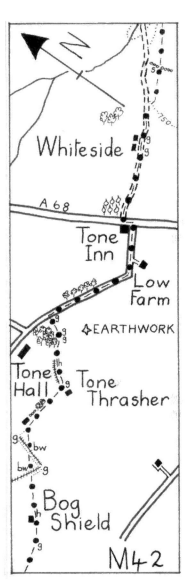

extension, with a cryptic sign which says, 'This is it'; it doesn't take much imagination to realize the meaning of the statement.

Continue over a hurdle and follow the fence on a bearing slightly east of north-east. To the left is a line of low crags, and through a gap there is a glimpse of the Cheviot Hills in the distance. Approach the corner of a fence where the stile should be, but walk further along to the right to a convenient gate. Proceed along the left-hand side of the barbed-wire fence in front to a point where the right of way should go. However, there is no stile, so aim for a gate at the top end of the field and turn right. Pass a stone barn, and follow the wall which quickly becomes a fence lined by mature trees. Note the wide-ranging views to the south. The imposing stone building ahead is delightfully named Tone Thrasher, and is important enough to be marked on the OS map.

Walk forward to the second metal gate, bear left and follow the tree-lined fence. The fine-looking house to the left beyond the fields is Tone Hall. Climb over a wooden hurdle, walk part-way along the fence, before slanting across to the right-hand corner of the wood. Go through two metal gates, and proceed up a track, with the deciduous wood on the left-hand side, to a gate. Turn right along the farm lane, a pleasant tree-lined way canopied with overhanging branches and bordered with grass verges. The Tone Inn is situated at the end of this lane on the main A68 road.

The frequent use of the word 'Tone' obviously refers to a locality of some quality. After all the map shows a Tone Well, a Tone Cottage, a Tone Thrasher, a Tone Lane and a Tone Hall. The landlord of the Tone Inn intimated that the word may come from *Toeland* or *Towland* – a toll house on a toll road. Alternatively, the name 'Tone', could be the surname of the original occupant of Tone Hall, the large house at the heart of the local estate. The Hall and the Inn appear to be of the same age, built in two periods from 1500 to 1700.

The A68 follows the line of Dere Street, one of the most interesting stretches of Roman road in Britain. This great highway cuts across the centre of the region from the Roman base at Corbridge, then across the Border Hills, the Tweed Valley and the Lammermuirs. It was the main artery of the Roman military presence, and connected such important forts as High Rochester in Redesdale and Chew Green high in the Cheviot Hills. Another interesting point is that the area in the vicinity of the Tone Inn is thought to be the site of a Roman crossroads, and some excavation might yield definite evidence of this.

Quickly cross over the busy main road to a lane above on the right. Follow the tarmac farm way to a metal gate. Continue through Whiteside Farm to another gate, and proceed to a point where a boundary comes close to the route. Slant off to the right across the pasture and then straighten out to a stone step stile in the wall. Aim for the farm buildings ahead; there is no indication of a path on the ground. Cross Dry Burn and rejoin the track at the edge of White House Farm. The next few yards will serve as a memorable part of the journey to be talked about in years to come. Pass the farmhouse and make for a gate ahead; there is no other way, so gird up your loins!

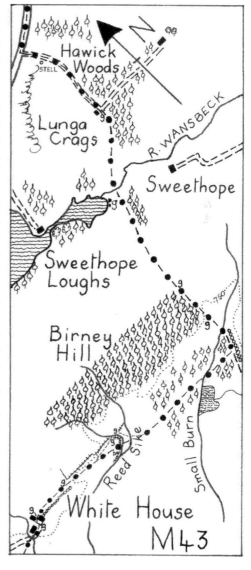

Enter a small enclosed stockyard and aim for a tall gate sheeted with metal in the far left-hand corner. Proceed through and walk to the right alongside a farm building. However, imagine an unsuspecting walker coming from the opposite direction and being faced with this tall sheeted metal gate, which effectively obliterates any view of the enclosure. The barrier has to be opened, and then one could be faced with a massed gathering of bovines plus bull, in order to reach the exit on the far side. There seems to be no other way round the farm at the present time.

Walk alongside the wall, topped with barbed wire, follow the track to a gate and continue through the field on the right-hand side of a fence to another gate. Bear right to a small gate and accompany a small watercourse for a few yards, before heading left to cross Reed Sike. This last section of the route is not as indicated on the OS map, due to barbed wire and the lack of a stile by the watercourse. Continue on a bearing just south of east, crossing drainage channels at intervals, to follow a wide grassy grack between young conifers. Keep straight on and cross Small Burn, noting a stretch of water away to the right. This area appears to be a favourite spot for seabirds; the birds become agitated, the cry goes up, 'Strangers in the House', and you are promptly seen off the premises. Continue through the area of young conifers to reach a stand containing fire beaters at a path crossroads. It is of interest to note the lack of a stile* through the wall on the line of the path to North Heugh; a waymarker would be helpful here. (*Problems resolved)

Turn left along the grassy public bridleway close to the wall, and then slant left to a wooden gate. The track, which is badly churned up, probably by the Swin Hope Light Horse, follows alongside a plantation on the left to a small wooden gate. There is a young plantation now on the right, as a clear grassy track approaches a gate. Note a good picture in the foreground, with the composition of a stone barn, a ruinous byre and two lonely trees surrounded by a dry-stone wall. Descend to cross the infant Wansbeck, which has its source on Fourlawshill; it issues from Sweethope Loughs, then flows easterly to Morpeth and on to join the North Sea. Fishing is available in Sweethope Loughs, and the entrance for visitors is from the Lake Wood road.

Ascend the grassy groove that swings to the right to join a track, and on to meet a second track emerging from Hawick Woods. Another badly churned up section leads to a gate that won't open; it is not a gate really, but a sliding barrier that is securely chained. Pass the large building, an animal shelter, and continue up the track. Note the beautifully crafted stell perched on rising ground; this outcrop is the tail-end of Lunga Crags. Proceed along the metalled surface to meet the Lake Wood road, and a sign indicating a public bridleway to Plashetts, 2¼ miles. Turn right, walk along the road for a short distance and bear left at the junction. It is then about half a mile (0.8 km) to the bridge over Middlerigg Burn, and a step stile by a metal gate on the right. A track soon peters out, so head across the pasture to a groove that descends to cross the Ray Burn, and then climb up to pass under the former railway line – two minutes' silence here!

The Wansbeck Line was authorized by Act of Parliament in 1859, and by 1865 the line was completed to link up with the Border Counties Line at Redesmouth junction. This particular section involved a moorland climb to 830ft (253m). at Summit Cottages, which

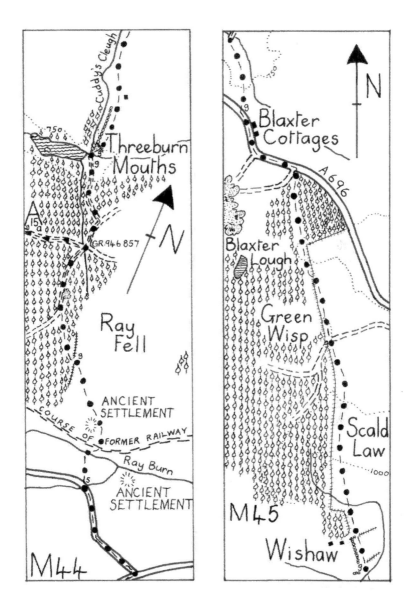

lie just 1 mile (1.6 km) to the west. All passenger services were
withdrawn between Morpeth and Redesmouth in September 1952,
although goods traffic continued until closure in November 1963.
There was a final nostalgic occasion when a special train, the

Wansbeck Piper, ran from Newcastle to Woodburn and returned via Scots Gap in October 1966; but this, sadly, was the end, and the metals were lifted in due course.

During the life of the line, the Army used it to move personnel and stores to bases in the Woodburn area. It is interesting to note that at the present time the Army is studying ways of developing a nationwide rail system for the transportation of tanks, guns and armoured vehicles; which, for example, includes the remaining 22 miles of the Wensleydale line in the Yorkshire Dales linking the Catterick Garrison. In Northumberland, the important Army ranges at Otterburn could use a revitalized Wansbeck line for the movement of heavy equipment. This would reduce traffic congestion and environmental damage on the road; and would also give the border economy and farming communities a boost from tourism. Maybe it's far-fetched or just pie in the sky; but some of the former railway routes need to be resurrected, in order that parts of beautiful Britain are not submerged by a tidal wave of motor vehicles and pollution.

Climb up the grassy slope, past the site of an ancient homestead, and walk through the heather, aiming for the edge of the forest.

'What was that?' A plaintive sound echoed against the mass of dark trees. Could it be the whistle of an ex-North British J36 class 0-6-0 struggling up over the moors between Woodburn and Knowesgate? I looked down, and there almost under my boots were three speckled, buff-coloured eggs in a scrape on the ground. Above, the mother bird wheeled and dived, sounding the alarm.

Aim for a gate in the fence and walk along the grassy ride to meet a forest track. There is the obstacle of a gully to negotiate, and a plank across at this point would be helpful. Continue straight ahead along the forest track with a felled clearing to the left, pass an old quarry on the right, and descend gently with a view of two tall masts on the horizon. There are now felled sections on both sides of the track followed by pines on the left-hand side. The line of the right of way indicated on the OS map is subsequently blocked by fallen trees, so keep on the forest track to meet an important crossroads of tracks at GR NY 946 857.

Walkers bound for West Woodburn, (see Alternative Route, p.152) should bear left at this point if the need for accommodation is the prime consideration; otherwise walk straight on ahead. Perhaps spare a moment to add to the as yet insignificant cairn.

The land on the right has been felled except for a small stand of growing timber. Descend gradually, with forest on the left and a cleared area on the right. The track swings left, and aims down to a metal gate with a lake to the left at Threeburn Mouths. Cross the bridge over the stream and bear right towards a stand of pines. The track veers to the right just before a gate, so cross the stream and proceed up the track to a fence. Climb over and follow up the side of a wall alongside a stand of pines. Pass an old wooden hut – definitely not on the shortlist as a cricket pavilion! The surroundings are now open moorland; so continue straight ahead, aiming for the right-hand side of two buildings in the distance below the afforestation. The direction of travel lies on a northerly bearing with only a vague impression in the heathery ground. Keep to the right of and above Cuddy's Cleugh, where there is a faint trod on top of the stream bank. Head for a metal gate beyond in the corner of a wall. However, at this point you are faced with a very boggy bit, and it is wiser to take avoiding action by hopping over a fence. Walk by the side of a wall and aim left to a gap in the corner at the top of another fence. Wishaw consists of a lonely house and barn.

Proceed up the slope alongside the forest fence, with open grass

Ravenscleugh near Elsdon

and heather moorland on the opposite side. Pass a small wheeled metal contraption that could possibly be converted to a cricket pitch line marker, and continue to follow the edge of the forest boundary. Occasionally, across Scald Law, there are patches of close-cropped turf to walk on, so enjoy this experience whilst you can. There is a young plantation on the left with more mature timber in front. Keep by the fence, which is helpful in misty conditions, and walk through the heather to reach a gate on the left. This spot goes by the delightful name of Green Wisp. A track, which leaves the A696 a short distance away, enters the forested area by the gate. This is an excellent viewpoint, looking westwards across a vast restless tide of woodland that rolls away to the far horizon.

Overhead, the dull dreary covering had cleared to become a north-west sky. Fleecy towers of cumulus were surrounded by pockets of blue, with an occasional stippled pattern of higher cirrus. Conditions on the ground mirrored the movements of the clouds; one moment a copse of trees were jet black, and just as suddenly they became clothed in a vivid green. Photographers must wait patiently to record these contrasts of sharp light and deep shade, as the effects are an attractive component of landscape photography.

The sight of the long purpled skyline of the distant Cheviots spur on many walkers, with the realization that beyond the hill barrier lie the lush valleys of the Rivers Till and Tweed and journey's end.

Continue straight on, climb the fence a little way ahead since there is no stile, and follow the heathery forest ride with no sign of a path on the ground. The way passes gorse bushes and descends with easier conditions underfoot to the main road. Turn left, and walk along the grass verge for half a mile (0.8 km), passing Blaxter Cottages to a wooden gate on the right. Descend the sloping pasture with expansive views to the north-west across Redesdale. Head towards the deeply-cut valley in front; continue along the cleugh edge, then follow the raised boundary bank and descend towards Ravenscleugh Farm. Cross the small footbridge over the stream, keeping to the right of the farmhouse, and accompany the wall. Slant left and descend to cross a footbridge over the Raylees Burn.

The immediate area is a pleasant place with a mini-gorge and attractive waterfalls. Climb up to Burnhead, a disused low building with two chimneys, and turn left through a metal gate despite barbed-wire decorations. Walk up the bracken covered rise straight ahead, and follow the boundary bank to meet a wall. From this point on

Gallow Hill there are glorious views of Elsdon, Harwood Forest and beyond to the Cheviots.

There is no stile through the wall in front, but walk a few paces to the right and cross at a hurdle. Descend the grassy slope, keeping to the right of the building Redshaw. There is a small area with young trees, and the line of the path should go through the left-hand gate to a fence in the corner which is now covered with barbed wire. An alternative way is through the right-hand gate and round the planted area; then a descent alongside the boundary bank lined with several trees, to a pair of gates, one on either side of the bank. The line of the path on the OS map (path 15) follows the boundary bank on the left-hand side. Note the old bath by the side of two ash trees.

Continue on to a hurdle, and bear down to the right across the field to meet the road. Turn right and walk over the bridge into the village of Elsdon.

NOTE: Walkers who have encountered problems on the main Ravenber route from Wark (up to the boundary of the National Park) to Elsdon, with reference to public footpaths in the parishes of Bavington and Birtley, should send details of the problems plus grid references to:

The Area Management Officer
Northumberland County Council
County Hall
Morpeth
Northumberland, NE61 2EF
Tel: (01670) 534089

Alternative Route

(1) Wark to West Woodburn
Maps A15a, p.147, A15b, A15c, p.153

(2) West Woodburn to Elsdon
Map A15d, p.156

Map	As per Main Route – p.139
Highest elevation	(1) Threeburn Plantation 958ft (292m) (2) Wether Hill 988ft (301m)
Height of ascent	(1) 1,092ft (333m) (2) 860ft (262m)
Distance	(1) 14½ miles (23.2 km) (2) 5½ miles (8.8 km)
Terrain	As per Main Route but including the valleys of the Lisles Burn and River Rede

As main route until crossroads of tracks in woodland at GR NY 946 857 Map M44, A15a (see p. 148). Turn left, walk down a good track with a felled area on the left, and then along a rough grassy way for a short distance. Go through a conifer plantation to a metal gate and proceed alongside a wall to another gate. Continue ahead past an old railway goods waggon and accompany a wall to meet a tarmac lane. Bear right, pass over a cattle grid near Pitt House and descend gently to a second cattle grid. There is a slight rise to Linnheads Pond, a trout farm, and on to a third cattle grid.

Walk along the farm lane to a metal gate; go through a yard to the left, to a step stile on the right by a gate, and forward to another stile and waymarker. Descend to cross a stream in a wooded dell and ascend to a tied-up metal gate. Pass through a small wooden gate with arrow to a metal gate, proceed to a gate and step stile, and follow the wall on the right to a stone step stile. Head straight across to a fallen ash tree in front of a derelict building, pass a marker post, and on to a ladder stile in the left-hand comer. Continue across a large pasture

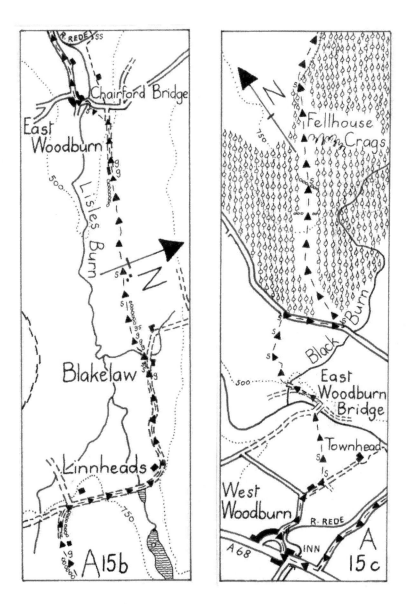

and accompany a wall to a wooden gate. Go through the farmyard with two gates and over a cattle grid. Carry on down the farm track, branching left to a stone step stile and FP sign above Chairford Bridge. Turn left, cross the Lisles Burn, and walk along the road into East

Woodburn; it is now a gentle mile down a quiet lane to the A68 and West Woodburn. NOTE: There is a footpath route from Chairford Bridge via Alder Hall, then the stepping stones across the River Rede, and by Townhead into West Woodburn.

After an undulating journey across the spacious uplands of southern Redesdale, the A68 plunges down to cross the River Rede, passing a row of terraced houses, before climbing steeply on its way north to Carter Bar. Though the area around the village is rural in nature, there were once thriving ironstone industries in the neighbourhood of Ridsdale and Broomhope Burn, together with coal pits and quarries. These industries and the local community were once served by the Wansbeck railway line.

Just north of West Woodburn, by a gateway on the west side of the A68, is a re-erected Roman milestone, the work of the Redesdale Local History Society. Close by is St Cuthbert's Church, Corsenside. Built in the twelfth century, it occupies a quiet place at the end of a farm lane with wide-ranging views; it is mainly Norman with a bellcote added later. An annual service is held in the church, with regular worship available at All Saints Church which is situated between East and West Woodburn.

The line of Dere Street passes a little to the west of the village. Close to the Roman road is the outlying fort of Habitancum (Risingham) and the marching camp on Swine Hill. What little remains of Habitancum is of third-century origin. A building stone records the name of the site, and states that the first cohort of Vangiones was the new garrison.

The village has a Post Office and general store and several establishments providing accommodation.

Just above the Bay Horse Inn turn right along the lane. Two steps on the right lead down to Brae Well (water unfit for drinking). Pass Peel Cottage with greenhouses to a stone step stile on the left. Climb up the field towards the top right-hand corner to another stone step stile. Walk across the meadow and descend the bankside to the River Rede and a magnificent wide-arched stone bridge. This is an idyllic riverside landscape of scattered trees, grassy banks, clear animated water chuckling over a stony bed, fish jumping, pied wagtails and dippers bobbing and curtsying.

The position of this fine important-looking bridge poses several questions. Was it an estate bridge for access to the big house? Did it lie on an important crossing point of the Rede en route for East

Woodburn? Was it built at the original crossing point of the river? Was the settlement of East Woodburn more important than West Woodburn at one time? This bridge is an enigma!

I would like to think that the landowners, farmers with horses and carts, stockmen and shepherds with lines of cattle and flocks of sheep, coaches and packhorse trains crossed the river at this point. There are two inscribed stones; one dated 1793, and the other signifying that a County Bridge was built in 1832. Today, it carries only a track, but passers-by will surely pay their compliments to its handsome appearance; the Ravenber Walk will once more make it feel important.

Cross over the bridge, turn left along a track of fine manurial consistency to a footbridge crossing the Black Burn, a tributary of the Rede. Proceed directly ahead up the steep slope, a mixture of rough grass and trees, and aim for a step stile. The way continues to ascend, as it bears right through a small pasture to a second step stile, and heads for another stile and FP sign by the road. Looking beyond to the skyline, a prominent stand of Scots pine indicates the next section of the route through the afforestation.

Turn right, walk down the road to a step stile and FP sign to Raylees on the left. Cross a plank bridge, enter a young forested area and

Elsdon

follow the well-waymarked path as it ascends on a grassy way. There are a number of plank bridges across drainage channels on this section of the route. Pass a walled compound containing a tall stand of Scots pine on the left and an old quarry on the opposite side. Ascend through trees to pass a circular ring of cleared heather edged by stones. Proceed through a gap in the wall, cross a plank bridge and rise through the heather to a marker post. Go forward to a stone step stile in a wall with its ends painted white.

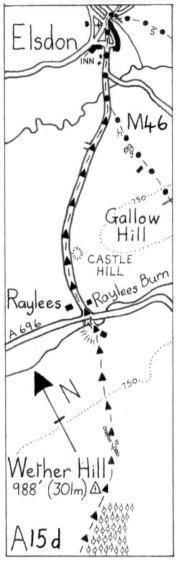

Continue through the plantation on a wide heather and grass-covered ride noting another marker post in front. Looking further ahead, there is a pile of stones on the ridge near an old sheepfold. Walk through an area of young trees and heather to reach a step stile over the forest boundary fence.

Aim for the ruined fold, and follow the forest fence, with pleasant grassy conditions underfoot, to the summit of Wether Hill. The OS survey column is placed at 988ft (301m).

Descend the grassy slope in an east-north-east direction to reach a ladder stile over a wall. Continue to descend the fellside on north north bearing, initially on a thin green track, then crossing a field drain, and on towards the left-hand side of a cottage. Pass through the banks and ditch of an ancient earthwork, descend to cross the footbridge to a metal gate, and climb up to meet an FP sign by the A696.

Cross over the main road to Raylees and ascend the minor road to Castle Hill. Continue along the road and descend to the village of Elsdon. The distance is 1½ miles (2.4 km) from Raylees to Elsdon.

10. Elsdon to Rothbury

Map	OS 1:25000 Outdoor Leisure, Kielder Water and Forest, Sheet 42
Highest elevation	Manside Cross 1,050ft (320m)
Height of ascent	1,158ft (353m)
Distance	13 miles (20.8 km)
Terrain	Remote area with rough walking along forest rides. Some good forest tracks. Moorland and hill paths with grass and heather

THE NAME OF 'ELSDON' derives from Eledene, probably meaning 'Elli's dene' or 'Ell's valley'. The village lies tucked away in a green bowl, at the foot of dark forested slopes and high open pasture. Around the settlement some meadows are enclosed by stonewalls, and scattered deciduous trees complete the scene. On the eastern side, massed battalions of the Harwood conifers seem to be marching nearer and nearer to the village. Roads depart in various directions, with some routes and tracks heading for the high wind-swept moors of the Otterburn Military Training Area. These ways are guarded by notices indicating strict safety rules, and supplemented by a network of red flags or red lamps. There are footpaths and bridleways open to public use at all times around the periphery of the military training zone.

Elsdon has an interesting past, and history is never far from the surface. After William's laying waste of the north, Northumberland became a deserted land. His representatives, the family of de Umfravilles, became Lords of the Liberty of Redesdale and upper Coquetdale. The Normans found a strong natural position at Elsdon and constructed a motte and bailey castle *c.* AD 1080. The artificial mound was raised on a spur of land commanding the Mill Dean gorge and the approach to the castle from the north. The motte platform measures about 150ft (46m) across, and would have contained a fortified timber-built strong-point, protected by a palisade. The approach to the motte was strengthened by a deep ditch, and the bailey was defended by more ditches and earthen banks. Elsdon's castle was abandoned *c.* AD 1157, in the time of Henry II, in favour of another motte and bailey site at Harbottle in nearby Coquetdale.

The unsettled nature of the conditions prevailing in the area, on both sides of the border, during the fourteenth to sixteenth centuries is reflected in the domestic architecture. Landowners and wealthier farmers built fortified houses or peles as a precaution against attack. They were often squarish towers built of heavy stonework, three or four feet thick, and were usually of three storeys above a stone-vaulted ground floor. The pele towers had a steeply pitched roof or a flat leaded covering, and many had crenellations and a walkway round the edge of the roof. Although some peles have been incorporated into later homes and adapted to suit the needs of the occupants, many are scattered about the border countryside and are now in ruins; they symbolize the stubborn spirit of our ancestors, and their determination to survive in this rugged landscape.

At the north end of Elsdon's large green is a fine example of a fourteenth-century fortified parson's pele. The ground floor room, 27ft x 15ft (8.2m x 4.6m) has a good lath and plaster barrel-vaulted ribbed ceiling. There are bedrooms on the first floor and another room above them. The title 'parson's pele' is derived from the fact that it was a defensive tower for the protection of a largely Catholic priesthood. Probably only a wealthy clergyman could afford this type of building. These pele towers could not withstand a heavy prolonged assault, but they were effective against lightly-armed raiders, and could survive until help came. The building was used as a rectory until 1962 when it became a private house.

At one time, Elsdon was situated on a meeting-place of ancient tracks converging on Redesdale, including a route from the Roman Dere Street and Gamel's Path via Leighton Hill, and would have been subject to frequent raids from border reivers.

St Cuthbert's church is set on the village green and dates from the twelfth and fourteenth centuries. It was built on the foundation of one still older, with the tradition that the body of St Cuthbert rested here in AD 875 on its wanderings towards Durham. The building has good plain windows, especially on the eastern side. The nave contains a fine Renaissance tablet set on a column together with other interesting monuments. The lawlessness of the border country demanded extra watchfulness, and the marks on the pillars near the door are said to be where men sharpened their weapons when they were suddenly called out from prayer to battle.

When the church was renovated in 1810 a mass grave was uncovered, containing the skeletons of young and middle-aged men thought to have been killed at the Battle of Otterburn in 1388. Otterburn was a typical border skirmish between the rival houses of Douglas and Percy.

Once considered the capital of Redesdale, Elsdon is a peaceful place of eighteenth and nineteenth-century stone houses set around the village greens. Looking around the village, there is the Victorian school building, which became a diocesan youth centre and is now a recording studio. There is also a circular pinfold where stray sheep and cattle were impounded, the site of a cock-fighting pit and a bull-baiting stone; it is interesting to note the names of the family and date of construction, 1729, on a door lintel with its attractive moulded hood and architrave.

The Elsdon area is good cycling country popular for touring and with clubs, who feature the village in their riding programmes. The local hostelry, the Bird in Bush, is situated at the southern end of the green. The nearest Youth Hostel is located at Byrness on the line of the Pennine Way. However, there are two or three establishments in and around the village that provide accommodation facilities.

Main Route
Maps M46, p.151 M47, p.160

Walk to the north end of the village, cross over the bridge and bear right to a metal gate across the road. Turn right by a small wooden bungalow and follow the fence; this is path 21. Keep towards the higher ground and head towards the corner of the wall to a step stile. Walk straight across rough pasture land with a fence on the left to the corner, bear sharp left and accompany the fence. Pass a thin strip of woodland descending the hillside on the right, and slant right to a step stile with a tall post. Cross a footbridge and head towards another strip of woodland. The OS map routes the path through the woodland, but there is no visible way on the ground, plus barbed wire. Go through the metal gate on the left, cross a stream, and turn right following the plantation boundary up the field. Slant left at the top and look for a small metal gate in the wall. Climb up the meadow towards the electricity pole and aim for a stile on the right-hand side of a wall. Turn left, pass in front of a farm, East Todholes (pronounced Toddles), and proceed along the faint track, with a spring on the right, to a gate and PB notice. You are about to enter Harwood Forest.

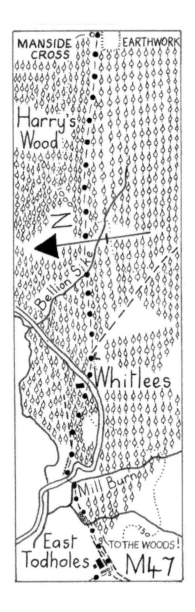

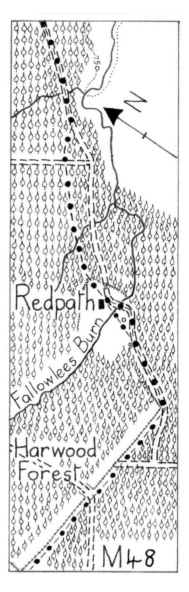

Northern Forests

The Forestry Commission was formed in 1919 with the aim of creating a national reserve of timber for the benefit of the country's economic needs. The area of upper Tynedale, Redesdale and Coquetdale stretching to the border hills was almost devoid of trees, and with the advent of tree-planting, the existing vegetation under-went a dramatic change.

During the early period of afforestation, the seedlings were planted in peaty, ill-drained soils on bleak hill slopes. It was soon realized that the young trees did not prosper when planted directly into the wet ground. A new method of planting proved much more satisfactory: the ground was cut with drainage channels and the young trees were planted into the lines of raised turves. The growth of the root system was then helped by the rotting vegetation, and the channels carried excess water away into the main drainage system.

Soon, dark regiments of young conifers began radically to change the traditionally open landscape. Blanket coverage of hill slopes and valley bottoms created a monotonous, uniform mass of woodland; a notorious example was Ennerdale in the Lake District. However, the Forestry Commission and private forestry groups, to their credit, have learned from their mistakes, and have brought about improvements and changes in forestry working methods and practices. For example, the idea of thinning and brashing trees has been modified; the felling programmes are now carried out with more careful thought about landscape features and the natural contours of the land; improvements have been made in the configuration of planting sections and blocks of trees, and larch has been planted to create an attractive visual aspect in blocks or along boundary lines.

Another imaginative project is to select the many watercourses, and to plant stands of broadleaved species such as rowan, alder, ash, sessile oak, willow and birch. Again, this is intended to add contrast to the forest as well as creating a habitat for wildlife; it is scheduled that these watercourse sections will not be grown for commercial timber production.

Five species of conifer account for almost all the afforestation: spruce, which produces high yields on peaty soils; Norway spruce the 'Christmas Tree', which will withstand harsher, more exposed conditions and poorer soils; Scots pine, which grows well on heathery, drier ground; lodgepoll pine, planted in areas where heather has flourished on deeper layers of peat; and Japanese larch, a versatile forest tree that grows well on land that supported bracken; it does not burn easily, and is therefore useful as a natural fire-break; it adds seasonal colour and softens the dull monotony of spruce.

The great northern forests include Kielder, Falstone, Redesdale and Wark; in the west there are Kershope and Spadeadam on the Northumbria/Cumbria border; in the east is the Rothbury Forest District, containing the main forests of Kidland, Uswayford, Harbottle, Thrunton and Harwood.

Since the first planting, the forests have produced timber for the mines, pallets, wood for the construction and building industry, pulpwood for chipboard, packaging and paper.

The landscape of dense forests, innumerable watercourses, reservoirs and lakes, craggy outcrops, grassy rides and heather moorland has produced a habitat for a wide variety of wildlife: birds of prey, such as the sparrow hawk and peregrine falcon, woodcock, green woodpecker, red grouse and red squirrel.

The Forestry Commission and Forest Enterprise are keen on landscape improvement. They wish to foster good relations with the public, and in the main, welcome visitors to walk the paths and tracks, to use the excellent forest drives, parking and picnic facilities, and generally to take an interest in the beauty of the forest.

There is a short boggy section to follow with conifers on the right. Cross over a small footbridge with a wall to the left, and continue along the forest ride; the trees are mainly larch and spruce. There's a FP marker and footbridge ahead, with a notice-board containing the following information: 'MILL BURN NATURE RESERVE': Information from the Secretary, The Hancock Museum, Newcastle-upon-Tyne.

Walk forward to a farm track with a finger post. Cross over to a larch plantation with no sign of a path on the ground. Follow the fence in front; it is rough going as far as the fence corner. There are two rides in front; be sure you take the right-hand one. Proceed through a carpet of heather and rough tussocky grass and climb steadily up the ride; the grassy surface improves nearer the top of this section. Look back at the view, as well as taking the opportunity for a breather. Emerge on to a road by a cottage called Whitlees. A marker post indicates the route to Manside Cross, 1½ miles, and Harwood Head, 1¾ miles. Walk for a few paces, then take the right-hand ride, with good conditions underfoot, to reach a broad forest track. There is a corner wall on the right with an area of mature conifers.

The route bifurcates: left towards Manside, straight ahead towards Harwood. Bear left, the harder choice, and head deeper into the forest along a carpet of heather and rough grass. There are some fairly deep gullies and drainage channels to negotiate. Emerge through an opening in the trees on to a track with a FP marker sign. Continue straight ahead up the ride and along another tussocky section of difficult terrain. At an intersection of rides go straight on to meet a gully and another track, but help is at hand in the form of a helpful FP marker. Whilst struggling through rough grass, I thought you would appreciate two pieces of information; firstly, that this part of the forest is called Harry's Wood – bless him; secondly, that you happen to be striving hard along FP 32.

Eventually, the way becomes easier underfoot, the ride opens out, the dark wall of trees slides away and a view appears ahead with a FP marker. The clearing contains two items of interest, a wayside cross and a defensive earthwork. The base and a shaft stub are all that remain of Manside Cross. During medieval times, crosses were erected at important junctions and along wayside tracks to protect and direct travellers. Similarly, in the packhorse era, guidestones were erected at strategic points on routes across wild countryside. Also at this point may be seen the considerable banks and ditch of an ancient hill-top earthwork.

Looking north from Manside Cross, a forest ride disappears into the dark mass of trees – thankfully that is not the way.

Thoughts on Forest Walking

Forests can be intimidating places; one needs to be psychologically prepared for the encounter with the massed ranks of conifers. Throughout the journey your mind and body constantly seek relief in the thought of verdant pastures, high moorland ridges with expansive views, and filtered sunlight dappling some canopied river bank.

When forest walking, it is important to use your compass at frequent intervals, since you can easily become disoriented. Monitor your position regularly as you follow a track or forest ride – the choice of an incorrect route can result in utter failure. There are few habitations along the way and no facilities for obtaining food and liquid, so a day's supplies will have to be carried. Full emergency rations are essential.

If you are walking with companions, the leader should be single-minded and concentrate on the matter in hand; it is so easy to miss a vital turn along some forest ride or track. Don't expect to find waymarkers on every tree; the challenge of navigating through a forest is itself a rewarding experience. There are compensations, such as an occasional clearing with colourful larch and glistening birch in harmony with the soft chuckling sound of a burn. There is also a chance of hearing or catching a fleeting glimpse of the forest's secretive wildlife.

Don't always rely on the line of the right of way as indicated on the OS map, as some routes have been impaired by trees and undergrowth. Although forest tracks give greater access, be aware that not all tracks and rides are shown on the map. Sometimes, all your counting and checking may be to no avail. A pedometer may be useful, and there are expensive satellite-linked tracking devices, but a good map and a firm trust in one's compass are essential points for forest walking.

Forests are fruitful places for story writers, as plots seem to emanate from the dark depths like resin oozing from a pine tree. There is mystery in the destination of some tracks and rides; secret clearings off the beaten track for anarchistic ecologists; lonely, isolated buildings with tales to tell; grass-covered metals of a seemingly forgotten railway line, and so on. But, ultimately, there are the scents and sounds of the forest: the silence and solitude, the varying hush and rustle of the wind through the trees, the movement, and somewhat eerie creaking of trunks and branches, the sighing sensation of pine fronds, the sharp cracking of a twig and the aromatic smell of pine needles and damp vegetation – the living forest adds fuel to the imagination.

There are solitary buildings you may come across in the depths of the northern forests, which are cared for by either the Mountain Bothies Association or the Forestry Commission. They are rightly unannounced and unadvertised, and make ideal shelters for explorers. A particular place encountered during one of my long walks was especially welcoming, on a day of intermittent rain and low cloud that drifted in and out of the sodden spruce; it was a haven, a stoutly-built refuge against the elements. During the evening the stone-flagged roof easily resisted the malevolent blasts of wind that rushed through the forest clearing. The door was firmly closed, a fire coaxed into cheerful warmth and the billy brewed on the portable stove. A restful night was spent in relative comfort in the down bag on the sleeping platform. The next morning the bothy was swept out, the grate cleared, wood re-stocked and an entry made in the log book. It is interesting to realize that these facilities exist in areas of remote and wild countryside. Users must be willing to observe the simple rules, and to support the associations and bodies that provide these basic shelters.

From Manside Cross, follow the fence ahead in an easterly direction, keeping on the right-hand side and accompanying a long strip of unplanted land – a most welcome visual contrast. A deer fence appears on the right, as well as a forest ride, but keep straight on. The deer fence slants away as the route reaches a hard-surfaced track. Bear left and walk easily to meet a slight bend and a horseshoe-marked post – yes, our friends of the SHLH are still in the vicinity! Continue to follow the fence to a FP sign, and notice the farmhouse of Redpath in the distance.

Proceed for a few paces, ignoring the forest track on the right, and keep straight on to a metal gate. The isolated building, with painted door and window frames, is set in a large forest clearing. The surrounding pasture looks in poor shape. Pass a ruined sheepfold on the left and cross the bridge over the stream. There is an FP marker on the right just past the farm indicating blue and yellow routes. The yellow way bears left and gently ascends to a fence and stile. The clear forest track, indicated by the blue marker, may also be followed at a quicker pace if time is short.

From the stile walk into the forest along a ride, cross over a bisecting ride and continue straight on. The way first bends a little to the right, followed by a straight section, then curves to cross a stream and goes on to meet another track. Do not go straight on. Turn on an easterly bearing for a few paces, then head in a north-easterly direction along the next ride. Negotiate fallen trees, drainage ditches and rough tussocky grass to reach a small glade prior to two rusted iron posts. Proceed across a bisecting grassy ride, and head straight on to a point where the right of way should continue – but the path is blocked. Continue along the ride to meet the wide track coming from Redpath and turn left. The route follows the track (note a boulder on the right approximately 140 yards above the exit from the forest), crosses over a bridge with deer fencing on the left to protect a young plantation, and climbs gently to Fallowlees.

Bear round to the left, well clear of the group of buildings, and walk for just over a quarter of a mile to a crossroads of tracks. This spot is marked by a blue horseshoe on a yellow background and signpost to Chartners – an intriguing location in the depths of Harwood Forest.

Turn right and follow the track, which bends round to the left and descends to cross the Font Burn. This watercourse becomes one of the main streams that drains the eastern side of the forest; others include Newbiggin Burn, Blanch Burn, Smiddy Burn, Chartner Burn and Jabeltrew Sike – now there's a fascinating name for you. What or who is Jabeltrew? Perhaps a character from a coven of witches; there's another plot and another story!

The immediate area around the Font Burn is a delightful contrast to the dense forest gloom. The clearing contains several broadleaf trees, a scattering of boulders, a carpet of bracken and patches of heather; it also appears to be a good spot for a large commune of amorous frogs.

The wide track climbs past old quarry workings, and continues in a northerly direction for about a quarter of a mile, with newer plantations on the left. Turn right and proceed along the ride with very pleasant walking conditions underfoot. Bear left at the next junction of rides, and walk for a short distance in a northerly direction, to reach a ride slanting off in a north-north-east direction.

This is Whittlestick Corner, GR NZ 0240 9628, an important turn for Coquet Cairn. I did carve three rings around the top of a stick and placed it in situ; but, if a hungry deer has eaten it, perhaps the Forestry Authorities or a handy Ravenber walker could replace it. Note, that the original right of way joined the ride at this point, but the route is now impaired. (Alternative Route from Whittlestick Corner, see p.172). Bear right and gently ascend the ride to reach the edge of the forest at Coquet Cairn, GR NZ 0252 9647.

It is with a feeling of release that you look out across rolling countryside. The view encompasses open heathery moorland that undulates towards the dark line of the Simonside Hills. Close by, to the west, a thrusting block of afforestation continues northwards, and then swings out of sight beneath the frowning northern crags of the escarpment.

This is the type of landscape that inspired the Northumbrian poet Wilfrid Wilson Gibson:

> *The ragged heather-ridge is black*
> *Against the sunset's frosty rose;*
> *With rustling breath, down syke and slack,*
> *The icy, eager north-wind blows.*
> *It shivers through my hair, and flicks*
> *The blood into my tingling cheek.*

From *Stonefolds*

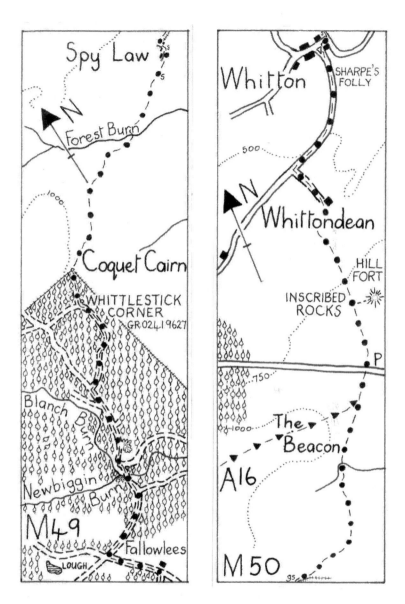

Fell Sandstones

In Lower Carboniferous times a thick succession of sandy sediments were laid down, originally as the vast delta of a river which drained an enormous land mass across the northern hemisphere. Tremendous earth movements folded and faulted this great thickness of sandstone into a series of blocks, to form a sinuous arc of high ground that curves southwards from just below Berwick towards the Cumbria/Northumbria border. The fell sandstones are a massive and uniform stratum up to a thousand feet in depth, and reaching a height of 1,411ft (430m) in the Simonside Hills south of Rothbury. Many people come to recognize the fact that these sedimentary rocks symbolize central Northumberland. Commercially, too, sandstone has been important as an excellent building stone that is noted for its durability and attractive appearance. The Romans discovered its qualities by using it for the facing blocks of Hadrian's Wall.

From the little knoll at Coquet Cairn accompany the fence and cross it at a step stile. Swing to the left opposite a gate, noting the sign 'Beware of Adders', and walk on a comfortable grassy surface past a line of shooting butts spaced out at intervals. Slant to the right as the track descends to a peaty section. A pleasant grassy surface appears again, with a grand view across the heather moorland towards the crinkled Simonside ridge. Bear left at an FP sign, and descend, passing a solitary post, to cross the Forest Burn by means of a primitive footbridge. This delightful tree-fringed spot is cool and shady on a hot day, with the stream having cut a groove across the open gently sloping moorland.

Climb up the far bank following the fence left to an FP sign, then swing to the right, and continue in a north-east direction, aiming for the isolated building ahead. The path is indistinct on the ground, but the line of progress is clear. Descend and cross a culverted stream and up to a ladder stile. Cross the pasture, with signs of old 'inbye' land boundaries, to reach a stone wall in front of the building called Spy Law.

The old farmhouse was undergoing renovation by volunteers of the Prince of Wales Trust. When I was there, a group of young people from Sunderland were busy repairing and refurbishing the structure, and making it watertight and habitable. I chatted for some time with this enthusiastic team, and received a scalding hot mug of tea during the conversations. I'm not quite sure of the purpose of the renovation, but it would make a splendid bothy on the Ravenber route. Another incident at Spy Law comes to mind. After saying my farewells, I had just rounded the corner when a Range Rover hove into view along the track. It stopped, and a gentleman in the passenger seat enquired, 'Are you Mr Brown?' I replied that I was not that person and continued on my way. It was only later during the evening that I learned that the gentleman was a near-relative of the Duke of Northumberland, and that Mr Brown was the name of the team leader working at Spy Law. You never know just whom you are going to meet!

Cross to a ladder stile, bear left, proceed between a wall and a small ruined building and turn right. Pass an FP sign on the left and walk towards a metal gate and ladder stile.

The sound of the wind through the copse of protective pines is distinctly audible, and seems to enhance the atmosphere surrounding this lonely place. Certainly, the name Spy Law should be included in some tale of forest mystery.

Negotiate a wet section and continue along the moor side of the fence, as far as an FP sign and tall pole near to a gate. Bear left and follow a pleasant wide grassy track; note an FP sign thus:

A grooved trackway descends, with a boulder-strewn hillside for company, to a wooden bridge over Grain Sike. Tread through a peaty section, pass another FP sign, and gradually ascend the heather-covered slope. There is another sign warning 'Beware of Adders' and a cairn to the right. A path veers off westwards along the Simonside ridge.

Continue straight on along the clear grooved way to descend the hillside, noting a boundary bank slanting up to the left. (The Alternative Route from Whittlestick Corner rejoins the main route here; see p.175*).

Cross over the minor road from the FP sign to the Lordenshaw parking area, where another sign indicates: 'Whittondean 1, Rothbury 2'.

A clear grassy path rises gradually in a northerly direction to meet a marker post on the western flanks of the Lordenshaw hill fort, thus:

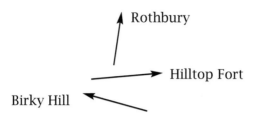

The arrow pointing to the right leads through the hill fort's western entrance towards the centre of the defensive earthwork. NOTE: The path has been routed through the original hill fort entrances to minimize the problem of erosion on the ramparts.

Lordenshaw Iron Age Hill Fort

Having a collection of stones handy is all too convenient for the construction of a twentieth-century cairn on the summit of the hill fort. Unfortunately, over the last few years, visitors have been using stones from the fort's three-thousand-year-old defensive walls. Under the guidance of the Northumberland National Park archaeologist and National Park warden, the children of Rothbury Middle School combined a live history lesson with a wheelbarrow exercise, and moved five tons of stones from the cairn and replaced them on the ramparts.

Lordenshaw, in the shadow of the Simonside Hills, is one of the best Iron Age hill forts in Northumberland, and has a spectacular view over the Coquet Valley towards the Cheviot Hills. During the Iron Age, from around 1000 BC, the climate became colder, reducing the amount of cultivated land, and hill forts were constructed to protect people and their flocks and herds. The fort site was occupied for about 800 years from around 400 BC, passing into Roman times. During the more peaceful conditions, the ramparts were demolished and circular huts built inside the fort.

The geographical location of Lordenshaw, allied with its commanding position, has always attracted human activity; it was used as a burial and religious site, a well-defended strong-point, and a settlement. Later on, the slopes were rig-and-furrow ploughed into arable land, and sections used as grazing pastures. In medieval times the area lay within the Forest of Rothbury, with the arable fields along the valley bottom, together with extensive tracts of upland grazing. A recognizable feature is a deer park pale or boundary wall which runs roughly north south through the area and slightly west of the hill fort site.

Another feature of great interest is the number of inscribed stones with cup and ring marks. The subject of decorated stones, and ornamented outcrops of natural rock, has frequently given rise to controversy. The markings are a language of signs, not pictures of actual objects. Most symbols are to be found on isolated boulders or on outcrops of rock that overlook wide landscapes. The main form of pattern design is a simple cup-like depression surrounded by one or more continuous or broken concentric rings. Occasionally, there is a duct running into the cup. Lordenshaw has a distinctive style of rock carvings, with large cups, some basins and very long ducts.

The marked rocks are found along natural routes used by people who were partly nomadic; it is conceivable that someone was marking the routes to indicate territorial divisions, hunting grounds, or the direction to sacred places. The evidence points to the Early Bronze Age people rather than Neolithic. The symbols are best viewed in conditions of strong, low-angled light.

Some Locations

West Lordenshaw (Birky Hill)	GR NZ 0512 9912
West Lordenshaw (Horseshoe Rock)	NZ 0502 9918 NZ 0524 9916
East Lordenshaw	NZ 0562 9909 to 0565 9935 NZ 0569 9938 to 0565 9950
Lordenshaw (hill fort)	NZ 0549 9922

NOTE: In 1992, a management agreement for Lordenshaw was drawn up under Section 39 of the Wildlife and Countryside Act 1981, between the National Park Authority, English Nature and the landowner, the Duke of Northumberland. This created an access zone including the Iron Age hill fort and nearby examples of rock carvings, to which the public will have free access at all times.

From the western entrance of the hill fort, descend the hillside on a northerly bearing, with a fine view across the valley to the wooded hillside surrounding the large house called Cragside. Keep to the

western side of a small plantation, and bear right to cross Whitton
Burn. Pass through Whittondean Farm, turn left, and continue along
the track to join Hillhead Road. Turn right along the rough-surfaced
track to pass Sharpe's Folly, which was built under the instructions of
Rev. Sharpe in order to provide work for local stonemasons in the mid-
eighteenth century. In Whitton the fourteenth century pele tower was
once the parsonage of Rothbury, and has modern portions built by
successive rectors. The vaulted basement would be used to hide the
frightened inhabitants during a Scottish raid, and the courtyard would
secure the cattle.

Take the right fork and then turn right at the road junction. Pass
the Horse Riding Centre with cheerful readiness, and the Whitton
Farm House Hotel, to reach a footpath in the extreme left-hand corner.
Proceed along a small fenced section to a step stile that leads into the
field. Rothbury lies ahead with Cragside Hall still half-hidden amongst
its protective girdle of trees.

Descend the grassy slope, and the Coquet Valley begins to open
out westwards. The compact, warm stone town fits comfortably in the
valley bottom and encroaches up the far hillside. The path descends
steeply to a metal kissing gate and FP sign. Walk down the quiet lane
to join a road at the foot of the slope and turn right. Proceed for a few
paces, turn left, and cross over the modernized four-arched stone
bridge into the town of Rothbury.

NOTE: For problems experienced with rights of way within the area
of the Northumberland National Park, contact:

National Park Headquarters
Rights Of Way Officer
Eastburn, South Park
Hexham, Northumberland NE46 IBS
Tel: (01434) 605555

Alternative Route
**Whittlestick Corner, GR NZ 0240 9628, via Simonside Hills to
Lordenshaw. Parking Area: GR NZ 0525 9879
Maps A16, p.174; M50, p.167**

From Whittlestick Corner, GR NZ 0240 9628, carry straight on up the
grassy ride to meet a track. Turn right, and proceed ahead to a
palisaded fence. Walk through the grass and heather in a northerly

Map	OS 1:25000 Outdoor Leisure, Kielder Water and Forest, Sheet 42
Highest elevation	Simonside 1,411ft (430m)
Height of ascent	1,555ft (474m)
Distance	14½ miles (23.2 km)
Terrain	As per main route with course along fell sandstone escarpment

direction towards the forest fence to the west. There is a felled area beyond the fence as a thin, intermittent path follows the boundary. Negotiate a swamp of sphagnum moss by taking avoiding action to the right, and then retracing steps back to the fence.

Continue on the thin trod through the heather to reach the edge of Selby's Cove, with a ruined building to the right. Keep to the fence overlooking an attractive boulder-strewn mini-canyon. Descend the peaty slope and slant across to the right to a stile in a fence. Long-jumping skills are required here to cross the stream, Ousen Sike. Ascend on a thin path through the heather, aiming for a gap between the trees and the fence, then bear left towards a small outcrop. Continue on a faint trod through rough grass and heather, with a line of burnt trees on the left standing like blackened skeletons. The going is boggy underfoot, but walk along the edge of the forest to meet a track with a marker post displaying a red triangle.

Turn right and commence the climb up the steep slope, passing a huge boulder on an outcrop of rock. Looking upwards there is an impressive rock picture of the western crags of Simonside – huge pock-marked weathered buttresses of fell sandstone. Pass a small pillar of eroded stone on the right, and continue the climb to the summit cairn of Simonside, 1,411ft (430m). The rock scenery looks very familiar, reminding me of the Roaches in my native North Staffordshire.

The stone cairn has a decorated top, and the escarpment edge drops down to meet the advance elements of the forest army. There are some well-cut letters chiselled into a hugh protruding block of stone, and the neighbouring outcrops are generally of interest to rock

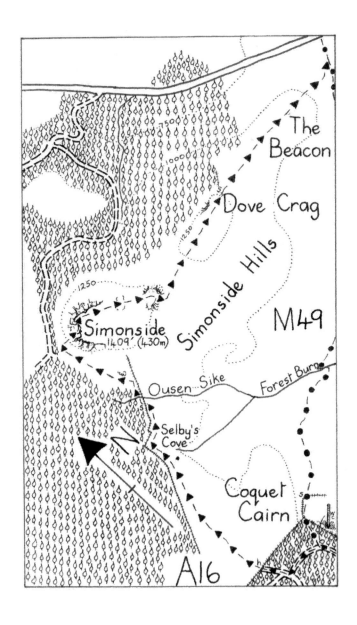

climbers. Walk along the ridge and pass through a line of posts to reach a cairn on a heathery and grassy top. Descend, and note another path slanting down left towards the forest. Pass by a rocky crest in front, and then past rounded tor-like crags away to the right. Continue through the heather to reach the summit of Dove Crag. A large cairn and circular shelter decorate the top and large outcrops of rock overlook the forest; it is another excellent belvedere for views to Coquetdale, Garleigh Moor and Cartington Hill. Descend a short steep slope; observe that another path leads off to the left from a marker post and descends towards the sea of larch, spruce and pine.

From a fence and step stile continue along the ridge on a wide path to reach the circular cairn shelter on the Beacon.

Descend the hillside following a bank cum wall, amidst surroundings of bracken, boulders and heather. Bear left at a path *junction and walk down the slope to meet the minor road. Cross over to the Lordenshaw parking area, GR NZ 052S 9879.

11. Rothbury to Alwinton

Map	OS 1:25000 Explorer, Alnwick and Amble, Sheet 332. OS 1:25000 Outdoor Leisure, The Cheviot Hills, Sheet 16
Highest elevation	Ship Crag 755ft (230m)
Height of ascent	1,171 ft (375m)
Distance	Direct: 12 miles (19.2km). Including Harbottle: 12½ miles (20 km)
Terrain	Hillside and moorland walking; river valley and upland pastures. Interesting villages

ROTHBURY, *Hrōpa's Burgh*, is a delightful township, and lies in the valley of the River Coquet about halfway between its source in the Cheviot Hills and the North Sea. In whatever direction you look the grey roofs of the little town are outlined against a background of hills. It consists essentially of three main streets, with Front Street and High Street running parallel with the river and Bridge Street leading off at right angles. Between the first two streets lies the attractive sloping strip of the green, bordered by mature sycamore, chestnut, beech and oak trees.

The parish church of All Saints lies in the angle of the three main thoroughfares, at the south-east corner of what was the site of the market place. The church, rebuilt in 1850 with a big west tower, has a thirteenth-century chancel and east wall of the transepts. The building contains an important font with a bowl dating from 1664, decorated with geometrical designs. The shaft is the lower part of an Anglo-Saxon cross-shaft, *c.* AD 800, and is carved with wonderful stylistic patterns. Amongst these are biting long-tailed monsters, a lion and the scene of the Ascension of Christ. This font is one of the most important of its date in England.

Being so close to the border, the settlement, and Coquetdale in general, were inevitably subject to Scottish raids. Even as late as the

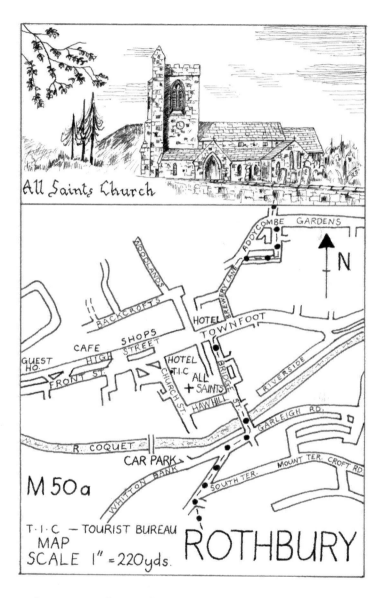

eighteenth century, the settlement was described as little more than a cluster of rude cottages thatched with heather, together with an inn and a church. As times became more peaceful and conditions for farming improved, so Rothbury became the market centre for Upper

Coquetdale. Cattle and sheep were brought into town, the drovers were provided with accommodation, and shops were opened to supply them with provisions. Today, stone houses and shops line the northern side of High Street, and houses lie along the southern side of Front Street. There are a number of establishments that offer accommodation facilities for visitors, who use the town as a popular centre for touring Coquetdale. It is also a convenient base for walking on the Simonside and Cheviot Hills.

Rothbury began to grow rapidly after 1865, when a wealthy industrialist, Sir William Armstrong, bought a desolate valley to the north of the town. A mansion, Cragside, was built and millions of trees and shrubs were planted. Armstrong was an ingenious practical engineer himself, and developed a system of lakes and power houses. The installation of piping and hydraulic machinery enabled Cragside to be the first house in the world lit by hydro-electricity.

The railway reached Rothbury in 1870, largely at Armstrong's instigation, but closed for passengers in 1952 and for goods traffic in 1963. Many stories were told about the sinuous Rothbury line, no doubt a bit more being added every time an incident was recounted. For example, it is related that, by mutual arrangement, the train was stopped in order for passengers to pick blackberries or even catch rabbits!

In 1977, the National Trust acquired the Cragside Estate, and the house opened to the public in 1979. Since then, the formal garden, the rose loggia, the Italian garden and clock tower have been opened to visitors. The full glory of flowering azaleas and rhododendrons are a tremendous attraction in June.

Main Route

From Townfoot, turn left off the main street immediately after the Queen's Head and walk along Brewery Lane. Slant to the right past a corner shop, then bear sharp right alongside a wall and a row of picturesque gabled terraced houses. There is a fence in front, so turn sharp left, and proceed to a small kissing gate, passing a row of neat semi-detached bungalows. Cross Addycombe Gardens road, continue ahead to an FP sign and ascend alongside a hedge and fence to reach a kissing gate. Slant up across the meadow to another kissing gate and proceed in this direction through a hedge gap and another kissing gate. Looking back there is an excellent view of the town and the

Simonside Hills. Turn left up a narrow path bordered by a hedge and fence to meet a road.

Turn right for a few paces, then bear left at a PB sign. Pass behind the end of a bungalow, then strike up to the right to walk alongside a stone wall to reach a track. Cross over and aim for a boundary stone ahead marked thus:

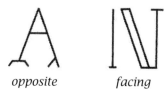

opposite   facing

There are a number of paths in the vicinity, but keep slanting up through the trees to reach a track on a bend. Bear left. The route gradually ascends to pass a stand of Scots Pines on the right, and then curves one way and another bordered by bilberry and heather.

A leafy section follows, edged by rhododendrons, and there are openings northwards through copses of pine, ash and birch. Pass a PB marker to reach a viewpoint by a large slab of sandstone and a huge knobbly boulder. The former has been liberally inscribed with names, initials and dates over a period of many years. There would be a good view overlooking Rothbury if it weren't for a proud silver birch hogging the scene. The pleasant track continues past birch, ash, and conifers standing amongst heather and bilberry, and descends to a kissing gate and a large gate.

The track is one of the old carriage-ways of the Cragside Estate which contours round the steep wooded hillside of Addyheugh, and now makes an excellent walking surface. Over thirty miles of carriage-ways and paths were laid down when William Armstrong converted his house into a mansion, created five lakes and planted millions of trees.

Pass a waymarker sign and note the tall WT mast in front on Ship Crag. There are dark conifer plantations away to the north against a backdrop of hills on the skyline. A footpath goes off left through bracken and heather heading directly for Rothbury. Opposite the mast is a copse of broadleaf trees and pines surrounded by huge boulders and rocky outcrops – a perfect natural rock garden. To the left a small rise overlooks the valley – a good coffee spot – and the open terraced track affords views along Coquetdale, the Simonside Hills and the purple line of the approaching Cheviot Hills.

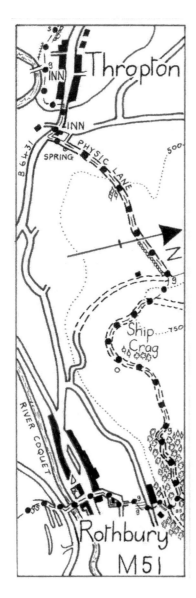

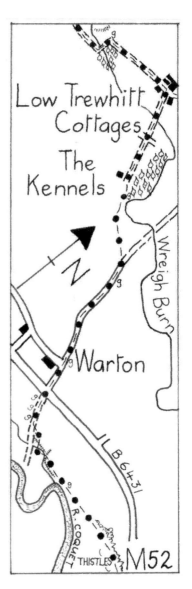

Downslope to the left lies the isolated building of Brae Head against a background of conifers, with a pattern of field boundaries beyond in the lush valley of the Coquet. Leave the track on a path to the left, and descend through the heather to a lower track. Go through a gate in the wall and walk down a grassy lonning with patches of gorse. Pass through a gap in a fence, still accompanying a wall on the left, and over a rusty metal grid. Continue to a metal gate, with two large stone posts.

Ahead the way narrows between ash, brambles, nettles, thorns, wild rose, elder and willow.

The village of Thropton lies below, and this delightful track descending from the moors is known as Physic Lane; its name may be derived from the fact that local monks gathered herbs and plants there.

As you pass beneath a leafy canopy a welcome seat appears in front, and the lane takes on a metalled surface. A cottage on the left has an interesting relic going back to the days when this old route leading to the moor was of some importance. Set into the wall is a pipe issuing spring water into a stone trough, complete with a metal cup and chain. The surroundings are decorated with pretty flowering rock plants, and the inscription engraved in the stonework reads: 'Drink, Rest and Be Thankful'. It is a feature that will be welcomed by Ravenber walkers, and great credit is due to the person who looks after it.

Continue down the lane to meet the road, turn right and walk to, or past, whichever is your inclination, the Cross Keys Inn at the junction of the road to Snitter. Another inn, the Three Wheat Heads, is situated at the other end of the village. It is believed that the large residence called Wreighburn stands on the site of a medieval guest house run by monks, and that one of the village dwellings contains a bastle house.

Walk across the narrow humped road bridge via the pedestrian way, and cross over to a path alongside the Wreigh Burn. Pass by a seat and bear right at the bottom to proceed by the Coquet through patches of butterbur. This creeping plant is widespread, and enjoys damp ground by streams and ditches. According to tradition, the large leaves were used for wrapping butter. In the Middle Ages the plant's roots were powdered and used to remove spots and skin blemishes.

Continue along a narrow trod where part of the path has fallen away; go past the footbridge to a small gate, and follow the fence away from the river bank. Cross a track coming in from the right and walk ahead below the line of the hedge to a step stile. Cross another track and keep straight on past overhanging thorn bushes. Remain on the grassy shelf by the hedge to approach 'Thistle Alley'.

Before you lies a dense mass of viciously prickly characters determined to bar all progress. Ladies and gentlemen with shorts and bare legs should be equipped with a scythe (rucksack folding model). Another form of protection is to wear long moleskin trousers; otherwise, simply beat a retreat to the road. .

Having battled on bravely to a gate above the river the line of the footpath is unclear. Proceed through long grass on the field edge, climb over a fence in the corner and then through more long grass. Negotiate another fence into a field where progress becomes easier. Aim for a metal gate on the left, then bear right up the track, and continue through a second metal gate displaying a notice 'Fishing Strictly Private': Go forward to another metal gate displaying the oft-met Northumbrian 'Beware of the Bull' sign. Cross over the road and walk up the land to where it turns sharp left to the hamlet of Warton. Go straight on to a gate with, you've guessed it, a 'Beware of the Bull' sign. Note the antique signpost.

The track is bordered by hedgerows and leads to another gate with a 'B_ _ _ _ _ _ o _ t _ _ B_ _ _' sign; it is a little game now, please fill in the above spaces. This track, by the way, is classified as a County Council road, which could be surfaced and used by lorries. Will they be fitted with bull bars?

Bear left round the field corner and slant across the large pasture towards the far boundary in order to avoid a swampy depression. Pass through a small gate, and through an area of newly planted trees with a cottage to the left. Continue straight on along the track, across a stone bridge, and on to a gate at Low Trewhitt Cottages. Take the track to the left, and go past the farm buildings towards a gate by a wood. The track is now rather muddy as it swings left round the edge of the plantation. The surrounding countryside is composed of pleasant undulating farmland, with copses, larger plantations, streams, lush pastures, and a good number of pheasants, lapwings and an inquisitive stoat. Away to the right is a fine twin-arched stone barn with a red pantiled roof.

Walk across a small stone bridge, bear right, passing the earthen retaining bank of the former Trewhitt Lake, and continue on to reach a double gate. Turn right, and proceed down the road for a few paces to the first gate on the left. The right of way, though not clear on the ground, assumes a westerly bearing, and climbs gently across a large open grassy pasture. Negotiate a metal gate, with barbed wire at the top, and head for the southern boundary line of Sharperton Edge

Plantation. From this elevated location there is a good view of the Simonside Hills and the high land of Holystone Common. Climb over a vague sort of stile in the fence, carry on along the woodland edge, and continue to a gate by the sharp angle in the road. Turn left and walk down the road for half a mile (0.8 km) to a large farmhouse called Charity Hall. Walkers in need of refreshment should follow the Alternative Route via Holystone (see pp.187-188).

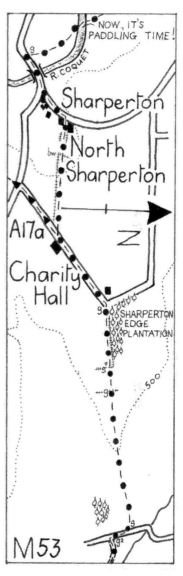

Go through a gap on the right-hand side of the road opposite Charity Hall and follow the fence on a westerly bearing; it is not easy walking as the field has been ploughed close to the boundary line. Climb over pieces of fencing with a barbed wire top and cross a small watercourse. NOTE: The line of a linking Roman road between High Rochester and Low Learchild near Whittingham crosses the right of way at this point, then descends to cross the Coquet and heads towards Lady's Well at Holystone. Proceed through a disturbed area with rough conditions underfoot and continue through two lines of fences. Bear slightly right at the top and go between a small housing development to reach the road at North Sharperton. This exit on to the road does not agree with the line of the path as shown on the 2½" OS map.

Turn left and walk down the road to Sharperton. Bear right and cross the new road bridge spanning the Coquet. The old structure with latticed metal sidework carried the following information: A. & J. MAIN & CO., BUILDERS, 1878 GLASGOW & LONDON. Proceed to a metal gate on the right and then aim for another gate across the riverside meadow. At this point the Coquet is fairly shallow with a gravelly bed, and, normally, there is no difficulty making the crossing. Head for a gap in the fence on the opposite bank, and walk on a north-west bearing across Peels Haugh, which may sometimes be under crops.

NOTE: In the event of flood conditions which could make it difficult to cross the river safely, it is advisable to choose from one of the three alternative routes:

1	From North Sharperton to Harbottle via Well House and The Peels. Distance: 2½ miles (4.0 km)
2	From North Sharperton to Harbottle via Holystone, North Wood and Seal Rigg. Distance: 3½ miles (5.6 km)
3	From North Sharperton via Sharperton and Wood Hall, along the valley road. Distance: 2 miles (3.2 km)

In the absence of a stile, walk along the fence to the top left-hand corner of the field to a gate. Bear left and proceed alongside a fence to a wall, then follow the track to The Peels. Keep left of the farm complex to a mini green, slant left past a line of cottages, and continue down the road for a short distance. The village of Harbottle lies on the south bank of the Coquet, and access is via a substantial footbridge. The name 'Harbottle' or 'Hirbotle' derives from the Old English *hȳra*, 'hireling', and thus means 'the dwelling of the hireling(s)'.

Overlooking the village is the site of the castle built in the reign of Henry II. As the result of worsening political conditions, the motte and bailey castle at Elsdon was replaced by another timber-built fortress at Harbottle. This distant border outpost was strategically important, but was soon sacked by the Scots. Rebuilt more strongly, it was partially destroyed after Bannockburn; the fragments of masonry walling which survive on its motte are probably of this later date. By 1515 it had been mostly restored to receive Margaret Tudor for her confinement. She was the sister of Henry VIII and the widow of James IV of Scotland; it was here at Harbottle that she gave birth to a

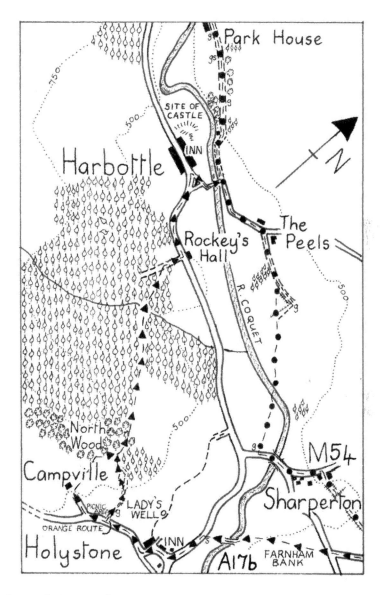

daughter, also named Margaret, who was later to become the mother-in-law of Mary Queen of Scots.

The village lies within the National Park on the fringe of the Otterburn Training Area, and at the foot of heather and bracken-covered slopes capped by impressive outcrops of rock. The River Coquet winds its way down the widening valley towards Rothbury. Harbottle is the main settlement in upper Coquetdale, and attractive stone houses line the main street. There is an inn, the Star, and nearby, a waymarked Nature Trail leads to the Drake Stone. There is a Forest Information Centre and car parking facilities.

Returning from Harbottle over the footbridge, the route now has a gravelly surface as it continues along the river bank. The track passes an attractive gabled stone house, and gently climbs into a wooded area containing ash, birch, oak, beech and sycamore. The way emerges into an area of open grassland with solitary thorn bushes, and approaches a wooden gate. As the track ascends note the signs of cobbling in its surface – a former coaching route perhaps? Pass two stone gate-posts and continue to ascend on a grassy surface lined with more thorn bushes, with good views of Harbottle Crags. The gradient eases to a gate and step stile and heads for another gate.

The ambition over many long miles of reaching the Cheviot Hills is now about to be realized. Ahead rise the smooth green slopes leading to the higher skylines – a tremendous thrill for all Ravenber walkers. Beyond Park House the track becomes a metalled lane, which goes past an imposing lime kiln, then across two cattle grids, to reach an FP sign at Low Alwinton. A short stretch of path climbs the slope to the beautiful thirteenth-century church of St Michael and All Angels; its unusual hillside position means a rise of ten steps from nave to chancel.

Walk up the road, crossing the bridge over the River Alwin into the village of Alwinton. The welcoming curlew sign of the Northumberland National Park is there to greet you.

The Northumberland National Park, designated in 1956, is one of eleven National Parks in England and Wales. It stretches from the border south to Hadrian's Wall, and encloses a landscape of rolling hills, lonely valleys and heathery moors. Additionally, a large section of the Border Forest Park lies mainly in Northumbria, so that over one fifth of the National Park is covered by Forestry Commission and Forest Enterprise afforestation.

National Parks are neither national nor are they parks. Most land within their boundaries is privately owned, with no automatic right of access. However, one of the most important duties of the National Park Authority is to ensure that visitors have adequate opportunities to explore and enjoy the surroundings. Access agreements have been made with landowners, and facilities such as toilets, picnic sites and car parks have been provided.

Alwinton lies within the National Park and also on the edge of the MOD Training Area. The live firing range, where public access is restricted, extends south of the River Coquet; it is one of the six principal Military Training Areas in the United Kingdom. The 58,000 acres of land owned by the MOD, which lie within the National Park, stretch from Coquetdale to Redesdale, and now comprise the largest single live firing range in this country. British and NATO troops come to fire their weapons, and warplanes practise air-to-ground attacks. The Training Area is particularly suitable for artillery and for infantry manoeuvre training.

There are 63 miles of public road, bridleway and footpath for public access, of which 40 miles are open at all times. The remaining roads, tracks and paths are only open to the public when no red flags are flown or red lamps lit. However, since firing or other military activity is carried out on most days of the year, a percentage of roads, tracks and paths are almost constantly out of bounds.

On the other hand, despite the clamourings of countryside pundits, the local people, farmers and landowners are keen to continue their good working relationship with the military authorities.

Alternative Route
Charity Hall to Harbottle via Holystone and North Wood

Map	OS 1:25000 Explorer, Alnwick and Amble, Sheet 332. OS 1:25000 Outdoor Leisure, The Cheviot Hills, Sheet 16
Hight	1,355ft (413m)
Distance	Rothbury to Alwinton via North Wood 13¾ miles (22km)
Terrain	As main route but including woodland

As main route to Charity Hall, then down the road to a junction. Take the path straight on over Farnham Bank, cross the footbridge over the Coquet, and walk along the road to the village of Holystone. This charming place is named after a priory of twelfth-century Augustinian nuns. Lady's Well, a short walk away, was used in early Christian baptisms. However, the local pub, the Salmon, may be more to people's tastes. Ravenber walkers can then continue to Woodland car park, where the Forestry Commission have provided an attractive information and display board, illustrating a number of waymarked colour-coded walks in the surrounding woods.

Proceed through a gate on the right. Follow the orange route and climb gradually with open pastures on the left. From a yellow marker go through an oak wood and along the woodland boundary. On reaching a forest track bear right to Rockey's Hall. Turn left and walk into Harbottle. From Charity Hall to Harbottle via Holystone 3½ miles (5.6km); main route from Charity Hall to Harbottle 2½ miles (4km).

Garleigh Moor near Rothbury

12. Alwinton to Westnewton Bridge

Map	OS 1:25000 Outdoor Leisure, The Cheviot Hills, Sheet 16
Highest elevation	Cairn Hill West 2,438ft (743m)
Height of ascent	2,930ft (983m)
Distance	Alwinton to Westnewton Bridge 19½ miles (31.2km). Alwinton to Uswayford 6½ miles (10.4km). Uswayford to Westnewton Bridge 14 miles (22.4km)
Terrain	Hill walking amidst grassy slopes and afforestation on clear paths and tracks. Peaty Border Ridge – some stone pathways. Delightful easy walking down College Burn Valley

ALWINTON (whose name derives from a British river name, Alwenton, and is pronounced 'Allenton') is a small village sheltered by the green foothills of the Cheviots, and situated at a point where the Coquet Valley broadens out. It faces the heather slopes and sandstone outcrops of the Harbottle Hills, and has long been the meeting place of ancient routes through the border uplands. It is normally a very peaceful place; a few dwellings line the burn and the green. There is a Post Office, an Inn, a car park and toilets.

Alwinton is famous for the Shepherds' Show held on the second Saturday in October, when farmers, shepherds and their families gather together. Sheep, lambs and sheep-dogs take pride of place, but there are fell races, hound trailing, stick dressing, wrestling and a whole host of rural skills. The mellifluous sounds of the local dialect mingle with the hauntingly beautiful melodies of the Northumbrian pipes; all complemented by the colourful rows of tables groaning under the weight of home-grown produce. There is the fine aroma of bread, cakes, scones and preserves, and if you are passing through on

Show Day you would be well advised to arrange your itinerary to include a rest day – those cakes are too good to miss! Afterwards, there is the splendid Rose and Thistle Inn; a good name for the pub here, reminding one of the Union of Crowns, and of the fact that the border is only a few miles away.

Upper Coquetdale is wild and solitary; a land inhabited by sheep, Blackfaced and Cheviots, and 'half breeds' of Cheviot and Border Leicester. From Makendon the tiny Coquet is quickly augmented by numerous streams. It passes long-deserted settlements, homesteads, sheepfolds and shepherds' cottages, where eighteenth-century farmers spent their spare time gambling and drinking illicit whisky.

The valley slopes steepen and tributaries like the beautiful Usway Burn join the Coquet after rising at the base of The Cheviot. An ancient route, the Pass Peth, follows this watercourse on its journey through the hills, and tempts the walker to explore these remote recesses.

At one particular point the dashing Coquet narrows, its voice echoing between lofty cliffs. Above, the high-level path was known to raiders from Scotland, who followed similar rough ways, and dodged their enemies in the clinging mists and boulder-strewn ravines. The confined Coquet issues from its narrow glen, and beyond Alwinton broadens out to continue its journey more sedately through a wide lush valley towards Rothbury.

The Otterburn Training Area extends north of the Coquet, but is not used for live firing. However, you may meet soldiers and military vehicles on exercises, as the land is used for tactical training using only blank ammunition and pyrotechnics.

WARNING: Do not touch or pick up objects lying on the ground.

NOTE: Only part of the Ravenber route along Clennel Street touches the boundary of the Training Area.

Before setting out from Alwinton, Ravenber walkers should be reminded that only limited accommodation exists at Uswayford, and at Kirknewton near Westnewton Bridge. All routes mentioned in Section 12 constitute long days.

Main Route

From the green, cross the footbridge over the stream; note the public bridleway signpost: Clennel Street to Border Ridge 8 miles. The track soon climbs, with hawthorns to the left, a fence to the right, and the

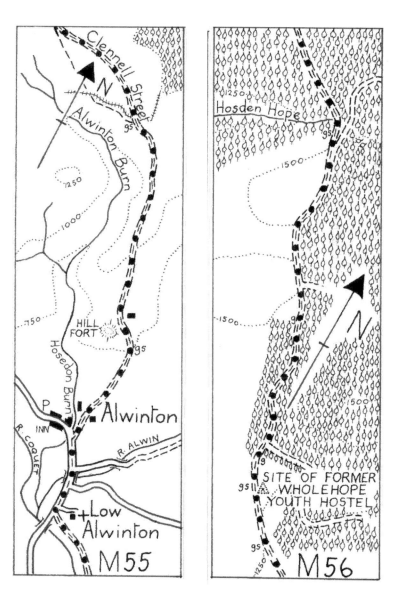

glorious sight of the enclosing hills. The track becomes fenced on both sides as it ascends to reach a gate and a ladder stile. Away to the right lies a low colour-washed cottage, with young trees on the west and north sides. Note the colour of the stone wall angling in to the track –

red Cheviot granite. The hill slopes rise on the left to the Iron Age fort of Castle Hills, and there is much evidence of past human occupation in the immediate vicinity: settlements, enclosures, homesteads, cairns and dykes.

Clennel Street continues to climb gradually, with the slopes on the eastern side falling steeply down to the valley of the Alwin. On the opposite side lies the deep V-shaped valley of the Hosedon and Alwinton Burns. A round stone stell appears on the right beyond the fence, and the dark mass of the Kidland Forest is evident behind the grassy foreground. The track, Clennell Street, runs over the hills to Cocklawfoot in Scotland. This ancient route was used by shepherds of long ago when taking their flocks up to the summer pastures. In the distance, northwards, may be seen a group of buildings now surrounded by afforestation.

Kidlandlee was at one time earlier this century a shooting lodge, but the whole Kidland area was a hunting ground from the time of the twelfth century. Approach the scant remains of a ruined building, the site of the former Wholehope Youth Hostel. Wholehope, pronounced 'Woolup', was a former shepherd's three-roomed cottage situated in an isolated position three miles from Alwinton. Open between the 1950s and early 60s, it was a popular starting point for walks on the Cheviot ridges.

Note the former hostel details:

MEN 6 WOMEN 6 NO M.P.
OPEN SATURDAY NIGHTS AND BANK HOLIDAYS ONLY.
OTHER TIMES BY ARRANGEMENT WITH REGIONAL SECRETARY –
TWO WEEKS' NOTICE NECESSARY.
Store: ALWINTON.

At Wholehope, the men and women who insisted on washing found the trek downhill to the stream something of a hardship. Later, a rainwater barrel was provided for washing purposes, although drinking water had still to come in buckets from the trickle of water in the burn. Sadly, the youth hostel was found to be too far off the beaten track to be properly managed, so it was abandoned. The building survived for a few years as an experiment by the Mountain Bothies Association, and was left open on trust for all who needed its shelter.

At one time, north-eastern Northumberland was well provided with a linking network of youth hostels: Wholehope, Rothley Shiel, Alnham

and Rock Hall. Now, only Wooler hostel provides accommodation in
that area. Ravenber walkers, with many long miles ahead of them, may
indeed look longingly at the tumbled walls of Wholehope, and wish
that this simple hostel could be resurrected into life. NOTE: There is
a **YHA bunkhouse** at Mounthooley in the College Valley, Kirknewton
NE71 6TX. Tel: 01668 216358.

Pass a corrugated iron shed and continue to a gate and step stile
in a fence. Beyond, there is a waterlogged section, but keep left and
proceed alongside a wall to a gate as the track enters the forest. A
track comes in from the right, but walk ahead to reach another gate
at the forest edge. Pass a footpath marker and keep straight on to the
crest of the rise, with grassland to the left and forest to the right. The
main Cheviot ridge comes into view with tracts of afforestation filling
the middle ground. Suddenly the aspect opens out, and there is a
splendid panorama of valleys, rounded hills and forests rolling away
into the distance.

The track forks, so take the left-hand branch to a gate and stile. A
nearby notice announces:

HOSDENHOPE FOREST
ECONOMIC FORESTRY GROUP
PLEASE PREVENT FIRES

Continue down a pleasant wide track through the woodland, keeping
straight on at a track crossroads. The way peters out into a path along
a ride, to meet the forest boundary at a gate and stile. A public
bridleway marker is fixed on to the gate.

Descend the grassy hillside slopes as the gradient steepens down
to the Usway Burn. The surroundings are photogenic, with a pretty
cascading waterfall and a nearby stell. Cross the footbridge, pass in
front of the sheepfold to a step stile and gate in a fence, and climb
the hillside with a view up the valley towards Uswayford. There is a
marker post with a blue arrow near the top of the slope, and a stout-
looking wooden shed by the fence. Make for the gate and stile with
three blue marker arrows, and continue ahead towards the finger post.
This point is an important track crossroads.

NOTE:		
	ALWINTON	6½
	BORDER RIDGE	1½
	USWAYFORD	¾

| | TROWS | 1¼ |
| | ROWHOPE | 1½ |

All miles of course!

Walkers who have booked accommodation at Uswayford should turn right here. From Uswayford take the bridleway through the afforestation and rejoin the main route at GR NT 8755 1555.

Cheviot colours and hill walking

The Cheviot range is a paradise for hill walkers and for those who enjoy exploring wild countryside; it's a land coloured with a broad canvas of silky greens and various shades of russet and brown. The main feature is grassland. The ground on the lower well-drained slopes is covered with sheep's fescue and bents; these give way to mat grass and purple moor grass on the higher flatter ground, where wetter and more acid conditions prevail. Heather flourishes on the drier areas of peat, and lower down bracken grows well on the deeper hill soils. The flat or gently sloping ground found on the smooth rounded summit of the Cheviot and the surrounding hill slopes, plus a heavy rainfall and a slow run-off, has produced blanket bogs and an abundant layer of peat; this is being furrowed by erosion into groughs and hags. The main rivers draining the area are the Tweed and Till on the northern side, and the Aln, Coquet and North Tyne on the eastern and southern side; all flow eventually into the North Sea.

In the Cheviot valleys springtime is heralded with the acid yellow of gorse, which stands out vividly against the duller greens of hill slope and conifer forest. Late August sees the moorland transformed into a purple splendour of flowering heather. But it is in autumn that you are recommended to visit the border valleys; here, the lower slopes are burnished gold with dying bracken, birch trees glisten in the sharp light, and rowan are ablaze with fiery red berries. In winter, snow lingers in the higher hillside hollows, and sharp frosts dust all surfaces with a coating of bejewelled patterns. Rivulets and streams of clear bright water slide between the branching spears of frozen fern.

Whatever the season, walking in the lonely valleys and on the high hills is the most satisfying way of becoming absorbed into the landscape. The sound of the wind, the elusive nature of clouds, and the ever-changing movement of hill grasses; the smell of wet earth, damp foliage, the faint chuckle of some shy watercourse and the sharp call of birds all combine to jolt the senses into an awareness of one's surroundings.

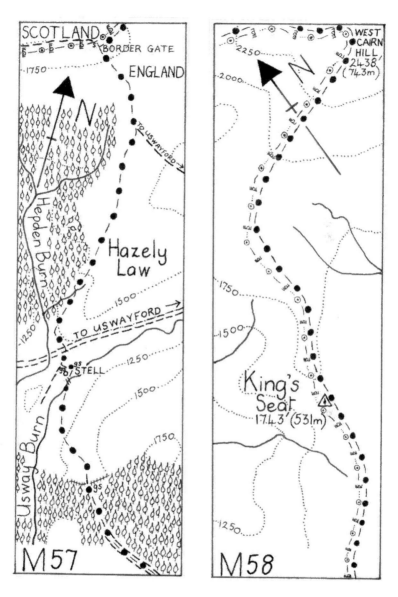

Continue ahead, climbing the slopes of Hazely Law above the stream Hazely Slack, with afforestation to the left, as the gradient steepens to reach the first rise. Don't forget to look back for another fine view. The forest edge now recedes as the track heads across rough moorland to a finger post pointing to Uswayford, I mile. This is the spot where the detour for accommodation rejoins the main route.

Bear left and ascend gently amongst surroundings of grass and heather to reach a gate and stile with a blue arrow. A finger post to the right indicates various destinations:

SALTERS ROAD, DAVIDSON'S LINN	¾
HIGH BLAKEHOPE	5
ALWINTON	8
USWAYFORD	1½

Proceed for a short distance to meet the Border Fence, and the point where the Ravenber meets the Pennine Way at the Border Gate, 1,778ft (542m). A sign shows the direction ahead for Clennell Street *en route* for Cocklawfoot in Scotland. Turn right and follow the Border Fence, where slabs of fine sandstone have been placed across the peaty sections. There follows a long gradual climb passing the OS Survey Column S7997 on King's Seat and on to Score Head to reach the sharp angle in the Border Fence on Cairn Hill west summit, 2,438ft (743m), GR NT 8960 1936.

NOTE: Walkers bound for Wooler and intent on taking the option of the Cheviot Route should continue straight ahead at this point. (see p.202).

Turn north-west along the Border Fence to Auchope Cairn, 2,379ft (725m), and descend the slope with the craggy fastnesses of Hen Hole, a place endowed with numerous tales and legends, but in reality a sanctuary for ravens, far below on the right. A railway goods waggon formerly stood on the col between Auchope Cairn and the Schil, and acted as a Mountain Refuge Hut for two or three persons. This windowless structure, with a sliding door, provided excellent shelter in severe weather conditions. The present smaller structure was erected in 1988 by Northumberland National Park Wardens and Voluntary Wardens, assisted by 202 Squadron RAF Boulmer; it is dedicated to the memory of Stuart Lancaster.

Cheviot Geology
The rocks of the Cheviot Hills are entirely igneous, derived as molten material from inside the earth from the earliest part of the Devonian period. Originating from a succession of volcanic eruptions, the debris fell as a thick layer of lava called andesite on to an ancient land

surface. The speckled purple or grey rocks produced from these lava deposits now form most of the Cheviot Hills.

Later in the Devonian period, another great mass of molten magma rose up from the earth's interior, melting as it did the rocks and solidified lavas which it encountered. This gave rise to an extremely hard, silica-rich granite, which became exposed on the subsequent erosion of the existing andesites. The area around the heights of Hedgehope and the domed plateau of the Cheviot are formed of this pink granite.

The andesitic lavas in the Metamorphic Aureole, that is, the zone around an igneous mass, were affected by the heat and pressure of the intrusive granite, and subsequently became toughened and more weather-resistant. The rock outcrops above the Harthope Valley, on the Schil, and the crags of Bizzle and Hen Hole, all represent exposures of these metamorphosed rocks.

At the end of the Carboniferous period, intervals of mountain building resulted in the igneous rocks being raised, and the development of fractures and fault lines in the surrounding sedimentary rocks. The later effect of these faults was to produce the long straight valleys of the College Burn and Harthope Burn.

The land forms continued to suffer intense erosion, and the whole area was finally covered by ice during the Ice Ages. The effect of the glacial ice was to smooth and shape the landscape into the familiar rounded hills of the Cheviot country. Glacial action and melt-water also deepened and widened the floors of the existing valleys.

From the shelter proceed to the head of Red Cribs, where a magnificent view awaits down the long valley of the College Burn. Also from this point there is the chance of another look into the dramatic rocky gorge of Hen Hole, where the College Burn runs through in a series of waterfalls and flows northwards to Westnewton Bridge.

Descend by a thin trod on the left-hand side of the gully, and aim for the bottom right-hand corner of the far plantation. Once on level ground, there is a metal hut in front, but keep to a line of rushes, and pass the corner of the plantation fence with a stell slightly to the right. The way ahead is indistinct on the ground through long grass, bracken and rushes before reaching a track. The track bends, crosses the stream under a hillside bank and continues as a grassy way. Pass a stell, proceed to a gate and step stile with an arrow marker and walk alongside a conifer plantation.

At GR NT 8807 2218, near to Mounthooly, a path slants down on

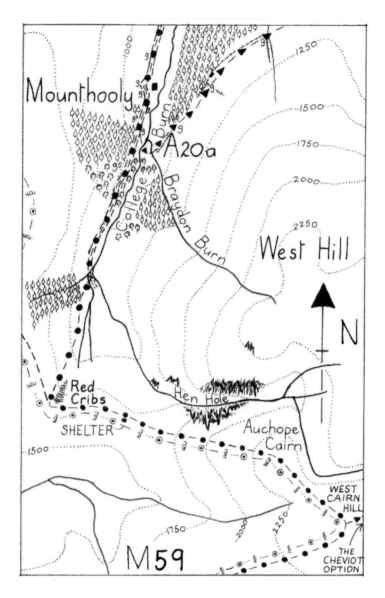

the right to cross College Burn. (This is the departure point for the Alternative Route to Wooler; p.205).

Proceed through a gate with a blue arrow marker passing an old stone-walled enclosure. Note a stell on the far bank of the burn and a private footbridge. Pass through a sheepfold with two gates, and continue along the base of another conifer plantation. Go through a gate with a waymarker arrow and on through a meadow to another gate. From this point the track becomes a thin ribbon of asphalt, and this surface continues down the valley.

However, in such delectable surroundings this is not too unwelcome, as it enables the walker to maintain a good steady pace. The Cheviot valleys have a beauty which is peculiarly their own. The College Valley is particularly attractive, wild and remote, the outlying hills sombre and brooding, with rounded expanses of seemingly white grass and patches of dark heather. A handful of dwellings lie scattered about on the valley floor, and some that are whitewashed stand out clearly against the background of dark conifers. The College Burn has increased in size and maturity from its many tributaries.

Pass a low white cottage on the right, then a black metal hay barn and a bungalow to a gate. The track bifurcates here and passes Mounthooly on the left and on through two gates. There is a notice here stating NO PARKING, NO VEHICLES BEYOND. Continue along the narrow road and cross two cattle grids, a stream and a third cattle grid to reach the white-painted farm building of Fleehope. There follows a wooden barn on the left, a series of gates and a small green hut on the right. Observe the notices – CAUTION, CHILDREN; better slow down! The farm dogs are quite friendly in these parts.

The little road is ideally terraced above the river with clear views of the afforestation on the opposite bank, and also of the side valley of the Lambden Burn. The latter joins the main stream just north of the tiny hamlet of Southernknowe, where there is a public telephone box. Pass the splendid community hall at the road junction (I bet some cut-throat games of whist take place here!), and proceed down the valley road to a cattle grid, just before a white chalet situated higher up the slope on the left. Cross the Whitehall Burn, pass the building Whitehall; (no, not the one of 1212 fame), and continue to a cattle grid before a zig-zag bend. Open grassland lies beyond the gate as the road approaches a small parking area. A notice supplies some important information:

COLLEGE VALLEY ESTATES LTD
NO VEHICULAR ACCESS EXCEPT BY PERMIT
VALLEY WALKERS WELCOMED
PRIVATE FISHING

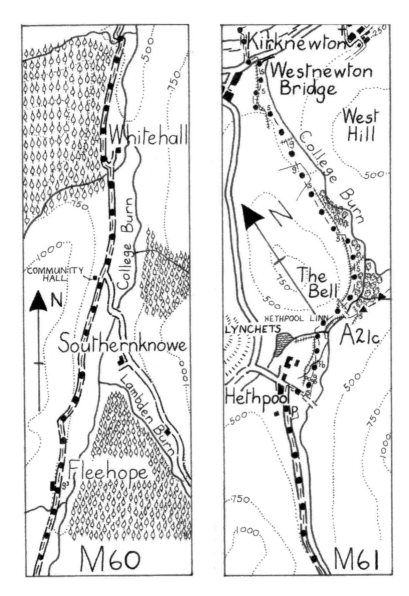

The College Valley is in private hands. The Estate allows just 12 cars into the valley a day, and permits must be obtained from the land agent in Wooler. Weekend permits may be reserved by telephone or in writing, and collected from under the office doormat when the office is closed: Sale & Partners Estate Office, Glendale Road, Wooler, Tel. 01668 281611.

Pass over a cattle grid; a footpath sign indicates a public bridleway to Mounthooly 3¾, Border Ridge 5½. Beyond, there is an attractive modern bungalow and a neat row of stone-built, slate-roofed gabled cottages with pleasant gardens. These dwellings together with the big house comprise the hamlet of Hethpool. NOTE: If time is pressing, it is a quick 2 miles (3.2km) by road from Hethpool to Westnewton Bridge.

A footpath sign on the right indicates the way to Old Yeavering, 2½. From the corner of the road proceed down the track for a short distance to a step stile on the left with waymarkers. Continue to a small gate at the far end of the pasture. Bear left over a footbridge and ascend to the fence with a clear view of Hethpool House. This is a grey, attractive-looking residence with a conical-topped round turret, solid chimneys, grey and red tiled roof, and bright red pantiles covering a lower part of the building. Slant slightly right towards two small gates, and take the one straight ahead. Cross the small stream issuing from Hethpool Lake, using convenient stepping stones, and follow the wall on the right. The path is now close to the banks of the College Burn which runs in a rocky channel. The water, at this point still and silent, contains large fish in its dark depths; an onlooker may be lucky to see one leaping clear of the surface. Descend to the footbridge.

Hethpool Linn is a beautiful and atmospheric place, where surely nobody could be reprimanded for lingering a while. On the northern side of the footbridge the water gathers momentum, and rushes down between rock slabs and moss-covered boulders in a tree-girt chasm.

NOTE: Do not cross over the footbridge. This is the point where the Alternative Route from Wooler rejoins the main route (see map M61). Ascend and return to the footpath, then proceed to a step stile over the fence with a yellow waymarker. Descend a little, with the sound of the river hurrying through its rocky channel below. Continue through bracken to a step stile where the path levels out, following a fence on the right. The way then gradually ascends through bracken, broom and newly-planted oaks to reach another step stile. Follow the fence with mature oaks lining the valley side above the river. At a gap in the trees there is a good view of Torleehouse Farm and Yeavering Bell across the far side of the valley.

The College Burn carved its gorge through the andesites to the south and east of the Bell, when the previous exit of the river was blocked by a lateral moraine towards the end of the Ice Ages.

Proceed towards a short length of fence on the left and to a ladder stile over a wall. Beyond, there is a pile of boulders with a pipe and metal drinking trough. Walk to the nearby metal gate and note the monument on Lanton Hill on the far side of the Glen Valley. Nearer, there is a glimpse of the former Kirknewton railway station situated to the right of a red-roofed house. Descend on a track passing two boulders to meet a gate in a fence. There is a waymarker on the far side of the gate. Walk across the grassy pasture above the gorse bushes towards a footpath marker. Continue along the river bank to a waymarker, and bear slightly left to another marker on the bankside. Bear right along the top of the bank following a fence and wall, with a view left to the hamlet of Westnewton.

Fromt a ladder stile walk alongside the fence through the meadow, and descend to a step stile. The path passes through broom bushes to another waymarker, and then through bracken, hawthorn and gorse to meet a short flight of steps. Continue by the fence on a narrow path above the river to a step stile. After another short stretch through gorse and broom, the path bears left to reach Westnewton Bridge. Climb the step over a low wall and on to the B6351 road. If accommodation has been booked in advance, bear right and walk along the road into Kirknewton.

The Cheviot Route
Cairn Hill, The Cheviot, Scald Hill, Hawsen Burn,
to Broadstruther and Wooler
Maps A18a, A18b, p.203; A18c, p.207

Map	OS 1:25000 Outdoor Leisure, The Cheviot Hills, Sheet 16
Highest elevation	The Cheviot 2,674ft (815m)
Height of ascent	From Alwinton 3,540ft (1,079m)
Distance	To Wooler 20¾ miles (33.2km). For other distances applicable to this route, see p.205

As main route from Alwinton to Cairn Hill west summit. Leave the main route at GR NT 8960 1936, and continue ahead on an easterly

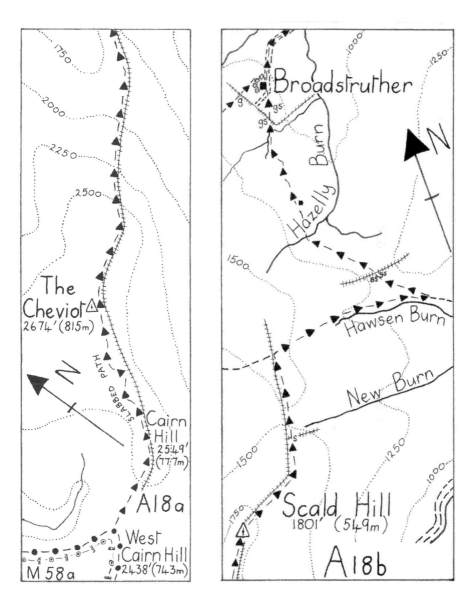

bearing following the fence to the summit of Cairn Hill, 2,549ft (777m). Pass a gate and stile giving access to a path down to the Harthope Valley. The stone shelter of Scotsman's Cairn lies on the eastern side of the fence. The path keeps to the northern side of the fence on a north-east bearing. After a short distance, a firm pathway of stone slabs, gleaned from redundant Pennine mills, weaves and dodges across the waterlogged peaty ground; it climbs gradually, taking advantage of the drier patches. Soon an object appears perched high on a concrete plinth; it is OS Survey Column S1560 marking the summit of the Cheviot, 2,674ft (815m).

The stone pathway terminates a short distance beyond the trig point. Follow the fence across the glutinous surface which soon improves. Continue by the side of the fence on firmer ground with a cairn on the right-hand side, and then pass a large cairn on the opposite side. There appears to be a way on either side of the boundary, although the line of the permissive path appears to lie on the northern side of the fence.

The grassy slope now descends steeply, and after a while levels out to reach the grassy expanse of Scald Hill, 1801ft (549m), where the path crosses over to the right-hand side of the fence. Walk along to a post, at which point the fence bends to the left. Continue to follow it down the slope to a stile and waymarker. Descend into a little depression and climb up the other side, still alongside the fence. Ascend steadily with a view westwards down the valley of the Lambden Burn. At GR NT 9349 2299 meet the path coming up from Goldscleugh.

Turn right, and follow the right of way that accompanies the rapidly deepening valley of the Hawsen Burn. At a path junction, indicated by yellow and blue arrows, turn left and ascend on a pleasant path through colourful bracken and heather. Looking back, there is a wide vista of green rolling hills and afforestation, punctuated by occasional rocky outcrops on the far slopes of the Harthope Burn; the whole scene is made all the more beautiful by a combination of sunlight and moving cloud patterns.

Proceed to a small gate and stile, and note the upright stone that appears to have the letters H and SH carved into its surface. Ahead, the isolated farm of Broadstruther is easily located by its sheltering clump of trees. A small rust-coloured nissen hut lies in the foreground of the wide grassy valley. Follow the path slanting left to cross the infant Hazelly Burn. Continue in a northerly direction on a direct line with Broadstruther. Beyond Rushy Gair, cross a watercourse and head towards a gate and stile. Walk a short distance to another gate and stile, and aim for the right-hand side of the buildings join the track as it descends towards Broadstruthers Burn. From this point, follow the Alternative Route to Wooler, Map A18c (see p. 207).

Other distances applicable to this route:

Alwinton To Uswayford	6½ Miles (10.4 Km)
Uswayford To Wooler	14½ Miles (23.2 Km)

Alternative Route
Alwinton to Wooler
Maps A20a, p. 198; A20b, A20c, p.207

Map	OS 1:25000 Outdoor Leisure, The Cheviot Hills, Sheet 16
Highest elevation	Cairn Hill West 2,438ft (743m)
Height of ascent	3,855ft (1,175m)
Distance	Alwinton to Wooler 22 miles (35.2km). Alwinton to Uswayford 6½ miles (10.4km). Uswayford to Wooler 16½ miles (26.4km). College Burn to Wooler 8½ miles (13.6km)
Terrain	Grassy slopes and afforestation. Peaty Border Ridge – some stone pathways. Delightful Lambden Burn Valley and lonely Broadstruther. Clear tracks and some indistinct path sections. NOTE: Allow sufficient time. Alwinton to Wooler constitutes a long day

As main route until College Burn, GR NT 8807 2218 (see p.198). Leave the track just south of Mounthooly. Bear right, slant down on a grassy way through bracken to ford the burn and head up to a stell. Walk beyond it to twin gates, take the left-hand one, cross a small stream and ascend the hill slope. Follow the left-hand side of the fence and go through a gate. Keep on a thin track through bracken and then swing left alongside the plantation boundary. Pass a hut to a gate in the left-hand comer of the fence and accompany the woodland edge. The faint track passes a corrugated iron hut and then a sheepfold on the forest edge. Continue to follow the fence with pasture to the left, and aim for a gate in a fence. Proceed straight on, cross a small watercourse, the Hebron Sike, and follow the forest boundary. After a short distance a track materializes, and at the point of descent, a ragged copse of trees appears on the slope to the right.

Ahead, the valley of the Lambden Burn begins to deepen on the descent to Dunsdale Farm. The way continues round the right-hand side of a black hut to a gate, and then across a paddock with another gate, to reach a tarmac road. Note the old wild cherry tree by a gate prior to the bridge over Bizzle Burn; this stream flows from the deep ravine of Bizzle Crags high on the northern slopes of the Cheviot.

Turn right at the junction, a favourite storage area of stone slabs for peaty paths, and walk up the valley following the Lambden Burn. Pass an afforested area on the right, and as the metalled farm road approaches Goldscleugh, go through a gate on the right and walk across the meadow. Looking back down the valley the prominent hill in the distance is the Schil, crowned with a rocky tor. Its isolated position ensures its importance as a splendid viewpoint, and for Pennine Way walkers the last summit challenge before Kirk Yetholm and the end of the journey.

The line of the path passes behind the farm buildings to a gate and on to a track. The right of way goes straight on, but one can turn right and walk a few paces to where the stream is bridged. Bear left down to a gate and paddle through the ford. There is a precarious footbridge fashioned from birch logs in imminent danger of collapse. Walk past a wooden hut, a sheepfold and a gate, at which point the track becomes a path. Look for a solitary tree on the opposite bank of the burn, and when opposite turn left on a thin trod up the slope. If you have a minute or two to spare, a cairn would be useful here. The way climbs gradually to a lonely gatepost, and continues past two birch trees, one by the path, the other nearer the stream. Note the stell below.

On reaching the end of the plantation walk along the top side of the fence to meet a small gate. Continue through afforestation for a short distance to meet a track junction, bear left, and ascend through conifers to reach a palisade with a yellow arrow marker. Follow the fence passing another waymarker on a fence post, with good views ahead to the North Sea – now stop jumping up and down, there's still some way to go yet! Although the line of the path probably goes through a gate on to the right-hand side of the fence, it is easier walking to continue down the left-hand side for a short distance, as a strip of heather has been cleared.

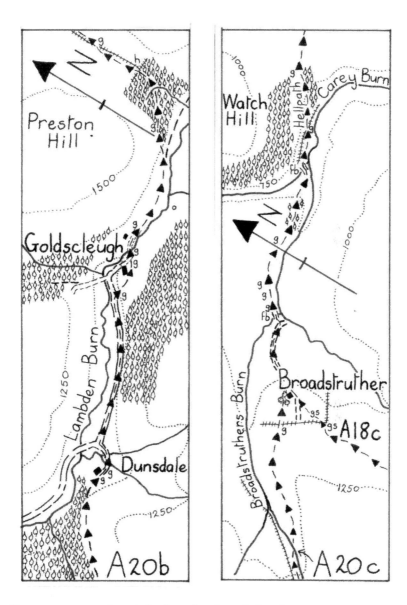

Cross over to the right-hand side of the fence and traverse the grassy slope on a bearing of 40° east following an indistinct path. Down below to the left is a sheepfold and sheep shelter. At the crest of the slope, walk on a bearing of 68° east towards a metal gate in a fence. Just ahead lies the uninhabited farm of Broadstruther with its distinctive clump of sheltering trees. Keep to the left-hand side of the farm buildings to join a track descending towards Broadstruthers Burn.

NOTE: Broadstruther is the point at which the Cheviot Route joins the Alternative Route to Wooler (see p.204).

Bear left, cross over the footbridge and up to a gate, and walk through grassy surroundings to another small gate in a fence. Looking ahead, on the left is a rusting nissen hut, a small stell and a dead tree with writhing tentacle-like branches. The way continues through open grassland to another gate and into an area of young conifers and heather. In retrospect, the lonely buildings of Broadstruther, the group of sturdy trees set in a grassy bowl and surrounded by green and tawny-coloured rounded hills, seems to be the perfect picture of the Cheviot scene.

Walk along past broom bushes and young trees, and descend to cross the footbridge over Carey Burn. Proceed along the fence side to a small gate and bear left. The lovely path that ascends through the trees is known as The Hellpath. Walkers should not expect to run the gauntlet of ghosts of reivers from past border troubles; it is just a corruption of the word *heilpath* or *hillpath*. Emerge from the conifer woodland at a small gate and follow a clear track across moor grass and heather. Looking back there is a good view of the deepening valley of the Carey Burn. Approach a gate and step stile, and walk alongside a plantation on the right and gorse bushes to the left. Follow the remains of a wall to a gate and step stile with waymarkers; then accompany a fence to another gate, and to a step stile on the left.

The right of way goes round the back of the house and heads for the footpath sign to the right at the far side of the open ground.

Walkers *en route* for Wooler should bear left at the footpath sign. The surrounding area is known as Wooler Common, which was enclosed in 1869. The nine freeholders were given less than one acre of land as compensation for losing their pasture rights on the common. Descend the track following a fence cum wall, then a fence, to reach a small gate. Ascend through trees to a pleasant picnic area attractively set out with tables. Continue through the afforestation on a delightful grassy way to a step stile in a fence. Cross an open area, bearing left down the slope to a boggy patch. Follow the blue arrow marker and turn right over a footbridge. Bear left to a kissing gate to pass Waud House, and continue along the track to meet Common Road. Turn right.

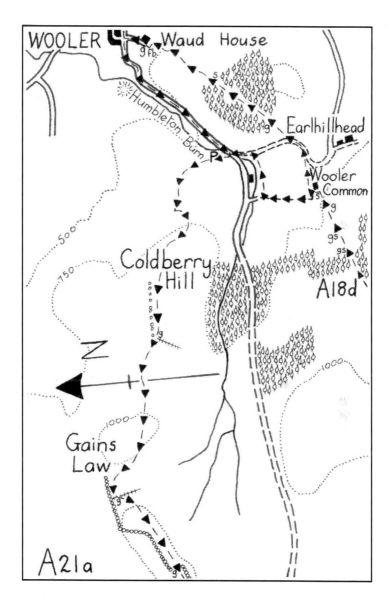

Ignore the seat, it's all downhill now and the rooftops of Wooler are beckoning. Pass a telephone box on the corner of Broomey Road, and descend Ramsey's Lane into the Market Place.

The name 'Wooler' (attested as 'Wullore' in 1187, 'Welloure' in

1196, and 'Wullouer' in 1212) apparently means 'bank of a stream', from *wella*, 'spring or stream'.

The quiet market town, granted its charter in about 1200, sits at the foot of the Cheviot Hills. Tower Hill, to the south of the present market place, was the site of the Norman motte and bailey castle of Robert des Muschamps, who was granted the barony of Wooler by Henry I.

To the north and east, the town faces the rich agricultural farmland of the Milfield Plain, once the location of a huge glacial lake. Wooler is the gateway to some of the grandest of the Cheviot Hill country, and is one of the best centres for exploring the remote hills and valleys.

The grey-pink stone houses with grey roofs are set round the small triangular market place at the southern end of the High Street. The latter was largely rebuilt after the disastrous fire of 1863. At that time the thatched roofs quickly caught fire, fanned by strong winds; it was several hours before help arrived, and by that time the town was totally

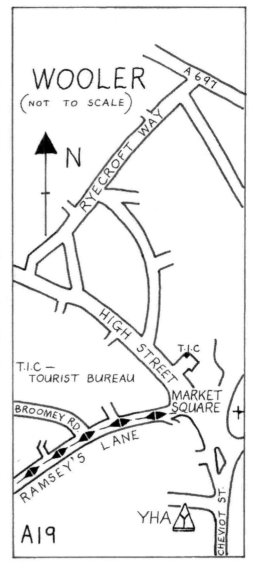

devastated. A fine Mechanics' Institute of red sandstone was built in 1889, and it is interesting to note that several nearby buildings show a distinct inward lean due to the draining of former marshy ground.

A mid-nineteenth-century trade directory listed a fine variety of occupations in the town: 14 tailors, 2 saddlers, 5 blacksmiths, 8 boot and shoemakers, 4 cartwrights, 2 coopers and 2 watch and clockmakers.

Wooler livestock market was established in 1887, and was also famous in the past for the many cattle fairs which were held there. The nature of the area, with its extensive tracts of hill country, has meant that the sheep market is one of the busiest in Britain.

St Mary's Church is externally Victorian, with a tower of 1856, but was in fact built in 1765 and has a broad aisleless nave and a narrower chancel. Nearby Tenter Hill above a sloping green recalls the town's eighteenth-century association with a thriving woollen industry.

The railway came to the town at the opening of the Alnwick to Kelso line by the North Eastern Railway in 1887. Passenger services were withdrawn in September 1930, but it remained open for freight until the line was breached by thunderstorms in 1948 between Wooler and Ilderton. Thereafter, the line was worked in two parts, but closed in March 1953, although the Wooler to Cornhill section kept operating until March 1969. Another sad chapter in the dismemberment of Britain's fine rural railway system!

The town has ample accommodation for visitors, with hotels, inns, guest houses and bed and breakfast establishments. The Youth Hostel in Cheviot Street is the most northerly in England, and provides accommodation and meals for members of the Association.

Alternative Route
Wooler to Westnewton Bridge
Map A21a, p.209

Map	OS 1:25000 Outdoor Leisure, The Cheviot Hills, Sheet 16
Highest elevation	Just south of Beater Cairn 1,099ft (335m)
Height of ascent	1,171ft (357m)
Distance	8¼ miles (13.2km)
Terrain	Easy walking, mainly on grass and heather-covered moorland. Clear tracks and some indistinct path sections. Expansive and beautiful views

From the centre of Wooler ascend Ramsey's Lane which in turn becomes Common Road. The road curves round the mound of Green Castle and continues to follow the Humbleton Burn to reach a parking area on the right.

Go to the far end of the parking area, cross a small stream, and turn left up a ride before a notice about Nesting Wildlife and keeping Dogs under Control. Ascend the grassy track through the afforestation to reach a small gate with a blue waymarker. Continue to ascend through a grass and bracken hollow to meet a gate and waymarker. (This section of the Ravenber route is also part of St. Cuthbert's Way.)

Turn left and then swing right to climb the track through bracken up the slopes of Coldberry Hill. Away to the right lies pointed Humbleton Hill, with the walls of the ancient hill fort still visible. Looking back, there is a view of Wooler and the countryside beyond to the sea. A ruined wall appears to the right as the track heads through a hilltop expanse of grass – lovely underfoot. Proceed to a gate in a fence with a yellow waymarker arrow and a notice:

PLEASE TAKE CARE
SOME GROUND NESTING BIRDS THAT BREED HERE DURING THE
SPRING ARE EASILY DISTURBED BY PEOPLE, AND IN PARTICULAR
DOGS. DURING APRIL, MAY, JUNE YOU CAN HELP MINIMISE SUCH
DISTURBANCE BY KEEPING DOGS ON A LEAD KEEPING TO THE
PATHS YOUR CO-OPERATION IS APPRECIATED ENJOY YOUR VISIT.

Walk along the grassy track through heather and climb gently to pass a marker post to the right on a small cairn. Pass across the slopes of Gains Law as the track swings left to a gate with a wall to the right. Continue to ascend easily on grass and heather to reach a solitary wooden post with artistically formed wire arrows – very unusual.

The track meets the corner of a wall and follows it to a little bend. Go through a gate, and accompany the wall to another small gate and simple step stile with a path marker. Walk by the side of the wall with the buildings of Commonburn House visible in the middle distance.

The path then swings away to the right through grass and heather opposite a gate in the wall – compass bearing 292° west. Follow a thin trod through the grass. Ahead, there is a clump of trees to the left, a gate, a track and a young plantation in front to the right. The indistinct path is clearer now through the heather leading to a cairn just before the plantation. Proceed to a track with a mini cairn and bear right to a gate. Looking round one can observe the larger cairn a short distance away, and the gate gap in the wall on the skyline.

A track soon swings off to the right on a right of way following Akeld Burn, but keep straight on along the fence. Bear slightly left towards a wall and gate with a waymarker. After negotiating the ladder stile keep to the right on slightly higher ground, as the area to the left is composed of deep tussocky grass. After a little progress the pole on Beater Cairn will be seen to  guide you to the track. Tom Tallon's Crag now lies behind to the right. Note that there is no path visible on the ground from the ladder stile to the track. Bear right and descend gently down the track to meet a cairn – a pile of stones with an old fire beater, and named by the author as Beater Cairn.

The twin-summited hill in front to the north is Yeavering Bell, 1,184ft (361m) and 1,165ft (355m) respectively. Both summits are surrounded by a stone rampart with a 13ft (4m) base, and with entrances on the north and south sides. There are also annexes on the east and west ends. This impressive defensive fortification, which stood 8ft (2.4m) high, enclosed an area of 13 acres (5.3ha), and excavations revealed that the eastern summit is ringed by a trench which formerly held a wooden palisade. It is likely that this airy enclosure held an unusually large community, with the identified foundations of at least 130 hut circles.

This Iron Age hill fort was one of a number of defensive enclosures concentrated on the foothills of the Cheviots. At that period it is certain that the Milfield Plain and the neighbouring river valleys were covered with fen marshes and thick forests. A fort like Yeavering Bell

commanded views of the Cheviot Hills, the
Milfield Plain and the Tweed Valley. As the
lowest ground was impenetrable, the best
grazing land would be on the lower hill
slopes, and in the summer, on the upper
hill slopes. The Iron Age people would
have been Celts and the Ottadini group of
Britons. They had settled in the region
before the Romans came, survived the
conquest, and continued their existence
into the Dark Ages after the withdrawal of
the Roman forces.

Descend gradually to a gate and step
stile with a waymarker. Then pass a
different form of route indicator at
ground level; it is presumably designed
with the idea that the hill top defenders
could not see it and purloin it for camp
firewood. The shrunken signpost
indicates routes west to Easter Tor 4 and
Wester Tor 2, and east to Yeavering Bell
½ and Gleadscleugh 2.

Continue to descend the slope to meet
a ladder stile over a wall, and pause to
admire the views of West Hill complete
with its hill-top fort, the College Burn
Valley and the green heights beyond. This
is an excellent vantage point – take a good
look, since you will soon be leaving the
delectable Cheviots. Proceed down the
track to meet the lane and turn left to
Torleehouse Farm. Pass through a gate, a
paddock and another gate, and walk along
the track with a tall copse of conifers on
the left. The way enters and leaves a young
mixed plantation with a gate at both ends,

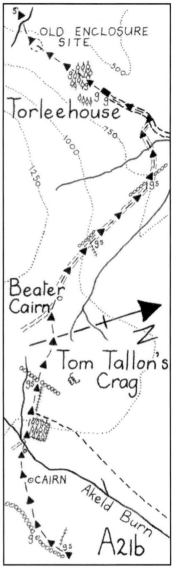

and gradually descends the hillside of rough grass, thistles and isolated
wind-blasted thorns. Humps and hollows on the ground indicate
ancient enclosure banks and ditches. In the middle distance there is a
fine aspect of Hethpool House in the valley of the College Burn.

A study of the map will reveal that the immediate area was fairly well populated in times gone by, with settlements, cultivation terraces, field systems, hill forts, cairns, homesteads and tumuli; a superb landscape in which to walk, observe and study.

Pass a rectangular stone sheepfold, then aim to the right of some isolated trees and down to a step stile with a waymarker. Descend a short bank, cross a small stream and continue on a beautiful path amidst leafy surroundings. Now the path runs along the edge of the deep cleft to the right, with one vantage point looking down into a deep pool. Proceed to a step stile and listen to the sound of rushing water in the tree-cloaked gorge of Hethpool Linn, GR NT 9023 2848. Descend some steps to reach the footbridge over the College Burn. Cross over and ascend to the footpath. This is the point at which the Alternative Route from Wooler rejoins the main route to Westnewton Bridge (see p.211).

Crookhouse, Housedon Hill

13. Westnewton Bridge to Norham

Map	OS 1:25000 Explorer, Kelso, Coldstream and Lower Tweed Valley, Sheet 339
Highest elevation	Slopes of Kypie Hill 656ft (200m)
Height of ascent	974ft (297m)
Distance	18 miles (28.8km)
Terrain	Gentle hill slopes, field paths and tracks; pleasant undulating countryside. Delightful riverside walking along the banks of the Till and Tweed. A scenic surprise in store

The church of St Gregory in Kirknewton, with a late nineteenth-century tower, was restored by Dobson after 1860. A chancel and south transept are survivals of the thirteenth or early fourteenth century, both with pointed tunnel-vaults. There is an interesting carving, probably twelfth century, of the Virgin and Magi, where the Wise Men are depicted wearing kilts.

The notable nineteenth-century social reformer Josephine Butler is buried in the churchyard under the shadow of Yeavering Bell.

Just to the east of Kirknewton is the supposed site of the inland capital of the seventh-century Anglo-Saxon king of Northumbria. Aerial photography in the 1950s revealed unusual crop markings in the field to the north of Old Yeavering Farm. Subsequent excavations indicated the timber post-holes of a succession of Anglo-Saxon halls, Edwin's Palace, and the foundations of a wooden amphitheatre. The site is named *Adgefrin*, which is evidently the old name of the prominent hill Yeavering Bell.

Main Route

Turn right off the road between Westnewton Bridge and Westnewton, through a gate signposted Crookhouse and West Flodden. Also, a notice board, Private No Through Road. Pass the old Wooler to Cornhill railway line and cross the bridge over the Bowmont Water. Follow the track as it swings to the right. Ahead, there is a clear view of the monument on Lanton Hill. Continue to the gate before the buildings at Lanton Mill and bear left. The part-metalled track climbs gradually to reach a stone wall, gate and cattle grid. Beyond a wooded area, there is a fine view of the valley of the Bowmont Water. The track passes through a small plantation and continues over a cattle grid to swing left round a plantation. Proceed to Crookhouse Farm and pass between the buildings to a gate. Ascend the track to another gate. Do not go through it, but negotiate the hurdle on the left – a waymarker would be useful at this point.

Keep alongside the fence to a gate, turn right and follow the fence and hedge to a gate. Turn left on a thin track that accompanies a fence across the flanks of Coldside Hill. Go on ahead to a small gate set in a wall cum fence beyond some gorse bushes. The Housedon Plantation lies to the west. Descend slightly, and follow up the right-hand side of a broken wall amongst pleasant hill scenery to meet a gate. Just beyond, bear left through a gate, and along the edge of a small plantation on Kypie Hill to another gate on the right – a very juicy patch of ground here! Turn right and follow the fence, but take a look back at the Cheviots. From now on the scenery changes to one of gentler slopes and rolling farmland; it becomes a landscape of hedged fields and strips of woodland.

Aim for a small gate on the right, and continue ahead to follow a fence and broken wall to a gate. Keep alongside a fence which is lined with pollarded thorn bushes plus a lone knobbly ash tree. Pass an animal drinking trough, and take 56 paces to reach a gate – those are my paces, not a standard unit of measurement! No doubt observant farmers will begin to wonder why walkers are striding about in a funny manner.

Pass down a short enclosed hedge section to a gate, with another animal trough immediately on the left. The route follows the fence and hedge side bordered with trees lower down. There is an interesting name attached to an area of woodland a short distance away – female walkers note. A thin wind break of woodland is passed as the path accompanies the field boundary down the slope. At the time of walking the route, crops in the field had been sown right up to the hedge. This makes for difficult progress, which would be easier if a space was left unploughed for the right of way.

At the bottom of the field make a grassy descent to a culvert and up to a palisade fence, which need a plank and stile respectively. Follow the hedge to a gate and on to the road opposite West Flodden Farm. There is a public bridleway sign, but it is conveniently hidden in the hedge. Turn right along the country road for half a mile (0.8km) to Flodden Farm and turn left at the footpath sign that indicates Crookham 2½. Walk along the track, which turns right and follows the hedge up the field. Bear left at the top, accompany a ditch and watercourse, and then ascend Flodden Hill along the fence past several trees and thorn bushes. Climb over a palisade to enter Floddenhill Plantation and on up to a track. Turn right, ignoring a track going off to the left. The route terraces round the hill through a delightful area of woodland with deciduous trees and mature conifers. Ignore another track going off to the right to reach the location of Sybil's Well, set at the base of a sandstone outcrop. This source of water was probably known to the Scottish soldiers who had camped on Flodden Hill in 1513. The well has a portal carrying the following inscription:

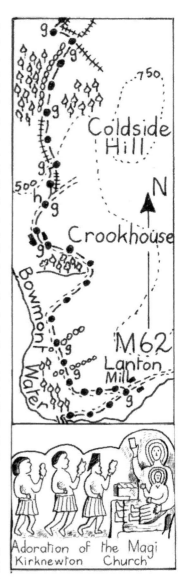

Adoration of the Magi
Kirknewton   Church

*Drink weary pilgrim drink and stay
rest by the well of Sybil Grey*

The design of the well is a bit like a stone fireplace with a canopy, and a round scalloped stone bowl at the base. Water issues from an ornamental stone rosette. The well needs tidying up and cleaning out, as the area in front is very boggy – the water is not too inviting either! STOP PRESS: The area has been tidied up.

Pass some fine specimens of beech in the wood, bear right, and follow the track down the side of a thin plantation to meet a group of ruined buildings. It would seem a pity that these substantial, but roofless, stonebuilt structures with good window mouldings could not be put to better use. They are part of the tiny community of Blinkbonny – what a lovely name. The track meets the road at a footpath sign, Flodden 1½.

As the crow flies, it is just 1½ miles (2.4km) to the site of Flodden Field.

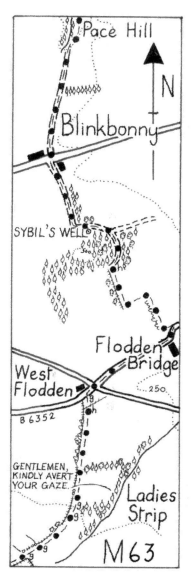

The Battle of Flodden
King James IV of Scotland had for some time been active with a strong army, making many raids into England. This served not only to create serious border problems, but also to act as a diversionary measure to help his French allies, whose country had been invaded by Henry VIII.

An English army under the command of the Earl of Surrey had been raised in the north of England to counter this threat. The Scots were encamped on the eastern slopes of Flodden Hill, and Surrey decided on a risky manoeuvre rather than attacking the enemy's strong position. He marched along the east bank of the River Till, having ordered his artillery over to the west bank via the Twizel Bridge. The rest of his force forded the river just north of Etal, probably unnoticed because of prevailing mist and drizzle, and he united all sections of his army near the village of Branxton.

There came a point when the king realized that he had been outflanked and moved his army to the crest of Branxton Hill. Thus, both armies were to fight facing their own homelands.

In the late afternoon of the ninth of September 1513, the Scots descended the slopes and formed squares of spearmen armed with long pikes. The English archers wreaked havoc, and in the fearful hand-to-hand combat that followed, the long pikes were no match for the English bills and battle axes that cut and hacked into the squares. As dusk fell the day was lost and the remnants of the Scottish army left the field of battle. The king died by his standard, along with his natural son, an archbishop, a bishop, two abbots, twelve earls, fourteen lords and perhaps ten thousand Scots. The English too paid dearly for their victory, as five thousand of their soldiers died.

Close to Branxton village, a path leads to a Celtic cross of grey Aberdeen granite which was raised in 1910. It carries the words:

FLODDEN 1513
TO THE BRAVE OF BOTH NATIONS

There is an annual commemoration service at the site, and the proceedings conclude with the moving pibroch 'The Flowers of the Forest' being played on the bagpipes.

Turn right for a few paces at Blinkbonny, and bear left at a footpath sign, Crookham 1¼. Walk along a good wide hedged track, cross a stream to meet some broom and gorse bushes near a conifer plantation. Where the hedged track ends, continue straight on along the gentle slopes of Pace Hill, with the little valley of Crookham Dean to the left. A track swings away to the right, but go on through thistles and nettles alongside the wood and down to a gate. Note that if you follow the track, it simply veers round a little eminence before descending to rejoin the line of the path. Accompany the fence to a gate, a footpath sign, and the busy A697. If accommodation has been booked at Crookham turn left along the road. Otherwise, bear right, and cross the road to a step stile on the left. Proceed through a small plantation to a footbridge, then along the left-hand side of a hedge to a ladder stile and small gate. Walk up the track, then left past a cottage to meet the B6353 road, and turn right. Walk along this quiet road for half a mile (0.8 km) to a footpath on the left to Old Heatherslaw. Go through a gap in the hedge and walk along the fence side. Descend to a footbridge and ladder stile, and continue on the right-hand side of the hedge on a gently ascending way to Old Heatherslaw. Pass between the buildings, bear right, and proceed along the farm drive to meet a minor road. Turn left. The road passes Heatherslaw Mill, which is one of the oldest water-driven flour mills in England, and has been preserved as a museum complete with car park and cafe.

A short distance to the south-east lies the settlement of Ford, a model village planned in the middle of the nineteenth century by Louisa, Marchioness of Waterford. At the end of its one long street lies the castle, surrounded by trees; parts of the building date back to Plantagenet times. The castle, which originally had four corner towers, was rebuilt in the baronial style. The school, built in 1860, now the Lady Waterford Hall, was decorated by Louisa with a series of nine watercolours and representations of themes from the Old Testament.

At Ford Forge, turn left – no sneaking off with the excuse of wanting to look at the steam train at the station. (You won't see the Flying Scotsman or the Duchess of Hamilton, but you will see the engine and coaches of the fifteen-inch narrow gauge steam railway running from Heatherslaw to Etal. The little train carries visitors from March to October on a journey along the banks of the Till.)

A footpath follows the road past Fore Hill to a point where a minor road joins the B6354. Then continue along this road into the village of Etal. Turn left, and walk down the village street, and bear right to a small parking area by the side of the River Till.

The River Till, which for the first part of its journey from its source on eastern Cheviot is the River Breamish, is joined by the considerable forces of Wooler Water, the Bowmont Water and the River Glen, to become the River Till at Bewick Mill. It then becomes a slow and sinuous river that creeps through the green water meadows or haughs past the villages of Ford and Etal. At Etal, it tumbles over the weir and becomes lively and joyous again, running lightly over its rocky bed; and on past banks lined with hazel, oak and conifer, and with sandstone buttressed sides, to its meeting with the mighty Tweed.

The name 'Etal' derives from *Eata's Haugh* or *Halh*, a *Halh* used for grazing. The village has a single street lined by eighteenth-, nineteenth- and twentieth-century cottages, a few with thatched roofs, including the Black Bull Inn. The impression is of a planned settlement, with an eighteenth-century Manor House set in parkland at one end and a ruined castle at the opposite end. The Manor House opens its gardens to the public on advertised weekends.

Following numerous Scottish raids by Bruce and Wallace, as well as from their neighbours, many landowners were given royal permission to fortify their manor houses. In fact, fourteenth-century

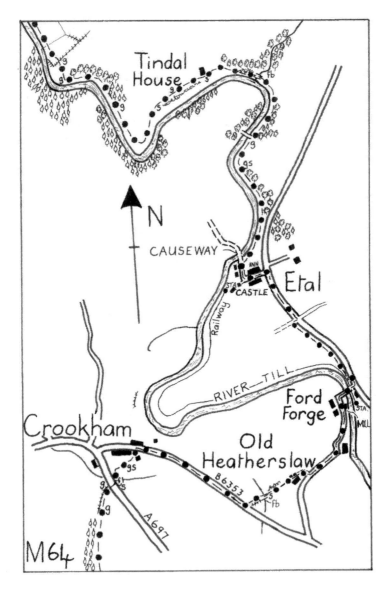

Etal Castle was once a fortress of some strength, strong enough to repel armed marauders but inadequate against an army. Needless to say, it never recovered from the assault by James IV Scots. The castle, which comprises a four-storey keep, a gatehouse and parts of its curtain wall and corner tower, is under the care of English Heritage.

Leave the small car park on the Etal side of the river, where there is a footpath sign to Twizel Bridge. The pleasant path pursues its way through leafy surroundings with conifers to the right and broadleaf to the left – a beautiful riverside walk. Continue through a gate with ladder stile, leaving the trees behind, and approach another gate. A private suspension bridge crosses the river; it would make an exciting prospect, but it's not a right of way. Proceed through a bower of leafy glades along the river bank, with a profusion of wild flowers carpeting the ground.

Pass over an ill-used ornamental stone bridge with a rock outcrop on the right, to reach a grassy part of the river bank with a seat for the weary. The path then ascends up the slope to a small gate, and along a grassy bank by a fence to the corner of a ruined building. There is a ladder stile and a waymarker in the comer. The right of way passes the outbuildings to Tindal House on an overgrown section with a flourishing nettle crop – you certainly won't want your shorts on here! People interested in the production of nettle beer should be advised that these are the finest nettles in Northumberland with a stinging quality of 98% proof.

Continue along the side of a thorn hedge with growing crops on the right, negotiate a fallen tree and proceed through a gap in a hedge. Approach a small kissing gate in the corner with a yellow waymarker – there is a glimpse of Scottish hills in the distance. Keep on along the hedge to a ladder stile and waymarker and descend to the riverside pasture. Go through a small gate into Black Bank Wood and continue to another small gate leading into a pleasant section of meadow. Slant gently up to the right and across to a small gate in a fence. Descend left to gorse bushes, and walk on the edge of the field with growing crops. Proceed to a gap in the fence in front and forward along a grassy track. Note the tall farm silo of Castle Heaton beyond on the opposite bank of the river. There are bushes on the left as the route passes a gate and on into mixed woodland. The track swings away from the river, crosses a stream and bears left again. Leave the track where a yellow waymarker indicates and pass through butterbur. The river at this point is variable in its movement, sometimes dancing, sometimes slow and ponderous.

Pass through a canopy of beech trees and walk quietly through the attractively named Tiptoe Wood; this is another charming and much enjoyed section of the walk. The way climbs a little, with tall pine trees to the right, plus some new planting, and descends once more to the river bank.

On the opposite bank a rocky outcrop becomes visible, together with the farm of Castle Heaton higher up the slope. An area on either side of a small tributary has been replanted with trees. Pass through a small gate on a grass track as the river begins to quicken its pace again. The weir across the Till is in a dilapidated condition and obviously past its former usefulness. In an area of more beech trees the path is signposted up to the right, as the way has been re-routed because of a landslip. Across the river lies the attractive dwelling of Heaton Mill House.

Ascend the track through the trees, and swing left to a footpath sign indicating the route downstream to Twizel. Proceed through conifers and over a ladder stile with the river now far below. This is an impressive aspect, reminiscent of the deep river valleys found in the tiny country of Luxembourg. Here at Heaton Mill, the river has cut a gorge, and the path continues along the top of the cliffs creating an outstanding viewpoint – a scenic surprise. Walk ahead to a ladder stile, and, peeping over the edge very carefully, note that the honey-coloured stone has been quarried at some time in the past.

The path goes through a small copse to another ladder stile, and then descends a grassy track to the left. A footpath sign announces the landslip on the riverside path for the benefit of walkers coming from the opposite direction. Walk through the meadow beneath a bank of gorse bushes as a track becomes discernible, but do not ascend, keeping to the riverbank instead. Approach a ladder stile, continue ahead to a footbridge and then past a hydraulic ram. Note that the river has carved out another gorge as it makes a sharp horseshoe bend. Go through a gate and pass beneath sandstone cliffs as the way descends to the river again. Beyond another small gate the grassy track passes through a newly planted tree area and leafy glades. A footpath sign indicates 'Riverside Path', which climbs above Twizel Mill to a hurdle and ladder stile. Proceed down the track to join a tarmac lane. A notice to the left states: PRIVATE, BEWARE OF THE DOG. At one time the group of buildings on the river bank formed part of a flourishing commercial enterprise. Across the river, situated on the high ground overlooking the valley, is the Tillmouth Park Hotel. Pass along the lane fringed with glorious beech trees and over a cattle grid to reach the A698 road at Twizel Bridge. The footpath sign indicates Etal 5½.

The medieval (early fifteenth-century) bridge crosses the gorge of the Till in one spectacular leap; it is a narrow bridge flung across the river with a span of 90ft (27.4m) – a beautiful shape in a beautiful setting. Over it on the fateful day of Flodden passed the Earl of Surrey's vanguard and artillery. However, the view of the old bridge is rather spoiled by the functional concrete and ugly railings of the modern structure. From the crossing point, beyond the wooded sides of the Till, can be seen the ivy-covered ruins of Twizel Castle, an eighteenth-century house that was never completed. From the footpath sign continue along the river bank, with sandstone outcrops on the right, to encounter giant 'triffid'-like plants. You hope they have already eaten – but, just to be sure, toss them a left-over sandwich! There follows another enjoyable riverside section to pass under the impressive railway viaduct carrying the former Kelso to Berwick line.

At the meeting of the Till and Tweed stand the remains of St Cuthbert's Chapel; a roofless building with window apertures. It was mentioned in verse as the chapel to which the heroine of Sir Walter Scott's 'Marmion' fled after the Battle of Flodden. If you think that the Tweed at the confluence is rather small, bear in mind that the shrub-covered land you are looking at across the water is in fact an island – there is a wider channel beyond on the northern side. One is also quite likely to see people fishing at this point; perhaps one in a boat, and a helper hanging on to a rope from the bankside, holding the boat steady in the strong current.

The leisure activity most often associated with the Tweed and its tributaries is salmon and trout fishing, which can be practised from Peebles down towards the Tweed estuary at Berwick. Fishing on the River Tweed above the sea fishing limit at Norham is controlled by the Tweed Commissioners. Salmon fishing can be achieved from the river bank, or from a boat or by wading out into the water, and can be done by spinning with bait or with artificial lures. A salmon fisherman's lure case may contain such fanciful names as Dusty Miller, Jock Scott and Black Goldfinch. If fishing for trout then the collection may include Greenwell's Glory, Grey Gnat, Knotted Midge and Waterhen Blow.

The season for salmon fishing on the Tweed is from 1st February to 30th November, and for brown trout from 15th March to 6th October.

River Tweed

The River Tweed rises at Tweed's Well Some six miles north of Moffat, and runs for 97 miles through the heart of the Scottish Borders. Its birthplace is set in an area of wild, rounded hills; the tranquil silence broken by the call of curlews, skylarks and lapwings. This high dissected plateau attains the heights of Hart Fell, 2,756 ft (808 m) and Broad Law, 2,756 ft (840 m).

The Tweed winds down from Tweedsmuir to Melrose, and at every turn, soft woodland colours of larch and spruce blanket the steep slopes, blending with the valley broadleaves. The closely growing trees hide the courses of myriads of small rivulets that race their way down the hill flanks to join the main stream. Above the trees, the higher slopes are roamed by flocks of hardy sheep.

In the central part of its journey, and around the main tributary valleys may be found the specialized knitwear industry that grew up at the turn of the century; this includes cashmere, tweed and hosiery manufacture.

Bordering the course of the river are many historic houses, castles and abbeys, such as Neidpath, Traquair, Abbotsford, Melrose Abbey, Dryburgh Abbey and Floors Castle.

After the border has run down the centre of the Tweed's channel for a length of nineteen miles, the Tweed becomes an English river for the last three miles of its journey to the North Sea.

Pass a green hut, then a cottage named Twizel Boathouse, and continue to a small gate and ladder stile. From now on your progress will be a most pleasant and satisfying experience: flower-bedecked grassy ways, lush water-meadows, occasional riverside cliffs and patches of woodland. Prior to each loop and bend, there is an expectation of what is going to be seen round the next corner.

Pass a small building with a pointed roof and solitary chimney which is opposite to a cliff on the other side of the river. Keep to the left of a house, follow the fence, and descend towards the river through trees. Note the large house on the far bank. The path through the trees, which includes some steps and a footbridge, is rather slippery, and particularly needs some attention alongside Dreeper Island. Cross over another footbridge and ascend a little, with a felled area to the right. The right of way was obstructed at this point by brash and tree litter which rather impeded progress. Pass a wooden hut and descend left to become clear of the island. As a matter of interest, Dreeper Island is in England, and its north-eastern end, Kippie Island, is in Scotland.

Approach a ladder stile in a fence and proceed along the river bank in an area now clear of trees. Walk by a small fenced off building, complete with TV aerial, lawn and kitchen garden. Follow a fence amongst grassy banks and pastures to pass a corrugated iron hut. Continue to a ladder stile, then go along the fence to another ladder stile with a footpath sign, Norham 1½, Twizel Bridge 3½. Struggle through a patch of rampant vegetation to a footbridge, bear left and negotiate a way impeded by fallen trees and undergrowth. Descend and cross a footbridge, with the old railway viaduct to the right crossing Newbiggin Dean. Ignore a gate, keep along the riverbank and pass round a metal gate that is lonely, unused and unwanted.

Looking back, there is a fine prospect of the river as it curves away. Pass a seat that is opposite to a small building on the far bank, and ascend through leafy surroundings to a gate. Proceed past houses on the right, the last dwelling called The Boathouse, and on to a footpath indicator with a nearly unreadable metal sign.

Walk along a tarmac lane to Bow Well, with a footpath sign on the left, Ladykirk Bridge ½. NOTE: Walkers not requiring accommodation at Norham should follow the path to Ladykirk Bridge and continue

Etal Castle

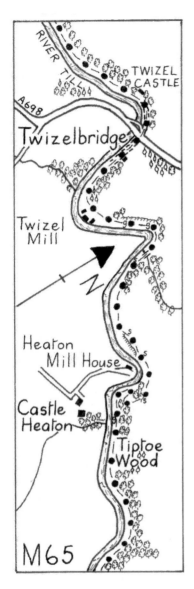

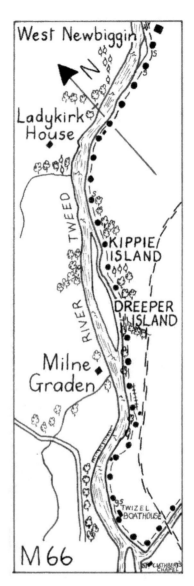

along the riverbank. Otherwise, the prospect of a bed for the night, chocolate bars and newspapers will tempt the Ravenber walker along the lane to meet the B6470, and then, only a short distance into the village of Norham.

14. Norham to Berwick-upon-Tweed

Map	OS 1:25000 Explorer, Kelso, Coldstream and Lower Tweed Valley, Sheet 339. OS 1:25000 Explorer, Berwick-upon-Tweed, Sheet 346
Highest elevation	Horncliffe village 98ft (30m)
Height of ascent	223ft (68m)
Distance	10½ miles (16.8km)
Terrain	Easy walking distance on attractive riverside footpaths along the banks of the Tweed. Journey's end at the fascinating and historic town of Berwick-upon-Tweed.

The name 'Norham' derives from 'Northern *hām*'; a homestead, an earlier name was Ubbanford or Ubba's Ford. The village is situated in the meadows in a bend of the River Tweed. It consists of one long side street leading down from the castle towards a triangular green, on which stands the Village Cross. The lower steps are medieval, and the Victorian shaft is surmounted by a vane in the shape of a fish to commemorate Norham's salmon fishing interests.

Until a few years ago a ceremony used to take place on the banks of the Tweed at Norham known as the Pedwell Blessing of the Nets. A service was conducted by the vicar which included the traditional Pedwell Prayer:

> *Good Lord, lead us,*
> *Good Lord, speed us,*
> *From all perils protect us,*
> *In the darkness direct us.*
> *Give us Good Lord*
> *Finest nights to land our fish,*
> *Sound and big to fill our wish,*
> *Keep our nets from snag and break,*

For every man a goodly take.
Give us, Good Lord.
Amen.

North from the Village Cross the road leads to the parish church of St Cuthbert, embowered in fine trees. It was built about the same time as the castle on the earlier site of a Saxon church. Although there is little left of the original Norman building after the nineteenth-century restoration (1846-52), what remains is truly magnificent. The arcade is exceptional for a parish church: five round-headed arches in the south aisle decorated with a zig-zag frieze supported on huge circular piers. The three-shafted piers of the chancel arch, and the beautiful windows in the south wall of the chancel, are also very fine. Particularly interesting are the vicar's stall and pulpit, with the carved coat of arms of late seventeenth-century work from Durham Cathedral.

Norham Castle
The magnificent situation of the castle, at the far end of the village street, emphasizes its former importance as the great northern

Norham

stronghold of the Prince Bishops of Durham. The castle is laid out on the normal motte and bailey plan, but the wards are larger than usual in order to fulfil its role as both fortress and bishop's palace.

Originally of timber construction, it was rebuilt in stone in 1158-74 by Bishop Puiset (Pudsey). At Norham the constable lived in the keep, and the bishop and his advisers lived in their quarters in the north-east corner of the inner ward. There are the remains of the great hall, with entrances to the kitchen, the great oven still in existence, and to the buttery and pantry, which were all part of sixteenth century rebuilding work.

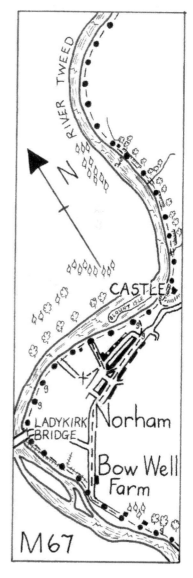

The splendid red sandstone keep was initially three storeys high, but was enlarged in the fifteenth century to a height of five storeys, with the addition of a spiral staircase built in the middle of the south-west wall. The east and south walls of the keep had to be particularly strong because they formed part of the curtain wall. The Norman keep was divided unequally by a cross wall, its basement constructed with barrel vaulting and supported by large broad arches arranged in a crosswise direction. Attached to the south wall of the inner ward are two towers: the one at the south-east end is a fifteenth-century oblong tower, and the other, Clapham's Tower, is of the sixteenth century, built with a pointed exterior and embrasures for artillery.

The West Gate, Marmion's Gate, is the main entrance to the outer bailey. Its masonry work is partly Norman, consisting of a tunnel-vaulted passage, which was closed in the fourteenth century and reopened in the fifteenth century, with a barbican and an unusual type of drawbridge. The north wall of the outer ward runs along the steep bank overlooking the Tweed, and where it meets the inner ward may be found the position of the fifteenth-century chapel. Water from the moat ran under the chapel and down to the river.

Norham was a very important point in the English defensive line against the Scots. By 1318 the fragile peace was again shattered when the castle was besieged for almost a year by King Robert the Bruce. The outer ward was captured, but was retaken after three days, and ultimately the blockade had to be lifted. The following year the Scots tried again in a siege lasting seven months.

It was at this time that a certain incident concerning Sir William Marmion was supposed to have taken place. The knight arrived at the castle with a new helmet given to him by his lady-love, with orders to prove his valour. The constable, Sir Thomas Grey, encouraged him to ride forth, after promising to rescue him – alive or dead! So Marmion charged out on his war horse and was promptly knocked out of his saddle by the Scots. He was rescued, sore and bleeding, but alive, by the soldiers of the castle garrison.

The event is used in Sir Walter Scott's *Marmion*. The opening lines of the poem contain a graphic description of Norham Castle at sunset:

> *Day set on Norham's castled steep,*
> *And Tweed's fair river, broad and deep*
> *And Cheviot's mountains lone;*
> *The battled towers, the donjon Keep,*
> *The loop-hole grates, where captives weep,*
> *The flanking walls that round it sweep*
> *In yellow lustre shone.*

The strength of the fortress was again put to the test in 1497 when the great cannon Mons Meg was employed by the Scots, but to no avail. However, in 1513, James IV attacked and captured the fortress on his way to Flodden, after bombarding it with heavy artillery.

Today, Norham Castle is a delightful place to visit, surrounded by fine beech trees and lawns rising to the remains of the curtain wall, turrets and keep. Although it is ruined, its beauty and spaciousness high above the Tweed can easily be admired, reflecting its long and eventful history.

Main Route

The short stretch of path from GR NT 8930 4665, from the footpath sign and small gate to Ladykirk Bridge, just before Bow Well Farm, was difficult to follow, due to the growth of trees, bushes, nettles and briars. After representations, the route has now been waymarked.

Climb over a step stile before Ladykirk Bridge and ascend steps up to the road; there is a footpath sign, Norham 1, Horncliffe 4. Higher up on the Scottish side of the river, opposite to Norham, is Ladykirk. It owes its name to a vow made by King James IV, who was in danger of drowning when fording the Tweed. The king declared that if he survived the crossing he would build a stone church in honour of the Virgin.

Cross the road and descend a long flight of stone steps to the riverbank. Walk along a clear and level path to pass through two kissing gates. A footpath sign indicates Norham to the right. NOTE: This right of way leads to St Cuthbert's church and into the village. A track now appears and so does a convenient seat. Pass a wooden hut on the right which is a River Gauging Station owned by the Tweed River Purification Board, and another seat. A track then leads off to the right with a footpath sign stating: bank erosion. rejoin riverside path this side of the castle. Turn right; this is obviously a diversion until work on the path has been completed. Continue along the track to re-enter the village by the War Memorial – walkers who have stayed in Norham take note. Proceed along Castle Street, and turn left to a footpath sign. Go through a small gate, with a sign stating RIVERSIDE PATH: Horncliffe 3, Berwick-Upon-Tweed 9. Pass a grassy area with more seats to reach another small gate. A footpath sign mentions the problem of bank erosion for the benefit of walkers coming from the opposite direction: THEY SHOULD REJOIN THE RIVERSIDE PATH AT THE END OF CASTLE STREET.

Descend steps, cross over a footbridge and climb up more steps; the castle appears on the hill in front. Walkers desirous of visiting the castle should continue along Castle Street to the site, and rejoin the riverside path that leaves at the bend in the road.

Continue along the grassy river bank to a ladder stile. Climb up steps under a rocky cliff and descend to cross a footbridge. Much time has been spent, and a good job done, on the next section of path, with steps and stabilization work. There is a footbridge to cross and forward to another ladder stile over a tree trunk. Climb up more steps, descend a zig-zag stepway and cross another footbridge. Note the interesting rock banding on the pathside cliffs. Approach a ladder stile and pass a corrugated iron fishing hut. Do not take the step stile to the right by a metal gate into a field; instead proceed along the riverbank as the Tweed makes a wide curve towards St Thomas's Island. Continue past a derelict fishing shiel with a red roof and a solitary chimney to draw level with the island which lies in Scotland. At this point the path seems to go to the right of the fence, and then returns to the north side at the next incoming field boundary. Go over a small footbridge, then through longer grass and cross another footbridge. When you are roughly half-way past the island the village of Horncliffe comes into view, standing on a red cliff high above the river.

Pass a small fishing shiel on the island which has red pantiles and a squat-looking chimney. Take the ladder stile on the right with a waymarker arrow, and slant left uphill to a hedge and ladder stile with an arrow. Climb the slope on some steps as the path swings left and terraces across the valley side. The route disappears into a thicket with verdant undergrowth, and emerges high above the river, level with the village of Horncliffe. This is a splendid view point of the sweeping course of the Tweed and the lovely riverside meadows and sloping banksides. Pursue a way through more thickets and then swing round to the right into a wooded section. Descend steeply to the left down steps to a footbridge over the stream at Burn Mouth. The surrounding area, including the Horncliffemill Burn, with its

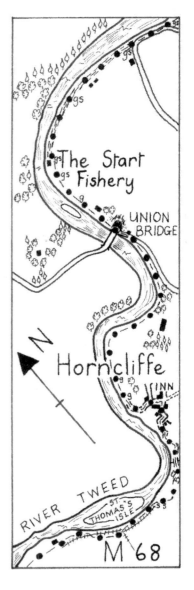

waterfall, is of great interest to botanists. Climb up the slope, firstly between hedges, and then along a gravelled track, to reach a footpath sign: Norham 3. Bear right into a road, incline left and proceed to the Old School House, built in 1833. This is Horncliffe; there is a small square to the right with a telephone kiosk at the end. Bear left at the top and continue to follow the road round to the Fishers' Arms – a very conveniently placed hostelry.

Turn left down the street at the side of the inn to a footpath sign at the bottom, indicating the riverside path to Union Bridge and Berwick-upon-Tweed. Go through a gate and descend on a track. Bear right, pass a building and then a wooden fishing chalet. Continue along by the fence to a kissing gate.

The River Tweed is now rapidly approaching the sea, and Horncliffe is the limit of the tidal reach and navigability.

There is a lovely grassy path now on which rapid progress can be made, and all previous struggles through rampant vegetation can be temporarily forgotten. Pass a ruined fishing shiel, then some mature trees, and continue alongside a stretch of pristine riverside sand. Walk to a footbridge and note the attractive situation of Horncliffe House, terraced on the hillside. The river begins to sweep grandly to the north towards the suspension bridge, as the tree-bordered path follows it round the curve. Cross a footbridge, continue along the leafy river bank to emerge on to the road by Chainbridge House and to a footpath sign: Horncliffe 1, Norham 4.

The Union Bridge was the first big suspension bridge built in the country. It was designed and executed in 1820 by Captain Samuel Brown RN, the inventor of the wrought-iron link, which he had patented three years earlier; it was improved and strengthened in 1902-1903 by the Tweed Bridges Trustees. On the southern side the chains start from a massive abutment built into the sandstone cliff and cross to a stone arch on the north bank. The crossing is 432ft (131.6m) long between the suspension points, 18ft (549m) wide, and 69 ft (21 m) above the surface of the water.

Continue straight ahead along the track, passing a white-painted house with shutters. Go through a gate, and walk along the grassy path to another gate and step stile. Ahead lies a pleasant mown area with riverside lights, slipway, and an attractive building with red pantiles and rendered walls – a notice indicates START FISHERY. Walk to a gate and step stile, and on a track to another gate and a ladder stile. Pass fishing cottages to reach a gate and step stile.

At this point a minor road comes in from the right, and just as it swings away from the river at GR NT 9472 5206, the border strikes north for two miles. For the last three miles of its course the Tweed becomes an English river.

Proceed ahead to a step stile, gate and footpath sign. Walk on a grassy track past a refurbished cottage to a ladder stile and more undergrowth. The path narrows to cross a footbridge and goes by another cottage and storehouse set into the bankside. The path remains narrow and close to the river, so watch out for planks across gullies hidden by vegetation – a hazard. Continue past a windowless shiel and approach a ladder stile submerged in rank vegetation. Cross the footbridge over the Canny Burn, ascend the steep slope partly to the right by means of wooden steps and emerge at a step stile with the bonus of a superb view above the river. The path has actually climbed up through the site of an ancient earthwork. Follow the fence, with the sighting of buildings in the distance, to reach a ladder stile. Now be calm, there's no need to leap about just yet!

The Royal Border Bridge lies beyond slightly to the left, and in the immediate foreground, the latest road bridge carrying the A1 crosses the Tweed at Whiteadder Point – the confluence of Whiteadder Water. Proceed to a step stile with a footpath sign and meet the busy main road. Turn right and cross over with due care and attention to the picnic area with toilet facilities. Aim for the far left-hand corner of the site to a step stile – you can now smell the sea. Walk to the right of a derelict building, climb up the slope and keep to the edge of the field, which may be under crops. Progress through a gap in the corner of the hedge, and continue through long grass along the field edge on top of the river bank. From a footpath sign the way emerges on to a road. Keep straight on through a kissing gate. Here, depending on the direction of the wind, the atmosphere is noticeably enriched by blasts of 'perfume' from the local sewage works.

Walk alongside the fence to a kissing gate in the right-hand corner. Follow the wire-meshed boundary and then a hedge to another kissing gate. Continue under a bank lined with trees. Here, on a small hill called Hang-a-Dyke Neuk, Edward III is reputed to have executed the son of Sir Alexander Seton, Governor of Berwick.

The Royal Border Bridge is the highest and longest of Berwick's three bridges. It stands 126ft (38m) above the surface of the water, with fourteen elegantly shaped arches of brick construction on stone-built piers. The viaduct was designed by Robert Stephenson, and was built between 1847 and 1850; it carries the main east coast railway line between England and Scotland.

Across the river lie the scant remains of Berwick Castle. Sadly, the Victorian railway engineers thought it necessary to demolish the medieval fortress, once one of the most important of border strongholds. In fact, Berwick Station stands on the site of the former Great Hall of the castle. The remains which survive are the White Wall, and a flight of steps which lead down to the White Tower.

Pass under the railway bridge and continue along the grass verge to emerge on to the road. The next bridge, the Royal Tweed Bridge, is a rather ugly concrete-spanned structure lacking the elegance and grace of the other two bridges. Designed and built in 1925-28, it spans 1,400ft (427m) in four giant leaps and formerly carried the Great North Road. It was opened by the Prince of Wales, later Edward VIII and Duke of Windsor.

Walk under the Royal Tweed Bridge to meet attractive rose beds at the entrance to the Old Bridge. This is still the finest way to approach the town. Built in 1610-34, the lovely graceful red sandstone bridge of fifteen arches links the town with the south bank of the Tweed. It measures 1,164ft (355m) in length and was a replacement for a wooden bridge which stood a little further upstream. There is a delicate inclining rise towards the northern side, with the second arch nearest to the town being the highest to allow for the passage of boats.

Stand a while in one of the projections and gaze at the town ahead to savour the lovely view – the afternoon sun highlighting the grey walls and red roofs of the town, with the prominent belfry of the Town Hall dominating the skyline; it is all reminiscent of a Tuscan or Provençal scene.

Berwick-upon-Tweed

The name 'Berwick' derives from *Berewic*, 'a corn farm', and suggests a small agricultural settlement, most probably founded by the Saxons. One of the first references concerning Berwick lay in the charter granted by King Edgar bestowing the settlement in 1097 to the Bishop of Durham. It became Scotland's most important port and was created one of four Scottish royal burghs by King David (1124-5 3). King John, brother of Richard I, burnt it to the ground after returning from a foray over the border. Rebuilding commenced and by the reign of Alexander III (1247-86) the town had become exceedingly prosperous from trading.

In 1292, Edward I gave Scotland to John Balliol in preference to Robert the Bruce, but soon after Balliol rebelled. The town was destroyed by Edward I, the inhabitants slaughtered, and it lost its importance as a fine trading centre. Resettled by English merchants, it was captured by William Wallace and occupied for a short time.

Royal Border Bridge

Again, the Scots took the town in 1333, but soon after were defeated by Edward III at the Battle of Halidon Hill on the 19th July 1333. One of the decisive factors was the introduction of the long-bow by the English, which was also used to great effect at the Battle of Crécy.

The town and its surroundings were the scene of constant strife for nearly 350 years, and changed hands thirteen times between 1147 and 1482, when Berwick finally passed to the English crown.

Berwick's first defences, raised by Edward I, consisted of a ditch, bank and palisade. Later, a wall was built by Edward II, and by the time of Henry VIII the wall had nineteen towers and five gates. The fortifications were constructed on an earthen embankment and strengthened at the rear by a retaining wall.

The town's second defences were constructed during two periods: the first between 1550 and 1557 under Edward VI and Mary Tudor, and the second between 1558 and 1569 under Elizabeth. It was during the latter period that the ramparts were constructed which are such a prominent feature of Berwick today. The fortifications were designed by two Italian engineers, Portman and Contio, at a time when guns and gunpowder dominated warfare. They used lower but thicker walls, and concentrated on providing the means to return fire in the most effective manner. Fundamentally, the essential features are a strong stone wall reinforced by an earthwork in the shape of an arrow-head. Artillery placed in the two 'flankers' could bring defensive fire to cover across the face of adjacent areas of the rampart, while guns on the outward segments provided offensive fire. The flankers were accessible by means of tunnels.

In front of the Brass Bastion is a low projecting wall, known as the Batardeau, which controlled the water level of the moat – look for the sluice grooves in the stonework.

It was intended that six of these bastions should be constructed to protect the central part of the town. However, only two bastions, Windmill and Cumberland, were fully completed. Another one, Brass, was finished in a non-symmetrical form; and two others, King's Mount and Meg's Mount, were only half completed.

Salmon Fishing on the Tweed Estuary
From the time of the first charters in the twelfth century, the River Tweed has been divided into fishing stations, each with their own titles and boundaries, on a length of river stretching from its mouth up to about ten miles upstream. It is believed that the earliest method

for catching salmon involved the use of nets or traps (stells), paid out from cobles or small rowing boats.

Through the Middle Ages, great numbers of salmon were caught in the Tweed, which were either sold fresh in the local fish market, or were salted, packed into barrels and exported to other parts of England and Scotland. Many sixteenth-century references are found concerning the purchase of Tweed salmon by the monks of Durham, sometimes fresh, sometimes salted.

There were times when the Tweed had no salmon at all, for various reasons – overfishing, disease, attacks by the Scots and poaching. It became necessary to lay down controls in order that fishing could be carried out in a fair and sensible manner.

In the eighteenth century, the method of fishing was by means of a flat-bottomed boat, square at one end, with the net making as large a circuit as possible. Helpers then pulled the net towards the shore to land the catch. This was later known as wear-shot netting, and after the Tweed Act of 1857 was the only method of salmon fishing used in the river.

In the nineteenth century there were still periods when the numbers of salmon caught in the Tweed diminished, and acts were passed to control legal fishing and to punish poaching. A gunboat was even stationed at the mouth of the Tweed, causing much resentment, with a number of incidents occurring between local fishermen and the authorities.

The Berwick Salmon Fisheries Company operated from fisheries near the mouth of the Tweed from 1872. After the Second World War, up to 150 men were employed in salmon fishing, but at the end of 1987 the Company sold its salmon netting rights and closed down.

However, the ceremony of crowning the Salmon Queen is still held in the third week of July, around the 20th of the month.

The town's football team, Berwick Rangers, are the only English team to play in the Scottish League. Their ground is at Shielfield Park on the south bank of the river. Their current home strip consists of a black and gold shirt, black shorts, and gold stockings with two black hoops.

Main Route – Journey's End

From the north end of the Old Bridge turn right down the flagged street signposted Town Walls, Fisher's Fort, Museum, to pass the Custom House. This area of the Quay Walls contains fine houses mostly built in the eighteenth and nineteenth centuries. Continue along the ramparts to reach Coxon's Tower and the projecting section of Fisher's Fort. A little further on is a gun captured from the Russians in the Crimea.

From Ness Gate walk along Pier Road, and just before Devon Terrace some steps lead up to the left and bear right behind the buildings. This way leads to a grassy area and car parks. Otherwise, proceed along Pier Road and turn left prior to the Pier Breakwater. The half-a-mile long breakwater was built in 1860 and has a lighthouse that is 60ft (18m) high. Walk ahead to reach the same grassy area, car parks and sand dunes.

There is now a little ceremony to perform. Stride forward purposefully to the strand facing Meadow Haven and dip your boots into the North Sea. You have completed the Ravenber Walk across

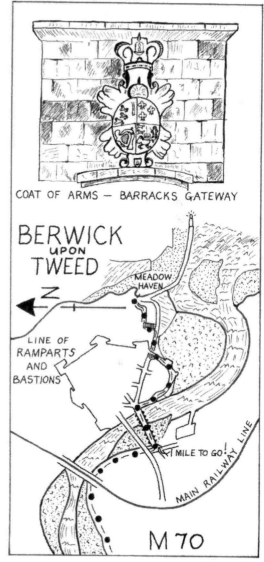

COAT OF ARMS — BARRACKS GATEWAY

BERWICK
UPON
TWEED

MEADOW HAVEN

LINE OF RAMPARTS AND BASTIONS

1 MILE TO GO!

MAIN RAILWAY LINE

M 70

northern England from coast to coast. Congratulations!

Local people may well react to this seemingly strange action. I was about to perform the ceremony when a passer-by called out: 'Haad on man, divent de it, tyek the boat from Newcassell' (translation: 'Hold on man, don't do it, take the boat from Newcastle').

If there is insufficient time left at the end of the day, or at the end of a holiday period, then, unfortunately, it's off to the railway station, or to a point where a friend or relation is waiting with a car to transport you home. Nevertheless, it would be a great pity to miss the experience of a quiet stroll around the walls of Berwick, in sight of the great river and of the North Sea,

Route Around the Berwick Ramparts:

Walk 1

Retrace your steps along Pier Road towards Fisher's Fort. From Ness Gate, built in 1816, continue north along the ramparts to the first bastion, King's Mount. Take care on the ramparts, as there are sloping grass-covered edges with a severe drop – it would be terrible to fall off your perch at this stage after completing the long journey from Ravenglass.

Proceed further and notice a tall house with stone lions at the front, followed by a sturdy, well-buttressed building surrounded by a high wall – this was the garrison magazine or armoury. The next fortification is the Windmill Bastion. Ahead on the left, the building with the massive gate-house and coat of arms is the Ravensdowne Barracks. Pass over the Cow Port, the only remaining original gateway. The gate has portcullis grooves and a heavy timber door, and was used by townsfolk to lead their cattle out to pasture. The parish church of Holy Trinity lies to the left as the route swings towards the town, passing Brass and Cumberland Bastions to reach Scotsgate. Descend the steps to the road. The original gate was a single-arched structure which was rebuilt in 1815 and again in 1858. Immediately beyond this point is Meg's Mount Bastion. Proceed along the ramparts, turning south-east alongside the river, passing the white statue of Lady Jerningham, to reach a flight of steps prior to the Royal Tweed Bridge. Turn left, walk along Golden Square to the junction with Marygate; the Town Hall lies to the right at the end of this street. Turn left opposite the bus station, and continue along Castlegate under Scotsgate. Turn left into Railway Street and bear left again to Berwick Station car park. Distance: From Ness Gate, 1½ Miles (2.4 km).

Walk 2

From Berwick Station car park turn left into Railway Street and left again into Castlegate. Proceed over the railway bridge and walk for a

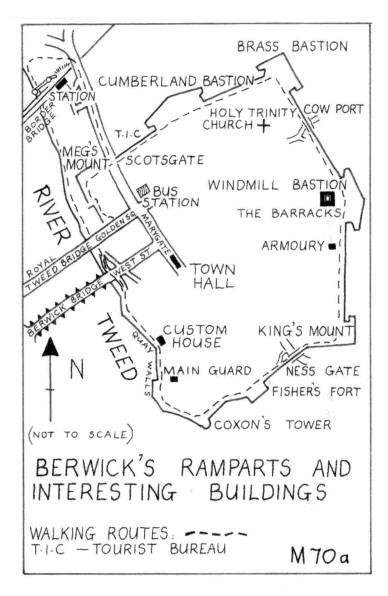

few paces along the A6105. Go left through a small gate and continue down through the park with an excellent prospect of the castle. Turn left along a path which passes through the castle walls, and on under the Royal Border Railway Bridge. The route continues beneath the

Royal Tweed Bridge and along Bridge Terrace to meet the Old Berwick Bridge. Bear left and walk ahead into West Street to reach Marygate; the Town Hall lies to the right. Turn left and return to Berwick Station as in Walk 1. Distance: From station back to station, 1½ miles (2.4 km).

Among the interesting buildings to be found in Berwick are the following:

Custom House, Quay Walls
An admirable building with its arched windows on the ground floor and Venetian doorway. Built in the late eighteenth century, an outstanding example of Georgian architecture.

Guard House, Palace Street
This eighteenth-century guardhouse originally stood in Marygate. The building has a low squat portico of four columns surmounted by a steep pediment.

The Governor's House, East Side Palace Green
A fine eighteenth-century building facing Palace Green, the home of the former head of the town garrison. It is three storeys high with five bays and two-storey wing sections. The centre bays are flanked by large projecting rectangular columns.

Ravensdowne Barracks,
Corner of The Parade and Ravensdowne
These imposing buildings with crow-stepped gable ends were probably designed under the supervision of Sir John Vanbrugh, and completed in 1721. The two three-storey buildings along the sides of a rectangular site provided accommodation for the men, and the rear block for stores. Later, in 1739-41, a third range of two storeys was built along the fourth side. A strong-looking gatehouse, with a pair of fine ornamental gates capped by a coat of arms, completes the picture.

The barracks were built due to public outcry concerning the inconvenience of billeting soldiers in local inns and private houses. They served as the joint depot for the Royal Scots and the King's Own Scottish Borderers. The buildings now serve as home to three museums: the Regimental Museum of the KOSB, the Borough Museum and Art Gallery and an Army Museum.

Holy Trinity Church,
Between Wallace Green and The Parade
This is a building of exceptional architectural interest: built in 1648-52, it is one of only two churches constructed during the Commonwealth times. The other is to be found at Staunton Harold in Leicestershire.

The west doorway is flanked by two large buttresses and two pepper-pot style turrets dating from the nineteenth century. The church has a nave, aisles and clerestory, but no tower. This is an elegant, restful building with an interior arcade of five bays on Tuscan columns. The south aisle and the north chapel are lit by fine Venetian windows patterned in a chequer-board of black and white, edged with blue and red. The original plain windows of the clerestory were replaced by Venetian lights in the mid nineteenth century. The west window contains splendid stained glass of Flemish or Dutch roundels dating from the sixteenth or seventeenth centuries. The grand Jacobean-type panelled oak pulpit originally belonged to the old parish church.

Town Hall, Marygate
The building is a fine example of Georgian architecture, complete with a portico at the head of an imposing flight of steps. It commands Marygate with considerable style, and its fine steeple rises to a height of 150 ft (46 m); it can be glimpsed from practically anywhere in the town. The belfry houses eight bells, four of which belong to the Holy Trinity Church, which does not possess a tower. Miscreants were put in the old stocks, last used in 1857, and the old gaol on the top floor still contains well-preserved cells.

Youth Hotels, on or near the route

Eskdale; Wastwater; Elterwater; High Close, Loughrigg; Ambleside; Windermere; Dufton; Wooler
www.yha.org.uk

Tourist Information Centres and Camping Sites

Tourist Information Centres

Ambleside: Central Buildings, Market Cross LA22 9BS. (015394) 32582

Appleby: Moot Hall, Boroughgate, Appleby CA16 6XE. (017683) 51177

Kirkby Stephen: 22 Market Street, Kirkby Stephen, Cumbria CN17 4QN. (017683) 71199

Penrith: Robinson's School, Middlegate, Penrith, Cumbria CA11 7PT. (01768) 867466

Hexham: Wentworth Car Park, Hexham NE46 1QE. (01434) 652220

Otterburn Mill: Otterburn Mill, Otterburn NE19 1JT. (01830) 520093

Rothbury National Park Centre: Church House, Rothbury NE65 7UP. (01669) 620887. March to September

Berwick-upon-Tweed: 106, Marygate, Berwick TD15 IBN. (01289) 330733

Wooler: Padgepool Place,Wooler NE71 6LQ. (01668) 282123

Camping Sites

Ravenglass: Walls Caravan and Camping Park, CA18 1SR. (O1229) 717250. March to November. GR 187 965

Holmrook, Boot: CA19 1TH. (019467) 23253. All Year. GR 178 009

Holmrook, Seven Acres: CA19 IYD. (019467) 25480. March-15 November. GR 073 018

Eskdale, Fisherground: CA19 1TE. (O19467) 23319. March to November. GR 152 001

Wasdale Head: CA20 IEX. National Trust Campsite. (019467) 26220. April to October. GK 183 076

Great Langdale: LA22 9JU. National Trust Campsite. (015394) 37668. All year. GR 286 059

Ambleside, Grizedale Hall, Hawkshead: LA22 OGL. (01229) 860257. March to September. GP 338 942

Low Wray, Nr. Ambleside: LA22 QJA. National Trust Campsite. (015394) 32810. April to October. GR 372 012

Windermere, Limefitt Park: LA23 IPA. (015394) 32300. March to October. GR 416 032

Hawkshead, Croft Camp Site: LA22 ONX. (015394) 36374. March to November. GR 353 982

Nentsberry, Alston: CA9 3LH. Horse and Wagon (01434) 382805. March to October. GR 763 449

NOTE: Many farmers and landowners along the route may permit the pitching of a tent for a single overnight stay; it is essential that permission is obtained before camping.

Tourism Associations

Cumbria Tourism
Tel: 0159 822222 golakes.co.uk

Eden District Council
Tel: 01768 212165 www.visiteden.co.uk

North Pennines Tourism Association
www.northernpennines.org.uk

North Northumberland Tourism Association
www.nnta.org

Rothbury and Coquetdale Tourism Association
www.visit-rothbury.co.uk

Hadrian's Wall Network
www.hadrianswallnorthumberland.co.uk

Bibliography

Beckensall, S. *Prehistoric Rock Motifs of Northumberland Vol 2*, S. Beckensall (1992)

Ekwall, E. *Dictionary of English Place-Names*; Oxford (1936)

Graham, F. *Berwick, A Short History*; Butler Publ (1987)

Graham, F. *Tynedale, From Blanchland to Carter Bar*; E Graham (1978)

Graham, P. Anderson, *Highways and Byways in Northumberland*; MacMillan (1921)

Grierson, E. *The Companion Guide to Northumbria*; Collins (1976)

Hunt, C.J. *The Lead Miners of the Northern Pennines*; Davis Books, George Kelsall Publishing (1984)

Johnson, P. *The National Trust Book of British Castles*; Granada (1981) (1983)

Millward, R., and Robinson, *The Lake District*; Eyre & Spottiswoode (1970)

Northumberland National Park and Countryside Dept. *A Field Guide to the Cheviot Hills* (1985)

Pearsall,W.H. *Mountains and Moorland*; Collins (1958)

Pevsner N. *The Buildings of England: Cumberland and Westmorland*; Penguin (1967)

Pevsner N., and Richmond, L. *The Buildings of England: Northumberland*; Penguin (1957)

Raistrick, A., and Jennings, B. *A History of Lead Mining in the Pennines*; Longmans (1965)

Rollinson W. *Life and Tradition in the Lake District*; Dalesman (1987)

Scholes, R., and Smith, R. *Scotland, The Lowlands*; Moorland Publishing Company (1990)

Scholes, R. *Understanding the Countryside*; Moorland Publishing Company (1985)

Sopwith, T. *The Mining Districts of Alston Moor*; Alnwick (1833)

Thackrah, J.R. *The River Tweed*; T Dalton Ltd (1980)

Trueman, A.E. *Geology and Scenery in England and Wales*; Penguin (1949) (1971)

Wainwright, A. *A Pennine Journey*; Michael Joseph (1986)

Wainwright, A. *Pictorial Guides to the Lakeland Fells*; Michael Joseph (1992);
    Westmorland Gazette: Book 2 (1957); Book 3 (1958); Book 4 (1960); Book 7 (1966)

Wainwright, A. *Westmorland Heritage*; Westmorland Gazette (1975)

Walker, J. and Cowe, F.M. *A Wake for the Salmon*; Northumberland County Library (1988)

Warn, C.R. *Rural Branch Lines of Northumberland*; F. Grham (1978)

White, J. Talbot *The Scottish Border and Northumberland*; Eyre Methuen (1973)

Wright, G.N. *The Northumberland Uplands*; David & Charles (1989)

Wyatt, J. *The Lake District National Park*; Webb & Bower Michael Joseph (1987)

In addition, tourist guides and brochures were read. A number of useful booklets and leaflets are produced by the National Parks Authorities, the Forestry Commission and English Heritage.

Index